Management

D0082472

The global business world appears to be changing and there is an ever-greater focus on developing countries. This change in the international business environment is not reflected in the range of management textbooks currently available, as most are written from a developed country perspective.

This book introduces and assesses the typical theories and management approaches that are popular in developed countries, from the perspective of managers in developing countries. A wide variety of countries, with many different environments and cultures, are explored and the book covers key concepts, such as:

- economic development
- planning and strategic management
- operations management
- HRM
- leadership.

With the added benefit of various pedagogical features and supplementary web materials, students taking classes requiring an understanding of management concepts will find Punnett's book adds serious value. It could be used as core reading for a range of classes, including international business, management, development studies, and managing in a developing country.

Betty Jane Punnett teaches at the University of the West Indies, Barbados. Her research focuses on culture and management, particularly in the Caribbean. She has published over sixty papers in international journals, and five books.

'BJ Punnett's book may well be described as a *tour de force* in the study and the practice of Management in developing countries. Written in an engaging and highly readable style, the book packs significant and relevant statistics, concepts, and theories. A unique feature is that it brings to the fore the challenges and nuanced realities as well as the economic and socio-cultural factors that contextualise the practise of management in developing areas. A must read for students, researchers and practitioners.'

Bill Buenar Puplampu, *University of Ghana Business School and Dean,*
Central Business School, Central University College, Ghana

'There is a growing importance of emerging and developing countries in today's global world. Betty Jane Punnett's book is the first of its kind. There's nothing like it available for the developing world. Although Punnett states it is not an international business textbook, I highly recommend it for international business students and scholars as well as anyone planning to do business in developing countries.'

Terri R. Lituchy, *Concordia University, John Molson School of Business, Canada*

'This is a fresh, innovative approach to Management from a developing country perspective. This book is current, relevant and engaging. The cases illustrate real life issues and the chapters are well structured, clearly written and have a depth of pertinent information. This book takes a realistic and holistic view of the issues faced today in developing countries and is written by an expert at the forefront of her subject.'

Spinder Dhaliwal, *University of Surrey, UK*

'This textbook approaches the study of Management in developing countries by utilizing developed countries' theories and models as well as consultants' experiences to analyze how factors defining developing countries affect management. Drawing on numerous examples from the BRICs, the Caribbean and other regions of the world, it is definitely a welcome publication that helps close the gap on the lack of available teaching resources on the topic.'

Maribel Aponte-Garcia, *University of Puerto Rico*

'As a Brazilian and an international academic I really loved this book. Its framework gives us an interesting way to profoundly engage with Management across cultures and different economic contexts. I am so glad to have been exposed to typical theories and management approaches that are popular in developed countries from the perspective of managers in developing/emerging countries like Brazil, Russia, India, China and South Africa. These countries face a different environment from that in developed countries, and this needs to be reflected in how management processes are carried out. *Management: A Developing Country Perspective* provides a valuable asset for lecturers in developing countries who want to ensure that students consider the realities of their environment.'

Neusa Maria Bastos F. Santos, *Fulbright Scholar, University of Michigan, USA and Professor of Management at Pontificia Universidade Catolica de São Paulo, Brazil*

'Our study of international business is becoming as obsolete as the old G-7 unless we expand our focus to include developing countries in their increasingly vital, central roles. This book promises to provide a very helpful introduction and analysis of that neglected sector of our global economy.'

Charles Vance, *Loyola Marymount University, USA*

'Betty Jane's insider perspective and view of management in the developing world is a welcome addition to instructional tomes on the new economy of the 21st century. Understanding Africa now and its complicated cultural, gender and value inter linkages is critical to claiming the 'last frontier' in human development. Her style, which includes practical examples and exercises for the management student is an inclusive way of helping students grapple with the complex issues that bedevil development in Africa and similar places.'

Samuel Sejjaaka, *Makerere University Business School, Uganda*

'Due to her extraordinary vision, Dr. Punnet always knows in advance what could be a great contribution for science and practice in management. This book enforces previous contributions on research, that management theories based on western developed countries will not be applicable for other different cultural environments. But her knowledge is not only based on her methodology, but on her personal professional life. This book is perfect not only for academics teaching abroad, or locally to global students, but also for practitioners who will be led to consider different options when dealing with organizations or people belonging to developing countries.'

Silvia Inés Monserrat, *Business School, Unicen, Argentina*

'This is not your typical Management book nor is it typical of an International Management book. The topics are covered nicely, but from a perspective that emphasizes "developing countries" (not the familiar term "emerging markets"). Here we're taken on a journey which vividly illustrates how the developing countries have springboarded the heavy infrastructure in land line ICT and are committed to newer technologies. She convincingly argues that they're not rooted in the past, but instead shows how many of these countries may be in positions to be innovative leaders of the future. This book is provocative and offers us a new perspective on Management in the developing world.'

Mary Ann Von Glinow, *AIB President*

Management

A developing country perspective

Betty Jane Punnett

Routledge
Taylor & Francis Group

LONDON AND NEW YORK

First published 2012
by Routledge
2 Park Square, Milton Park, Abingdon, Oxon OX14 4RN

Simultaneously published in the USA and Canada
by Routledge
711 Third Avenue, New York, NY 10017

Routledge is an imprint of the Taylor & Francis Group, an informa business

British Library Cataloguing in Publication Data
A catalogue record for this book is available from the British Library

Library of Congress Cataloging in Publication Data
Punnett, Betty Jane.
Management : a developing country perspective / Betty Jane Punnett. – 1st ed.
    p. cm.
Includes bibliographical references and index.
1. Economic development–Developing countries. 2. Strategic planning–Developing
countries. 3. International business enterprises–Developing countries–Management.
4. Personnel management–Developing countries. I. Title.
HC59.7.P776 2012
658.009172'4–dc23   2011023979

ISBN: 978-0-415-59068-6 (hbk)
ISBN: 978-0-415-59069-3 (pbk)
ISBN: 978-0-203-15205-8 (ebk)

Typeset in Perpetua and Bell Gothic
by Cenveo Publisher Services

MIX
Paper from
responsible sources
FSC® C004839
www.fsc.org

Printed and bound in Great Britain by
TJ International Ltd, Padstow, Cornwall

To Don with Thanks for Everything

Contents

CONTENTS

Figures

Acknowledgements

There are many people who have assisted in the preparation of this book. In particular, I would like to acknowledge and thank the following people: my husband Don Wood for reading and re-reading each chapter of the book and making valuable suggestions, changes and additions and for patiently giving me the time and space to work on this project; Nyzinga Onifa for assisting with the preparation of the Chapter Objectives, Discussion Questions and Exercises; Mike Kirkwood for preparing the Index. I would also like to thank the University of the West Indies for granting a semester's leave to devote to writing many of the Chapters, and the Department of Management Studies for providing financial support and a research assistant for work on the book. Finally, I appreciate Routledge's interest in publishing a needed book in an underserved field.

Chapter 1

Introduction

At the beginning of the twenty-first century, there is much discussion of the global nature of business and the need for management to be aware of the impact of globalization on business. There is little question that factors such as the relative ease of movement around the globe, innovations in communication and transportation technology, regional and international free trade agreements, international investment, continuing migration, and so on, all contribute to a sense of the world being a global village. The reality, however, is that when we talk of globalization and international management, we are usually talking about management in the developed countries of the world. These are the richer countries that account for a large majority of global trade and investment. These rich countries also account for most of the world's gross domestic product – GDP (the richest 20 percent of the world earn about 85 percent of the world's GDP, and the poorest 20 percent only 1 percent), however, they represent only about 20 percent of the world's population. Interestingly, over the past decades, there has also been discussion of the "myth" of globalization (Rugman, 2001) and there is substantial evidence that most large firms are regional and not in effect global (Rugman and Verbeke, 2008); Kolk (2010) calls this (semi) globalization.

For many years, Britain and the British Empire dominated the world, and the saying "the sun never sets on the British flag" was true because there were British colonies around the world. With this economic domination went a dominance of British businesses in many parts of the world; then the world changed. In the early twentieth century, mass production in the USA meant that American business became dominant globally, and "American management" was lauded and respected almost everywhere; then in the 1970s, the Japanese became the world's largest car producers, and "Japanese management" became the style to emulate. For many years trade and investment was dominated by the aptly named "triad" of Europe, Japan and North America. It seems, however, that the world may once again be changing. Some evidence according to Columbia FDI Perspectives (Kekic, 2009):

- foreign direct investment (FDI) inflows to the developed world declined by one-third in 2008, while flows to emerging markets increased by 11 percent;
- in 2009, for the first time, emerging markets were set to attract more FDI than developed countries;
- the economic performance of emerging markets has been better than that of developed countries during the recession beginning in 2008;

- companies with investments in emerging markets report better performance than those with very little investment in these countries;
- emerging markets are improving and liberalizing their business environments.

UNCTAD's *Global Investment Trends Monitor* (www.unctad.org/diae, April 28, 2011) found that global FDI had risen by 13 percent in 2010, with flows from developing and transition economies reaching a record high, both in absolute terms and in their share of total global flows (the global flows were, however, 40 percent lower than the levels recorded in 2007). The report noted the strength of developing and transition economies, the dynamism of their international companies, and their growing desire to compete in new markets. Their outward FDI reached $377 billion, almost a 25 percent increase over the previous year. Their share of global outflows reached 28 percent, up from 15 percent in 2007. Most of the investment from developing countries is directed to other developing countries; according to the report, 70 percent of the investment is developing country to developing country. Gokgur (2011) raised the question of the influence of state-owned enterprises (SOEs) in this equation. According to this report, emerging markets, led by China, are encouraging their SOEs to expand globally as multinational enterprises. These SOEs have taken the lead in Chinese expansion, supported by state-owned Chinese banks. The question that remains unanswered is how these SOEs affect consumers, labor, enterprise performance, owners and operators, taxpayers, competitors, communities, and the environment. Nevertheless, the report says that the international development community is promoting public–private partnerships, expecting the private sector to bring private investments and technical know-how, and to deliver competitive tenders and development outcomes. The report concludes that this result is doubtful if state-owned enterprises and banks hinder competition.

The Economist Intelligence Unit carried out a survey in 2009, which included 548 companies from 19 business sectors around the world. They found that close to 60 percent of the companies surveyed expect to derive more than 20 percent of their total revenue from emerging markets in five years' time. In contrast, only 31 percent reported currently deriving this level of revenues from emerging markets. This suggests that the shift in FDI flows may be a longer-term development and not simply an immediate reaction to the recession. According to *The Economist* (April 17, 2010):

- emerging countries are competing in ways that can be expected to change the way businesses everywhere are run;
- their companies are competing on the basis of creativity as well as cost and they are no longer happy simply to be the source of low-cost production and raw materials;
- they are becoming a source of innovation, in every field from cars to health care to telecommunications;
- they are redesigning business processes to perform better and faster than their rivals in the West.

This sounds surprisingly like the Industrial Revolution in the United Kingdom, mass production in the United States, and Japan's innovative approaches to manufacturing. It may indeed be the reality of the future that the economic powerhouses will be from the developing countries, and that we will look to these countries for the new management approaches.

The President of the United States, President Obama, in an address to the Millennium Development Goals Summit in New York (September, 2010) emphasized the importance of the developing world to everyone, everywhere. He said:

In our global economy, progress in even the poorest countries can advance the prosperity and security of people far beyond their borders, including my fellow Americans…

When a child dies from a preventable disease, it shocks all of our consciences. When a girl is deprived of an education or her mother is denied equal rights, it undermines the prosperity of their nation. When a young entrepreneur can't start a new business, it stymies the creation of new jobs and markets in that entrepreneur's country, but also in our own. When millions of fathers cannot provide for their families, it feeds the despair that can fuel instability and violent extremism. When a disease goes unchecked, it can endanger the health of millions around the world…

So let's put to rest the old myth that development is mere charity that does not serve our interests. And let's reject the cynicism that says certain countries are condemned to perpetual poverty, for the past half century has witnessed more gains in human development than at any time in history. A disease that had ravaged the generations, smallpox, was eradicated. Health care has reached the far corners of the world, saving the lives of millions. From Latin America to Africa to Asia, developing nations have transformed into leaders in the global economy.

He went on to say:

We also recognize, though, that the old ways will not suffice. That's why in Ghana last year I called for a new approach to development that unleashes transformational change and allows more people to take control of their own destiny. After all, no country wants to be dependent on another. No proud leader in this room wants to ask for aid. No family wants to be beholden to the assistance of others…the purpose of development – what's needed most right now – is creating the conditions where assistance is no longer needed. So we will seek partners who want to build their own capacity to provide for their people. We will seek development that is sustainable [and] we're making it clear that we will partner with countries that are willing to take the lead. Because the days when your development was dictated by foreign capitals must come to an end.

Perhaps the world is indeed changing in terms of the way it views development as the following illustrates.

The United Nations urged a gathering of global business leaders in June 2010 to invest in developing countries (*UN Daily News*, 2010). Secretary-General Ban said that investment in developing countries was to promote global growth. He said essentially that the world could not afford not to invest in the developing world – because that's where the greatest need is, but also because that is where some of the greatest dynamism is. The Global Compact was launched in 2000, and is a project to foster socially responsible business practices. Ban said that the financial crisis, climate change, poverty, and resource constraints test the world's capabilities, and needs business as a partner more than ever.

Another change is underway, this time to do with climate change and the carbon footprint that countries account for. The United Nations World Investment Report 2010 is subtitled "Investing in a low carbon economy." The report recommends promotion of low-carbon foreign investment. The report suggests that developing countries consider implementing policies that "reward" low-carbon investors. The report supports the idea that developed countries should actively pursue low-carbon initiatives in developing countries. Further, the report argues that the international financial institutions (IFIs) should encourage public–private partnerships in the area of carbon reduction, they should enhance assistance for cross-border investment and technology flows, particularly from developed to developing countries, and set up a low-carbon technology assistance center to support developing countries formulating and implementing climate change mitigation strategies and plans.

The report's focus on climate change suggests new opportunities for developing countries. In the coming years there is clearly going to be a great need for new technological developments in this area. Even climate change skeptics recognize that the world's growing population is putting stress on the planet's limited resources. Developing countries can be in the forefront of identifying these new technologies and bringing them to markets, at home and in the developed world. The developing countries, in many instances, are not wedded to existing technologies, for the very reason that they have not reached a high level of economic development dependent on these technologies. Because many developing countries have jumped over the heavy infra-structure investment in land-line telecommunications and are committed to the new cellphone and other wireless technologies, their technologies and institutions are not rooted in the past. This puts them in an ideal position to explore alternatives. Many developing countries are in areas of the world where power from alternative energy sources, such as the sun, the tides, vol-canoes, and wind may be feasible. This provides many possibilities for these countries to be the leaders of the future.

Just as we have seen management approaches reflect national leadership in technology and in the markets (British, then American, then Japan) we should expect new approaches to manage-ment to emerge with the growth of the emerging markets. Each generation of management approach has added to, not substituted for, its predecessor. In this book, we will explore the ways management in the future globalizing world can be enhanced by incorporating the new ideas coming out of many of the diverse and ancient cultures newly becoming important players in the game of global business.

In an interesting book entitled *"Why the West rules – For now"*, Morris (2010) takes an historical look at economic and social development over the long term. He says that throughout human history, development has been erratic, sometimes retreating in one place for a millen-nium or two before moving forward again elsewhere. Civilizations have grown and developed then declined and disappeared, usually for reasons their leaders were powerless to influence. In this context, he considers the West's current dominance of the world economy and concludes that it is in no way likely to continue far into the future. He believes that power, influence, and commercial dynamism are shifting eastward, and that if Eastern and Western social development continues rising at current rates, Western "rule" will end early in the next century. Most interest-ingly, however, he argues that if we survive the next 100 years, the quantum increases in comput-ing power and bioscience, are so exponential that humankind itself will be profoundly changed, making distinctions between East and West seem anachronistic.

Morris's (2010) analysis of the British ascent to power in the 1800s, and the consequent dominance of Western countries in today's world, is insightful. He asks why it was British boats that shot their way up the Yangzi in 1842 rather than Chinese ones up the Thames, and why many more people from the East speak English than Europeans speak Mandarin? The answer seems to be that the Industrial Revolution began in the West in the late eighteenth century thanks primar-ily to the efforts of British engineers and entrepreneurs who sought to exploit the energy from the country's abundant coal stocks and use it to harness the power of steam to drive ships, trains and machines in factories. The rapid march of technology gave Britain a temporary edge over other countries and allowed it to project both economic and maritime military power on a global scale that remained virtually unchallenged for most of the next 100 years. This established the ascendancy of the West that continues today. The changes occurring in the developing world today suggest that these countries may be poised to take over this ascendancy. Now, however, the world may be changing. The shifts in power may not be simply West to East, but also North to South. The development of the so-called BRIC countries (Brazil, Russia, India, and China), as a group to rival the groupings of more developed countries, is an indication of the changing nature of the world. In April 2011, the news was about the BRICS (a group including South Africa) meeting in South Africa to discuss, among other issues, their role in representing the economic interests of the countries of the developing world.

An Economist survey in 2010 (results emailed to the author, a participant) illustrates business interest in the developing countries (or emerging markets as they were called in the survey). Results showed that companies that already invest in emerging markets had deepened their investment over the previous three years; 79 percent reported an increase in investment, 14 percent expected their level of investment to remain the same, and only 7 percent reported a decrease. Respondents to the survey appeared to think that the risk–return ratio is becoming more favorable; 55 percent thought that the risks were increasing but 64 percent said that the rewards had increased. Overall, it seems that the interest in "doing business" in the developing world is increasing. At the same time, companies from the developing world were increasing their international activities.

In recent years there has been a dramatic increase in commerce among developing countries; it has doubled from about 8 percent of world trade in 1990 to over 16 percent in 2007, and the share of developing countries' exports to developing countries increased from 29 percent in 1990 to 47 percent in 2008 (Broadman, 2011). A substantial portion of this has been Chinese and Indian investments in Africa. According to Broadman, many observers believe that Chinese and Indian firms dominate Africa's economies, but this is incorrect, because 90 percent of the stock of FDI originated from developed countries; however, Chinese and Indian investments have dominated African inward FDI in recent years.

The previous discussion suggests that it is timely for students in management to pay greater attention to management issues in developing countries. It is timely for people around the world to understand issues of management from a global perspective rather than simply from a Western or developed perspective. The objective of this book is to provide a basis for such understanding.

The focus of this book is on "the rest of the world"; that is, the developing countries of the world. It is also on management in and from these countries. This book is not intended to be an international business text, but rather a book on management, from a developing country perspective. Because most well-accepted approaches to management, and theories of management, have been developed in what we call the West, these often serve as the basis for discussion in the chapters of this book. We take these established approaches and theories and ask how well they are likely to work in developing countries. I identify the characteristics of developing countries, and companies in these countries, to explore the effectiveness of various approaches and theories. Where possible, I identify and discuss research that has been done in developing countries, and use the results of this research to further explore various facets of management.

Before we address management issues, in order to provide the context for that discussion, definitions of development and the characteristics of developing countries are considered, particularly in contrast to the more developed. This discussion sets the stage for the introduction of a traditional model of management. This model is used as a guide for the rest of the book. I take each management process – planning, organizing, staffing, leading, controlling – and discuss it in the context of development. The final chapter looks at some issues of special concern in developing countries, which were not previously discussed in depth. The rest of this chapter provides an overview of the book, with a brief outline of each of the chapters to come.

Chapter 2 considers the terminology of development. In this chapter various terms that have been used over the past century are examined and explained. A major concern has been the negative connotations of classifying countries as "more developed" and "less developed", and people have sought alternative classifications such as "North" and "South". None of these has proved satisfactory to the global community. Chapter 2 settles for developed and developing as the most common usage to be incorporated into this text.

Chapter 3 considers the characteristics of developing countries. This chapter looks at demographic issues such as population growth and gender, cultural comparisons, politics, corruption, ethics and corporate social responsibility, and convergence and divergence among countries. The chapter also looks at a new index – the Happy Planet Index – which attempts to incorporate environmental issues into measures of development.

Chapter 4 introduces a model of management, which includes planning, organizing, staffing, leading, and controlling. This model is examined in the context of the previously described characteristics of developing countries. Two countries, the People's Republic of China and India are used as contrasting examples of how management takes place in different developing countries. The similarities as well as differences between these two countries are examined.

Chapter 5 focuses on explanations of economic development. Various traditional and development economic theories are considered, and the role of institutions and policies are explored. Some current thinking is also examined. The chapter concludes that while there is some evidence to support various ideas on economic development, we do not understand the whole picture regarding development.

Chapter 6 looks at planning and strategic management in developing countries. This chapter discusses the concepts associated with planning. Planning encompasses longer-term and strategic decisions, its vision and its mission. It also guides shorter term and daily decisions that keep the organization running. It introduces a variety of models for developing an effective strategy, outlines the elements of strategy, and defines terms commonly found in the literature. It considers these in the context of the environment in developing countries. The chapter also introduces a model of internationalization, and discusses various international entry options from a developing country perspective.

Chapter 7 considers organizing and operating an international company. A fictional product is used to track the reader through the internationalization process. Using the model from the previous chapter, a product called "Tanty Goodluck's Sauce" is traced, as it goes from a purely domestic base into a global company, to illustrate the realities of expansion. The chapter considers the reality of this progress, including changes in organizational structure, and the need for establishing a control system. This chapter also considers organizing and operating an international company from a developing country base. The challenges of operating from such a base are explored as well as ways of overcoming these challenges. The chapter also includes a brief consideration of organizational structures and how they change in response to expansion.

Chapter 8 looks at human resource management (HRM) from a developing country perspective. This chapter addresses issues of managing people in organizations – HRM – and how this takes place in developing countries. In the management model in Chapter 4, the function was called staffing. Staffing involves filling positions and making sure that the people can and do carry out the work needed for the organization to continue over time. This is essentially HRM. Formal HRM is often largely non-existent in developing countries, and this probably works quite well; nevertheless, the chapter argues that understanding fundamentals of HRM can help companies manage their human resources effectively.

Chapter 9 considers issues associated with managing an international workforce. In this chapter, issues associated with HR management are examined for international companies.

This is an area where newly internationalizing companies can learn from the experiences of international companies who have gone before, and avoid some of their costly mistakes. The information presented in this chapter can help firms from developing countries avoid failure problems experienced by developed country companies, and they can learn to seek to be more culturally sensitive as they internationalize. The chapter particularly looks at companies from developing countries going to developed countries.

Chapter 10 examines issues of motivation in developing countries. This chapter addresses motivation from a developing country perspective. A firm's success and profitability are directly related, to a large extent, to the performance and productivity of the people who work for it; this means that managers are concerned with how motivated employees are at work. This is as true in developing countries as it is in developed countries; however, what motivates people may differ. Particularly when one considers the differences between developing and developed countries, such as poverty, lack of education, lack of infrastructure, and so on. One can expect that these factors will all influence motivation.

Chapter 11 focuses on leadership issues in developing countries. This chapter looks at leadership and explores what we know about leadership in developing countries. It also uses the characteristics of developing countries to consider what might be most effective in terms of leadership in these countries. It begins with a general definition of leadership and differentiates between leadership and management, although the two terms are often used interchangeably. It examines Western leadership theories and considers whether these will be effective, given the characteristics of developing countries using literature from developing countries whenever possible.

Chapter 12 examines some of the special issues associated with managing in developing countries which were not considered in depth in earlier chapters. The issues selected for discussion were ethical considerations, differential treatment based on personal characteristics, and age dispersion. These were selected because: many indices have identified systems in developing countries as more likely to lead to ethical questions; there appears to be more differential treatment on the basis of characteristics such as age, gender, and sexual orientation; and, finally, the age dispersion in developing countries is such that there is a relatively young population, whereas the reverse is true of developed countries, where the population is aging. This chapter concludes with a brief review of the material covered in the book.

SUMMARY

Chapter 1 introduced the reader to some of the developments in world trade and investment over the past decade. This discussion served to illustrate the growing importance of developing countries in the world economy. The statistics and reports discussed point to a changing balance in the world, where developed countries will no longer dominate the world of business. There has been little attention to management in developing countries, and I believe this changing world means that it is increasingly important for academics, managers, and students to explore what it means to manage in these countries. Much of the world's management literature is based on research on management in developed countries. In this book I look at this literature and ask how it applies to developing countries. Ideas based on research in developing countries are also incorporated where ever possible.

The countries that make up the developing world are very varied, and they account for about 80 percent of the world's population. Clearly there will be many differences among these countries, and it is not possible to explore very many individual countries here, or to identify many of these differences. Where individual countries are explored in upcoming chapters, they tend to be those that are currently seen as having most influence; for example, China and India. Readers who are particularly interested in countries which are not discussed in this book, should seek country-specific information, and use that to consider how traditional management approaches are likely to work or not work in these specific countries.

In the next chapters, understanding what developing countries are like is the focus of attention. I consider various definitions for development and how these have changed over time. I also examine the main characteristics that distinguish developing countries from developed ones. These discussions set the stage for the rest of the book, which considers the processes of management and how managers can be effective in developing countries.

Chapter 2

Terminology of development

OBJECTIVES

The purpose of this chapter is to provide a context for the rest of the book. The objectives of this chapter are as follows:

- To familiarize the reader with the terms that have been used over the past century to denote levels of economic development.
- To explore the meanings associated with various terms used to denote levels of economic development.
- To identify the wide variation that exists among countries classified as "developing".
- To identify the specifics of the gap between the richer countries and the poorer ones.
- To consider the role of the developing countries in the changing world of the twenty-first century.
- To examine events in 2011 and their implications for managers in developing countries.
- To give the reader an overall appreciation of the issues associated with economic development.

INTRODUCTION

This chapter begins with the suggestion that the world is changing, and that developing countries are playing a larger role in world affairs. In turn, companies from developing countries are becoming more important on the world stage. In contrast to this, I also argue that there is still a large gap between the rich countries of the world and the poorer ones, and that this gap is important for both sets of countries. Growing out of this gap a need has arisen to classify countries according to their wealth and income. In this book we use the distinction of "developed" and "developing", but this terminology is not very satisfactory, so this chapter explores issues around the terms that have been used in the past, and those that are currently in use. The chapter also identifies the major differences between the developed countries and the developing ones. The chapter closes with a discussion of the current situation in developing countries, and how this is changing, particularly in the face of the relatively recent economic expansion of countries such as India and the People's Republic of China (PRC). The chapter briefly describes current events around the world, and their implications, in 2011, when the book was being written.

While developing countries are often discussed as a group, as they will be here, in reality it is difficult, if not impossible, to talk of them as a group because the group is made up of such diverse countries – ranging from very large (for example, India and the PRC) to very small (for example, Samoa and St. Lucia); including relatively well-off countries (such as Singapore,) and very poor ones (such as Haiti); covering a multiplicity of languages, religions, histories, and geographies, and representing all continents. This means that any discussion of these countries as a group must be tempered by a recognition that there will be as many differences among these countries as there may be similarities. Nevertheless, there is value in looking at these countries as a group and considering how their level of development, income, and wealth may influence management styles and practices. In the next section, a number of trends in developing countries are considered. In addition, within the overall larger group, there are subsets that can be discussed, such as the countries known as the BRIC group (the economically fast-growing countries of Brazil, Russia, India, and China) or the BRICS – the BRIC group plus South Africa, the countries that used to be called the Asian Tigers, and so on.

DEVELOPING COUNTRIES: THE NEW FRONTIER?

Chinese-owned businesses are investing around the world, India is at the forefront of techno-logical developments, Dubai is a global financial center, Brazilian banks are among the largest in the world, and companies, (small and large) from developing countries around the world are now investing in other developing countries as well as in the developed world. The developing world is now the focus of interest for scholars alongside business managers, the public sector and nongovernmental organizations (NGOs). The interesting aspect of all this is that the new focus is not just from a developed country perspective, but from the perspective of people and manag-ers within the developing world itself. The developing world itself has lessons for the rest of the world. Some quotes follow which illustrate how the world is changing (note that the following quotes all refer to the countries as "emerging" rather than "developing"):

- "Emerging-market banks have raced ahead despite the financial crisis", and "not only are they well capitalized and well funded, they are really big – and enjoying rapid growth. By profits, Tier 1 capital, dividends and market value they now account for a quarter to half of global banking industry" (*The Economist*, May 15, 2010, "They may be giants" p. 3 of a special report on banking in emerging markets).
- "The emerging world, long a source of cheap labour, now rivals the rich countries for business innovation" and "The United Nations World Investment Report calculates that there are now around 21,500 multinationals based in the emerging world" (*The Economist*, April 17, 2010, "The world turned upside down" p. 3 of a special report on innovation in emerging markets).
- "The new decade started on a sour economic note"; but "Emerging markets turned out to be the bright spot in the new economic order" and "not only the big emerging markets such as Brazil, China, India, but also smaller, more economically advanced markets such as Israel, Slovenia, Singapore, and Taiwan" (Ilan Alon, AIB Insights, 2011 10(1): 2 "Emerging markets' evolving role in the new economic order").

In 2006 *The Economist* (November 25, 2006, p. 64) in an article entitled "Steel the prize" dis-cussed the takeover battle between Tata, an Indian conglomerate and CSN a Brazilian Steelmaker, for Corus – Corus is the Anglo-Dutch company that absorbed British Steel. This may be a harbinger of the face of the future – two giant companies from developing countries, fighting over a developed country asset.

In spite of this changing world of business, what literature there is on management interactions between developing and developed countries implicitly assumes that managers from developed countries will be adapting to the environment in developing countries. The reverse, that is, developing country managers adapting to the environment in developed countries, may be more and more the reality of the management challenges of the twenty-first century. In many ways this is contrary to traditional thinking about developing countries. Until quite recently, the developing countries were seen only as the recipients of aid and investment from the developed world.

Although the world of business may be changing, the developing countries remain the poorer countries of the world. The French have a saying that roughly translates into English as 'the more things change, the more they remain the same'. In many ways this is true of the development situation. While there are many positive things happening in the developing world, there is still a major gap between rich and poor countries.

Developing countries make up about 80 percent of the world, and the gap between the rich and poor countries is striking (see Figure 2.1). In fact it has been growing substantially over time. This growing gap is of concern to many, hence the focus on finding ways to encourage development in poorer countries. Maddison (1982) estimated economic growth and income levels for the world back to A.D. 500 and concluded that rapid economic growth did not really begin until about 1820. His estimates suggest no growth from 500 to 1500, and then a growth rate of 0.04 per year from 1500 to 1820. Madison's estimates show growth rates for all countries accelerating after 1820, with the richest countries exhibiting the fastest growth rates and the poorest the slowest. As a result the ratio between average incomes in the richest region to those in the poorest region increased from about 3:1 in 1820 to 12:1 in 1950. According to Perkins et al. (2001), since 1950, the poorest region at that time, Asia, has recorded high levels of growth, thus narrowing the gap. Other relatively poor countries in 1950, including southern Europe, have grown relatively rapidly in the latter half of the twentieth century. African growth rates have been relatively poor especially after 1980, but there is some evidence that this is turning around, and in 2011, the International Monetary Fund was forecasting growth rates of 5.5 percent for the continent. Latin America has experienced mixed rates of growth, but growth rates in 2010 were around 4 percent for the region and growth was forecast to continue at this level or higher in 2011 (International Monetary Fund, 2011).

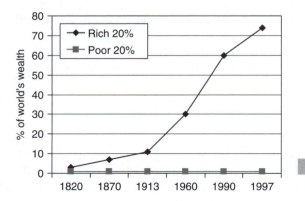

Figure 2.1 *Gap between rich and poor countries*

A Global Policy Study in 2000 (Davies et al., 2011) which looked at global household wealth concluded that global wealth amounted to $125 trillion, approximately three times the value of total global production; or to $20,500 per person. When they adjusted for differences in the cost of living the value of wealth was about $26,000 per capita. The per capita wealth for different countries was however dramatically different. Average wealth was $144,000 per person in the USA, and $181,000 in Japan compared to $1,100 in India and $1,400 in Indonesia. The report said that wealth is heavily concentrated in North America, Europe, and high-income Asia-Pacific countries; and that people in these countries account for almost 90 percent of total world wealth. This study illustrates the gap between the rich and poor countries of the world and again reinforces the need to understand these differences and how they can influence effective management practices. The *level* of average household wealth in the countries in the report is estimated via the determinants of assets and debts for thirty-nine countries which have balance sheet or survey data. The *distribution* of wealth in all countries is inferred from information on the pattern of wealth ownership for twenty countries (covering 59 percent of world population). Combining the level and distribution figures suggests that median global wealth on the basis of purchasing power parity (PPP) was PPP$8,635 in the year 2000, and that PPP$518,361 belonged to the top percentile. The top 10 percent owned 71 percent of world wealth and the global Gini value was 0.802 (the Gini index is a measure of inequality of income, and the higher the value, the greater the levels of inequality), showing that there is substantial inequality of wealth distribution on a global scale.

In the following section, the terms we have historically used and those we currently use are discussed.

TERMINOLOGY OF DEVELOPMENT

Over time the terminology used for development has varied. In the early 1900s, the poorer countries were often referred to as "traditional" and the richer ones as "modern". In the mid-1900s the poorer countries were referred to as "underdeveloped" or "less developed countries" (LDCs); sometimes they were referred to as the "third world" (in contrast to the first, rich world, and the second, communist world), and sometimes a distinction was drawn between the North (where most rich countries are) and the South (where most poor countries are). Reflecting the level of industrialization that accompanies development, sometimes the richer countries have been referred to as industrialized or advanced countries. More recently, the terms that have become popular are developing countries, transition economies – the countries of East–central Europe, the Balkans, the Baltics, and the Commonwealth of Independent States (CIS) – and emerging markets (Economist Intelligence Unit, 2006). As some of the highest-income countries have become heavily reliant on services (finance, research and development, medical services and so on) rather than manufacturing, these countries are sometimes now be referred to as post-industrial countries. In this chapter developed and developing are used, because these are terms that are likely to be familiar to most readers. In the following sections, some of the terms used are discussed in more detail.

Traditional and modern

The poorer countries were considered to be traditional in their approaches to government, economics and so on – that is, they used approaches which were considered "old fashioned". The richer countries, in contrast, were believed to have adopted modern approaches, such as democracy and free markets. Traditional countries were seen as being held back by their adherence to traditional ways, whereas modern countries progressed and advanced because of their adoption of new and innovative – modern – ideas and ways of behaving. At the extreme, traditional countries were considered backward and modern countries advanced.

Underdeveloped countries and LDCs

Poorer, developing countries were often called "underdeveloped" some fifty years ago. This terminology has been described as a carryover of colonial condescension and was changed to "less developed countries" (LDCs) in order to be less demeaning. This term has also been considered negative and is seldom now used for the developing countries as a group. The term LDC now describes the "least developed countries," the poorest nations in the world, which receive particular development attention from the United Nations.

Third World

The Third World designation for developing countries was used in contrast to the First World (the Organization for Economic Cooperation and Development – OECD – countries), and the Second World (communist countries). The Third World encompassed the countries that were not aligned with either the First or Second Worlds. Since the collapse of the Soviet Union, this terminology is less frequently used, but "Third World" is still in common usage, usually referring to the poorer countries of the world.

North–South (East–West)

The majority of the richer countries are north of the majority of the poorer countries (of course, there are countries such as Australia and New Zealand in the south). The North–South distinction began through an attempt to be neutral and North–South terms are used by many development organizations in the context of a North–South divide. People in the North are seen as the "haves" and those in the South seen as the "have-nots." People quite often also talk of the "West" versus the "East". Particularly in the management field, many management theories are described as originating in the "West". The West is thought of as Canada, the USA, and Western Europe, and the rest of the world as the "East". The Academy of Management's theme for 2011 – "West meets East: Enlightening, Balancing, Transcending" – illustrates the use of this terminology in the management field. Neither North–South nor East–West is very satisfactory, because it does not describe the reality of the world. There are rich countries in the South and poor ones in the North, and the countries of Africa, Latin America, and the Caribbean do not think of themselves as "East".

Transitional or industrializing countries

As some countries have embraced new economic forms, they have recently been considered as becoming developed or industrialized. The countries of the former Soviet bloc are often described as "transitional economies," and countries with substantial industrial bases, such as South Korea, Taiwan, and Brazil, have been described as "industrializing" or "newly industrialized countries" (NICs).

Emerging markets/emerging countries

The terms emerging market and emerging country are relatively recent and these terms have been seen as more positive than many of their predecessors (van Agtmael, 2007). The industrializing countries are also often called "emerging markets" to indicate the substantial potential markets that they represent. Recently, the so-called BRIC countries have been the focus of attention – these are Brazil, Russia, India, and China, all of which are having a substantial impact on the world economy and world trade and investment. In 2011, BRICS came into use, when South Africa hosted a meeting of the BRIC countries, the focus of which was economic issues in developing countries. Recently, many authors have switched from emerging markets to emerging countries to reflect that these countries are important as investors and producers as well as markets. The terminology "emerging markets" or "emerging countries" is seen by many to have optimistic connotations, as it is action-oriented and seems to imply a positive movement.

The difficulty with this terminology is that almost all terms, especially from a developing country perspective, are pejorative and demeaning – that is, to be "traditional and backward" implies that you are stagnant and unmoving, to be "less developed" suggests that you are a child, to be "developing" that you are seeking to be like the more developed, to be "third world" that you are third class. Even the current favorite "emerging" suggests that you are coming out of some undesirable state. The terminology also suggests that there is a good and desirable state, i.e., a developed one, that all countries are seeking. Many people in the developing world, although they certainly want to be better off, do not necessarily see the ways of the developed world as being the perfect end state of societies, particularly in light of the widening prosperity and wealth gaps that exist within these developed countries.

Definitions of "development" are sensitive because the concept of development is value-laden, and managers need to be aware of these sensitivities. Different groups interpret the word "development" differently at different times. Being classified as "developing" can be advantageous for a country when, for example, it wants to receive development aid or other donor assistance. At other times a country may want to think of itself as developed; for example, when it wants to attract foreign investment and high-technology firms.

The varying terminology of development stems from attempts to wrestle with several concerns. There are clear differences among countries in terms of their economic resources and level of industrialization. The United Nations and various development organizations, as well as the general population, want to recognize these differences. Much as with the term "development" itself, words used to recognize differences in development levels are inevitably value-laden. Newly devised terms were intended to offer value neutrality; as this neutrality faded and embedded connotations took over, other new terms arose. For example, less developed was used in the 1950s to describe poorer countries. Eventually this term was thought to be as demeaning as "underdeveloped," so "developing countries" became its more acceptable replacement, because it was thought to have a positive sense of moving forward. "Developing" versus "developed," however, suggests that one set of countries has reached a desired level of economic achievement to which the other set should aspire. The North–South terminology sought to differentiate without judging, but this approach did not succeed either. In effect, the rich and powerful North was usually depicted in a negative light as exploiting the poor and powerless South, both with mutual antagonisms.

The terrorist attacks in the United States of America (USA) on September 11, 2001, have made people everywhere more conscious of the way words can have different meanings to different people. Hence, sensitivity in the use of language is often important when people relate to others of different backgrounds. Clearly, "Jihad" does not mean the same thing to all Muslims, as it can be interpreted as a religious duty or a struggle, or a holy war, and it often has negative connotations for non-Muslims. Similarly, "crusade" is used commonly in English to mean any concerted and continuing effort, but to Middle Easterners it usually refers to the Christian holy wars against the Arab Islamic world. Development terminology is no exception. Managers should be aware of the diverse terminology used to describe countries that fall into different economic classifications and be conscious of the various implications these terms may carry.

In a radio talk-show, broadcast in Toronto, Canada (September 14, 2010), the host discussed the use of the word "Oriental" to describe a group of people. Apparently some people felt that it was "racist". In the ensuing phone-in discussion, it was evident that some people did in fact consider the term racist, and reminiscent of imperialist European policies and practices. Others considered it simply a way to describe people from different countries in the Far East, much as one would talk about Europeans, Latin Americans, Middle Easterners, and so on. The interesting distinction seems to be that "Oriental" does not refer to a continent or region, but comes from a European word "orient" that was used when the Europeans were sailing in the early colonizing years, and their maps were "oriented" towards the countries of the Far East (that is, these countries were at the top of the sailing map). Political correctness may sometimes be carried to extremes, and it is not possible to please all of the people all of the time. This sort of discussion does serve, however, to remind us all that the same words can be interpreted in a variety of ways, depending on your own background and "orientation" or experience.

The issue of describing differences without making judgments is likely to continue. The term "developed world" will be used here to refer to the OECD countries and the rest of Western Europe, and the term "developing world" will refer to the rest of the world. The major distinctions between "developed" and "developing," in this context, are that developed world countries, have, on average, a higher per capita income than the developing world countries, and they rank higher on the United Nations Development Index. What these distinctions mean for managers is that the business environment can be substantially different in the two regions. The next sections provide an overview of some of the main characteristics that differentiate the business environment of developing countries from that of the more developed ones.

DIFFERENCES BETWEEN DEVELOPED AND DEVELOPING COUNTRIES

Whatever terminology is used, the developed countries are the richer ones, and the developing are the poorer. Of course, within each group, there is a range of GDP per capita and a range of incomes and wealth. Especially in the developing countries, the range is large, with some countries being quite well off, and others very poor (the poorest are often now called the Least Developed by the United Nations to identify their special needs).

The United States Council for International Business (1985) used the following definitions, which are still helpful in understanding the most commonly accepted distinctions between developed and developing countries.

Developed countries

Industrialized countries are distinguished from developing countries or less developed countries (LDCs). Generally, the term "developed" is understood to refer to countries with the per capita incomes greater than US$10,000 in 1999. At that time, according to the CIA World Factbook, developed countries included members of the OECD, which comprised Australia, Belgium, Canada, Denmark, Finland, France, Germany, Ireland, Israel, Italy, Japan, the Netherlands, New Zealand, UK, and USA and in some cases the industrialized countries of Eastern Europe. In 2010, the following thirty-four countries were listed: Andorra, Australia, Austria, Belgium, Bermuda, Canada, Denmark, Faroe Islands, Finland, France, Germany, Greece, Holy See,

Iceland, Ireland, Israel, Italy, Japan, Liechtenstein, Luxembourg, Malta, Monaco, the Netherlands, New Zealand, Norway, Portugal, San Marino, South Africa, Spain, Sweden, Switzerland, Turkey, United Kingdom, USA. The CIA Factbook notes that this listing is similar to the new International Monetary Fund (IMF) term "advanced economies" which adds Hong Kong, South Korea, Singapore, and Taiwan but drops Malta, Mexico, South Africa, and Turkey (CIA World Factbook accessed at www.cia.gov/library, July 16, 2010). Note that Hong Kong is not a country, but is in fact a part of the People's Republic of China (PRC) (but it is often listed as a country, because of its special economic status within the PRC); the PRC does not recognize Taiwan as a country, and Taiwan does not currently have a seat at the United Nations.

Developing countries

This term is used most commonly at the United Nations to describe a broad range of countries including those with both high and low per capita national incomes and those that depend heavily on the sale of primary commodities. These countries usually lack an advanced industrial infrastructure as well as advanced educational, health, communications, and transportation facilities.

Wikipedia (www.wikipedia.org, accessed June 9, 2010) says simply "a developed country is one that has a high income per capita" and "a developing country is a country with a relatively low standard of living." Although I would not normally recommend Wikipedia as a source of information, this definition captures the major distinction between the two groups. The specific measure that is usually used for determining a country's status is income per capita.

Using this measure, income per capita, according to the Economist Intelligence Unit (2006) the twenty-five developed countries of the world are: Australia, Austria, Belgium, Canada, Denmark, Finland, France, Germany, Gibraltar, Greece, Iceland, Ireland, Israel, Italy, Japan, Luxembourg, the Netherlands, New Zealand, Norway, Portugal, Spain, Sweden, Switzerland, United Kingdom, USA. All others are classified as emerging markets or transition economies.

While income per capita is traditionally used to classify countries as developed or developing, there are limitations to this measure, and it does not capture the quality of life that may be experienced in a particular country. An alternative is the Human Development Index (HDI), which incorporates a variety of additional measures, such as health care, education, social benefits, and so on. By and large, the countries that score high on per capita income also score high on the HDI and vice versa. Nevertheless, the HDI provides a better sense of what one will experience in a particular country. For example, Barbados, although a developing country, was number 30 on the HDI list, indicating a relatively high standard of living.

The following countries were classified (2009) as having a very high development level (again, note the inclusion of Hong Kong, which is part of the PRC):

> Andorra, Australia, Austria, Barbados, Belgium, Brunei Darussalam, Canada, China (SAR), Cyrus, Czech Republic, Denmark, Finland, France, Germany, Greece, Hong Kong, Iceland, Ireland, Israel, Italy, Japan, Korea (Republic of), Kuwait, Liechtenstein, Luxembourg, Malta, New Zealand, Norway, Portugal, Qatar, Singapore, Slovenia, Spain, Sweden, Switzerland, the Netherlands, United Arab Emirates, United Kingdom, USA.

There is a great deal of overlap between this list and the list of countries classified as "developed". Not surprisingly, because the developed countries are richer, they naturally can spend more on education, health care, and the other factors that contribute to the quality of life.

THE IMPACT OF LEVEL OF DEVELOPMENT

The developing world is characterized by fewer economic resources than the developed world. Simply, developing countries are poorer than developed ones. From a management perspective, the consequences of poverty are clear:

- People are concerned with basic needs or, in the "better-off" of these countries, with achieving economic stability.
- Infrastructure is limited; roads, railways, ports, and other physical facilities are nonexistent in some locations and only adequate in the "better-off" developing countries.
- Social services are limited; education, health, and other social services are nonexistent in some locations and only adequate in the "better-off" developing countries.
- Resources are scarce, and projects need to be clearly justified to warrant governmental or nongovernmental support.

In spite of the relatively high rating for some countries on the United Nations Development Index, the economic disparity between the developed and developing countries is startling in many ways. Some statistics illustrate the level of disparity that exists:

- The richest 20 percent of the world earns 86 percent of the world's GDP, the middle 60 percent earns 13 percent, and the poorest 20 percent only 1 percent.
- In 2007, the highest reported GDP per capita (adjusted for purchasing power) was in Luxembourg with $80,800 and the lowest was Congo with $300.

Of even greater concern is the growing disparity between the rich and poor countries. Comparisons of per capita GNP for the top and bottom 20 percent of all countries over the past almost two centuries show a dramatic increase in wealth disparities. In 1820 the ratio was 3:1; in 1870, 7:1; 1913, 11:1; 1960, 30:1; and in 1997, 74:1. There is no question that the rich have been growing richer, and the poor have not been catching up. This disparity is important from a management perspective, and managers in the developing countries feel disadvantaged by it. The lack of economic resources in the developing countries means that there are few resources for government expenditure on infrastructure.

The following examples illustrate the differentials in selected resources between the developed and developing countries:

- High-income countries consume 5,783 kilowatt hours of electricity per capita per year; middle-income countries consume 1,585; and low-income countries consume 188.
- High-income countries have 92 percent of their roads paved; middle-income countries have 51 percent paved; and low-income countries have 19 percent paved.
- High-income countries have 286 newspapers per 1,000 people; middle-income countries have 75; and low-income countries have 13.
- High-income countries have 1,300 radios per 1,000 people; middle-income countries have 383; and low-income countries have 147.
- High-income countries have 269 personal computers per 1,000 people; middle-income countries have 32; and low-income countries have 4.

- Developed countries have 253 doctors per 100,000 people; developing countries have 76.
- Tuberculosis rates are 15 percent in developed countries, 79 percent in developing countries.
- Low-birth-weight babies have incidence rates of 6 percent in developed countries, 18 percent in developing countries.
- Enrollment in primary school is close to 100 percent in developed countries and about 86 percent in developing countries. Enrollment in secondary school is 96 percent in developed countries and 60 percent in developing countries.

These comparisons illustrate the dimensions of the gap between the rich and poor countries. Richer countries have more to spend on infrastructure, both physical and intellectual. Developing countries have less to spend on infrastructure; thus they often lack roads, railways, and ports; their people have limited training; and medical care can be limited, as is access to information.

Access to information through the Internet is often identified as contributing positively to development and providing a means to overcome economic constraints. The Internet can potentially provide everything from basic schooling to contact with the best medical authorities and research scientists. There is little question that the Internet can provide substantial benefits for the poorer countries, but, as Bill Gates, founder of Microsoft, has noted, Internet access is not helpful when you have no water or electricity. The richest 20 percent of the world accounted for about 90 percent of Internet users. As long as that imbalance continues, one cannot think of the Internet as a tool for development. Yet the development of wireless communication technology may provide increased opportunities for the developing world, and some developing countries are doing well in terms of improving technology (United Nations 2000). This suggests potential for the developing world. Interestingly, low-technology products also provide opportunities. Wind-up radios have given low-cost easy access to information and news media in parts of Africa that had no such access previously. Cellphones are being used increasingly by poor farmers and people working in the fishing industry, in various parts of the developing world, to identify where the best markets are for their farm produce or fish catch.

An additional area of interest is the economic or income equality/inequality that exists within a country – that is, the disparity between the rich and the poor in a given country. This will be discussed in the next section.

INCOME INEQUALITY

Income inequality is measured by the Gini (named after an Italian researcher who first presented the idea of measuring the differences in incomes across countries) index or coefficient. Scores on the Gini index range from zero (perfect equality) to 100 (theoretically, complete inequality), therefore the lower a country's score, the less disparity there is. In the most recent Gini index published, the "better" countries included Bosnia-Herzegovina (26), Canada (32.6), Croatia (29), Czech Republic (25.4), Finland (26.9), Hungary (26.9), Japan (24.9), Norway (25.8), Romania (31), Slovakia (25.8), Sweden (25), Uzbekistan (26.8) – essentially eastern European and Scandinavian countries plus Canada and Japan. The "worse" countries were Argentina (52.8), Bolivia (60.1), Botswana (63), Brazil (58), Colombia (58.6) Costa Rica (49.9), El Salvador (52.4), Gambia (50.2), Haiti (59.2), Honduras (53.8), Lesotho (63.2), Malawi (50.3), Mali (50.5), Namibia (74.3), Niger (50.5), Panama (56.4), Papua New Guinea (50.9), Paraguay

(57.8), Peru (54.6), Swaziland (60.9), Zimbabwe (61) – essentially Central and South American and African countries plus Haiti and Papua New Guinea. The USA had a score of 40.8, higher than the "better" countries but lower than the "worse" ones, probably reflecting a large, relatively well-off middle class combined with very high executive salaries and a growing number of billionaires.

The Economist (May 15, 2010, "Banyan – the elusive fruits of inclusive growth", p. 50) discusses Asia's rapid economic growth over the past two decades and notes that since 1990 the number of people living in extreme poverty has been halved to less than 20 percent. On the negative side, the story goes on to say that poverty remains entrenched in these countries and that inequalities are rising fast. The real challenge, according to the story, is that economists are unclear about how to achieve inclusive growth. The assumption that growth in income would in time "trickle down" to the poorest has not proved to be correct. The Gini coefficient shows inequality rising in Asia in Bangladesh, Cambodia, China, Nepal, and Sri Lanka.

In addition to purely economic differences, there are demographic differences between the rich and poor countries. The following section summarizes some of the most important of these.

A NEGATIVE VIEW OF DEVELOPING COUNTRIES?

A poll of Europeans showed a negative view of developing countries, predominantly focused on poverty and illness (BBC Report, April, 2002). In many ways this is the reality of developing countries. As defined previously, these are the poorer countries of the world, so they exhibit the effects of being poor. These are also the aspects of developing countries that tend to be in the news, so most people in the developed world do not hear of the positive side of life in developing countries.

There is a more positive side to the equation, however. For example:

- per capita incomes have been growing in developing countries, and there is a growing middle class in many of these countries;
- some developing countries score quite high on the HDI, indicating that they are good places to live;
- several developing countries are experiencing high rates of growth;
- the developing countries represent a very substantial and growing market, and source of supply;
- concentrations of wealth in developing countries have allowed them to engage in outward international foreign direct investment.

Hans Rosling (www.gapminder.org) has argued that we should stop calling a group of countries developing. He presents information on GDP per capita (adjusted for purchasing power parity) and life expectancy to illustrate the changing picture of the wealth and health of nations over the past two hundred years. His statistics show a dramatic convergence among countries in terms of both wealth and health (as seen in life expectancy). While the poorest countries still lag behind in terms of both measures, most countries have moved upward in terms of both quite dramatically in recent decades. He says that the distinction between developed and developing was useful in the past, but that the distinction is no longer clear in today's world.

The next sections consider the positive side of developing countries and events of 2011.

THE NEW REALITY: THE NEW FRONTIER

The Economist (September 16–22, 2006) had a cover which proclaimed "Surprise! The power of the emerging world." A special report entitled "The new titans" is headlined by the following "China, India and other developing countries are set to give the world economy its biggest boost in the whole of history" and goes on to ask "what will that mean for today's rich countries?" (p. 3). As this chapter pointed out at the outset, the developing world includes most of the world's population. Improvements in these economies can therefore have an enormous impact on the global economy. The *Economist* article indicates that in 2005 the combined output of emerging (developing) economies reached a milestone of more than half of total world GDP (measured at purchasing power parity). In addition, their share of world exports had increased to 43 percent from 20 percent in 1970, they consumed over half the world's energy, and accounted for four-fifths of the growth in oil demand, and they hold over 70 percent of the world's foreign exchange reserves. A comparison on GDP percentage increases over a year earlier shows the emerging economies growing at a higher rate than the developed economies.

This is all good news for the poorer people of the world, suggesting that the gap between the rich and the poor, identified at the beginning of this chapter, may now start to move in the opposite direction. As the people of the developing countries become better off and have greater access to the goods and services that are now common in the developed world, what will this mean for management? From a management research perspective it is likely to mean that there will be more interest in these countries and their management. This chapter will need to be revised in a decade's time, and, there will be more literature to draw on, and perhaps quite different views on developing countries by then. Students concerned with management in developing countries should watch their progress with interest. It may be that the weight of China and India is such that these two countries need to be considered separately from the rest of the developing world.

Of particular interest today is the impact that the People's Republic of China will have on the world economy, as well as particular economies around the world. Cheap Chinese exports have been flooding around the world, to the delight of consumers in both the developing and developed world, but equally of concern to producers. Producers in developing countries may be particularly disadvantaged because they cannot compete with the reputedly artificially low wages and currency exchange rate maintained by the Chinese communist government. The growth in Chinese manufacturing and industry has been accompanied by a need for raw materials and resources and the People's Republic of China has moved globally to source this need. The Chinese have been investing around the world, including in Africa, the Caribbean, and Latin America, to ensure access to the supplies that it needs for its own manufacturing. This is changing relationships around the world. Developmentgateway.org, a website devoted to development issues (accessed November 29, 2006), noted that the potential impact of China's rapid growth on the USA and European Union has been well documented, but that less is known about its impact on the developing countries. An OECD working paper (number 252) by Blázquez-Lidoy et al. (2006) concluded that Latin America would benefit most from China's expansion.

At the same time as China is expanding, India is as well, and it was announced in late 2006, that WalMart, the American retailing giant, would open a chain of stores across India. This, too, changes world relationships. As China and India become more global, and companies such as Walmart (as it is now called) open in more countries, the question arises, will the countries of the world simply become more and more alike, as influences from one country or region spread across the world?

EVENTS OF 2011

The Middle East and North Africa became the focus of attention of the world in early 2011. This attention began with a relatively small event in Tunisia when a Tunisian street vendor set himself on fire (News Reports, December 17, 2010) in protest of the confiscation of his wares, and harassment and humiliation that was attributed to a municipal official and her aides. His act became the catalyst for the Tunisian Revolution, inciting demonstrations and riots throughout Tunisia, which led to President Zine El Abidine Ben Ali stepping down on January 14, 2011, after twenty-three years in power.

Protests in Egypt began on 25 January and ran for eighteen days. The Egyptian government briefly attempted to eliminate the nation's Internet access, in order to inhibit the protesters' ability to organize through social media. However, as tens of thousands protested on the streets of Egypt's major cities, President Mubarak dismissed his government, later appointing a new cabinet. Mubarak also appointed the first vice president in almost thirty years. On February 10, to the world's surprise, Mubarak ceded presidential power to Vice President Omar Suleiman. He announced that he would remain president until the end of his term, but when protests continued the next day, Suleiman announced that Mubarak had resigned from the presidency and transferred power to the armed forces of Egypt. The military dissolved the Egyptian Parliament, suspended the Constitution, and promised to lift the nation's thirty-year "emergency laws". It further promised to hold free, open elections within the next six months, or by the end of 2011 at the latest.

At the time of writing, the overall events of early 2011 can be briefly described as a wave of demonstrations in Tunisia and Egypt, a civil war in Libya, civil uprisings in Bahrain, Syria, and Yemen, major protests in Algeria, Iran, Iraq, Jordan, Morocco, and Oman, and minor protests in Djibouti, Kuwait, Lebanon, Mauritania, Saudi Arabia, and Western Sahara. The protests have included strikes, demonstrations, marches and rallies, and, perhaps most importantly, the use of social media, such as Facebook, Twitter, and YouTube, to organize, communicate, and raise awareness in the face of state attempts at repression and Internet censorship. These events are still progressing as this book is being finalized. We cannot know what the final outcome of these events will be, but we can say, with some certainty, that they will influence the way business is done in the Middle East and North Africa, and that managers in these countries will have to consider the protests, and the desires of the protestors, in their management approaches.

Some people would argue that it should have been easy to predict that the Arab world was ready for revolution, because of a history of political repression, economic stagnation and, interestingly, because of their youthful populations. Nevertheless, the unrest was unexpected to many, and the spread through the region was a surprise for many people. The protests had a major immediate impact on businesses in the region, as well as on those considering doing business there. Managers with an interest in the region are watching events with interest, and will continue to do so.

SUMMARY

This chapter has given the reader a broad overview of the situation that exists in developing countries, and has contrasted developing and developed countries. The chapter began by looking at some recent developments in global business activities that show a changing business world from a developing country perspective. The chapter looked at terminology of development and reviewed how these have changed over time. The chapter concluded with a look at the new reality in developing countries, especially in light of developments in countries such as India and the People's Republic of China. Throughout, it was stressed that within the group of countries classified as developing, there are vast differences from country to country. It is therefore simplistic to discuss "management in developing countries"; nevertheless, there are some characteristics which these countries share, and these can provide a basis to think about management issues. Readers are encouraged to explore the characteristics of a wide array of the developing countries to develop a better understanding of specific countries. In conclusion, readers are also reminded of the changing and dynamic nature of the business management environment – nowhere is this more the case than in the context of the developing countries today. This chapter has introduced the characteristics and dynamics of economic development; these characteristics and dynamics will be used in later chapters to explore the implications for managers and the practice of management.

LESSONS LEARNED

Having completed this chapter, you should feel comfortable discussing issues of development. You should be familiar with the terminology that has been used in the past to distinguish between developed and developing countries, as well as the current terminology. You should also understand the connotations of the various terms and why they have been seen as negative. You should appreciate the characteristics that generally distinguish developed countries from developing countries, and the implications of these characteristics for businesses operating in developing countries. You should also be aware that the world is changing and that these changes may have a major impact on the world of the future.

DISCUSSION QUESTIONS

1   Review events of 2011 and identify an event that you feel is especially relevant to managers in developing countries. Discuss the impact of the event on developing countries and managers in these countries.
2   Select a country in the developing world and review its economic performance over the past decade. Compare this performance to that of a developed country. Discuss what the comparison suggests.
3   Review the performance of each of the BRICS countries over the past year. Discuss how their performance compares to that of a developed country, such as the USA, and the implications for managers in these countries.

EXERCISES

1   Students are asked to review the terminology related to development and identify any "new" terminology. In small groups, students discuss the terminology in terms of the positives and

negatives of various terms. Each group is asked to develop its own terminology and be prepared to share this with the class, and explain why this terminology is appropriate.

2   Students are asked to review the events of 2011 in the Middle East and North Africa. In small groups, students discuss these events in terms of their likely impact on business and management in the region. Each group is asked to share its findings with the class.

Chapter 3

Characteristics of developing countries

OBJECTIVES

The purpose of the chapter is to examine the ways in which developing countries differ from developed ones. It also takes into account cultural differences, and examines how people in different cultures think and act. The objectives of the chapter are:

- To give the reader a better understanding of differences between developed and developing countries.
- To explore the demographic differences, including population growth and dispersion, age distribution, literacy and numeracy, and gender roles.
- To examine cultural values, using the Hofstede cultural values, and how they differ between developed and developing countries.
- To identify the political systems and how they relate to developments between these countries.
- To consider issues and perceptions of corruption and social responsibility between the developing and developed countries.
- To question whether countries are converging or diverging in terms of the concepts discussed in Chapter 2.
- To present the Happy Planet Index concerns about the environment and examine some of the findings and the implications of the research.

INTRODUCTION

Chapter 2 focused on the terminology of development, and how this terminology is essentially related to income per capita and the results of income per capita. There are several other ways in which developing countries differ from developed ones. These differences may also be related to income and poverty, but the relationship is not always clear-cut. In this chapter, these differences are examined. We begin with demographic differences, including population growth, population dispersion, age distribution, literacy and numeracy, and gender roles. We then look at cultural values and how these appear to differ between developed and developing countries, and also at political systems as they relate to development. In addition we examine the issue of perceptions of corruption, social responsibility, and the question of whether countries are converging or diverging in terms of the concepts previously discussed. Finally, we present a relatively new index, the Happy Planet Index, and discuss some of the findings of this research and the implications of these findings.

DEMOGRAPHY AND DEVELOPMENT

There are several important demographic differences between developed and developing countries. These include population growth, population dispersion, age distribution, literacy and numeracy levels, and gender roles (United Nations, 1998, 2000, 2005).

Population growth

Population growth rates were substantially higher in the developing world, at 2 percent, than in the developed, which grew at a rate of 0.6 percent for the period 1975 to 1997 (Figure 3.1 shows United Nations Population growth estimates from 1998). This is also evident in fertility rates in the developing world, which are at five conceptions per woman as compared to 1.9 in the developed world. These differences are expected to continue for some time. Combined with the increasing income disparity previously outlined, this means a growing proportion of the world will be poor and a smaller percentage of the world's population will control an

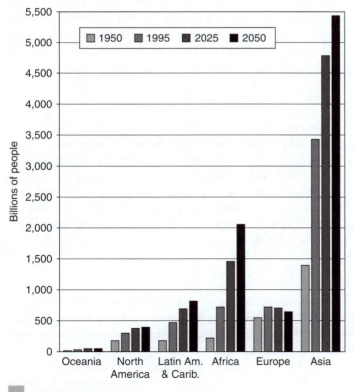

Figure 3.1 *Population growth estimates*
Source: adapted from United Nations (1998)

increasingly greater share of the resources and wealth. This situation does not sound like one that is sustainable, and managers need to be aware of the tensions that are created by such a situation, even at the individual or local level, as the apparent level of wealth and standard of living of foreigners from the developed world are increasingly resented. For example, the news of billion dollar bonuses in the developed world's financial industry was news in the developing world as well as the developed. It is difficult when you earn a dollar a day and can barely survive, to accept that elsewhere in the world people are enormously wealthy. Among other results, it fuels a desire among some in developing countries to leave home and attempt to get to a developed country, no matter what the cost (often, even the possibility of losing one's life). At the same time, the developing world's positive attributes of a large potential market and workforce are increasing as its populations and economies grow.

Population dispersion

The world as a whole is becoming more urban. About 50 percent of the world's population lives in cities, but the developing world is still substantially more rural than the developed world. According to www.globalchange.umich.edu, the human population has lived a rural lifestyle through most of history; however, the world's population is quickly becoming urbanized as people migrate to the cities. In 1950, less than 30 percent of the world's population lived in cities. This number grew to 47 percent in the year 2000 (2.8 billion people), and it is expected to grow to 60 percent by the year 2025. Developed nations have a higher percentage of urban residents than less developed countries; however, urbanization is occurring rapidly in many less developed countries, and it is expected that most urban growth will occur in less developed countries during the next decades. In developing countries, the cities are seen as the places where opportunities exist, and major movements of people from the rural areas to the urban often result in cities that are overcrowded and underserviced, with a substantial number of people living in very poor circumstances.

Age distribution

The average age of populations in developed countries is increasing while that in developing countries is declining. In 1995 the over-65 population in developed countries was about 15 percent compared to 5 percent in developing countries. This gap was predicted to widen by 2015 to 18 percent over 65 in developed countries and a constant 5 percent in developing countries. About one-third (33 percent) of the population in developing countries is under fifteen compared to one-fifth (20 percent) in developed countries. Developing countries thus have an increasing abundance of younger, less experienced workers. If education and training are available for these workers, they could provide the base for a productive workforce for the globe.

Literacy and numeracy

Literacy and numeracy rates are higher in the developed countries. Yet there are developing countries with good educational systems, and there is concern about the deterioration of education in North America and Europe. Nevertheless, on average, people in developed countries have access to better education, which results in functional literacy and numeracy as the norm. This is not the case in the developing world. The lower literacy and numeracy rates in the workforce of the developing world has major implications for the type of work that can be done, the use of technology, the testing and training that is needed, the need for supervision, and the opportunities for advancement.

A U.S. company with a subsidiary in a small island state hired a local manager to run the subsidiary. The local manager came well recommended by local contacts, was intelligent, articulate, and related well to the local workers. She was interviewed by a representative from headquarters and seemed to be an ideal choice for the position. Initially, operations went well, but it soon became clear that there was a problem as major discrepancies surfaced in terms of inventory levels and accuracy counts of parts shipped. The underlying problem was finally uncovered: The manager could not do the basic arithmetic of adding and subtracting, and operating the subsidiary relied on these skills. No one had thought to ask about these skills because they were simply assumed.

GENDER ROLES

Gender role distinctions are more pronounced in developing countries. In some places, laws discriminate against women in terms of land ownership, family inheritance, education, and a variety of other factors. Women often do much of the work within the family household and receive little, if any, compensation for their labor. Where there are minimum-wage regulations, these may favor men. The United Nations computes a gender-related development index that incorporates male/female differences in life expectancy, education, literacy, and GDP per capita. Countries that score high on the overall development index also score high on the gender development index. The richer and more developed countries thus appear to provide more equal opportunities for women than do the poorer, developing countries. These differences in how women are viewed and treated can cause problems and obstacles to success. For example:

- Where women are in a subordinate position, it is often impossible to make full use of their expertise and experience. Managers from developed countries working in less developed ones may have problems implementing the equal opportunity policies that they feel are appropriate because people in these countries may be offended by such policies.
- Male managers from developing countries may have difficulty interacting with women counterparts from developed countries and may feel compromised, both religiously and socially, by such interactions.
- Women from developed countries working in countries where women are treated differently may face barriers to effective performance.
- When women's role is defined as homemaker, it is difficult for women to work outside the home.

Although there is still substantial discrimination in favor of men, particularly in the business and professional world, the role of women is changing in many developing countries. Women are playing an increasingly active role in business. These women are often especially committed, hardworking, and innovative. They can be seen to provide an additional benefit for those who do business in these countries. An example of successful women in developing countries is offered by the Grameen Bank of Bangladesh, which has made a series of small loans to women to support their developing businesses. The Grameen Bank has found that their small businesswomen clients are successful and meticulous about repaying their loans. Interestingly, in the English-speaking Caribbean, there is substantial concern over the marginalization of young men, with the vast majority of university graduates being women.

27

A recent book entitled *Successful Professional Women of the Americas: From Polar Winds to Tropical Breezes* (Punnett et al., 2006) illustrates the potential of women in spite of the challenges they often face. This book surveyed and interviewed women in Argentina, Brazil, Canada, the Caribbean (Barbados, Jamaica and St. Vincent and the Grenadines), Chile, Mexico, and the USA. In all countries, the women interviewed and surveyed were found to be both professionally and personally successful and satisfied with their lives.

CULTURAL COMPARISONS

People in developing countries, in general, are more collective than those in developed countries, power differentials are more pronounced in many developing countries, and people are somewhat more averse to uncertainty and risk. In addition, there is some evidence that on average people in developing countries are lower on need for achievement and more external in terms of locus of control than people in developed countries (Punnett, 2009). Figure 3.2 compares developed and developing countries on masculinity/femininity, uncertainty avoidance, individualism, and power–distance based on Hofstede's (1984) measures of cultural values. As this comparison illustrates, the clearest distinctions are lower individualism and higher power–distance in the developing countries.

Of course, these value dimensions were measured in the early 1980s, and we can expect that they may change over time, particularly in response to the changing environment of the twenty-first century. As countries become wealthier, and their middle classes increase in size, their cultural values will also likely change. Conversely, cultural norms and values are slow to change, and they can be expected to influence behavior for several generations as they gradually tend to adapt to changing development conditions.

POLITICS AND DEVELOPMENT

There also appear to be some political differences between developed and developing countries. Generally, the developed countries have more well-established democratic processes, while the developing countries are more likely to be ruled by a powerful individual or an elite group, possibly a coalition of tribal leaders; in addition, developing countries with democracies are often new democracies. Market approaches are also somewhat different between the two sets of countries. Developed countries, to a large extent, separate government and business, and support free markets and free enterprise. In developing countries there is often a closer link between government and business, which is considered appropriate, and the state is seen as the agent of economic change. Linkages between prominent business leaders and government policy-making bodies, likely regarded as conflicts of interest in developed countries, are often common in developing countries where the ruling elite comprise or are linked with the main players in the private sector. There is an interesting link between economic freedom and income levels as well. Gwartney and Larson of the Fraser Institute (2002) described economic freedom as encompassing personal choice, voluntary exchange, freedom to compete, and protection of person and property. The Institute reports that as incomes increase, economic freedom also increases. Consequently, the developing countries have scores which are lower on economic freedom than the more developed countries.

The United Nations reports that the percentage of "some form" of democracy in country-level governance has increased worldwide from 28 percent in 1974 to 61 percent in 1998.

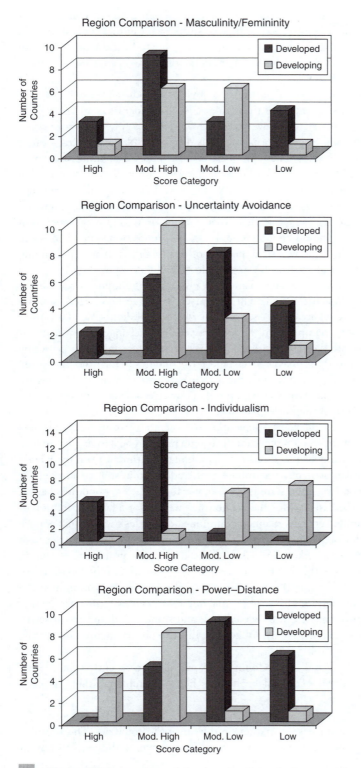

Figure 3.2 *Comparison of developed and developing countries on cultural values*

This increase suggests a substantial move toward democracy; at the same time it confirms that this is a new movement. Thus, many countries classified as democracies in this context are still in the formative stages of implementing democratic principles. Prior to World War II, most of the poorer countries were colonies of the richer countries. In the thirty years after the war, most of these countries became independent.

Democracy emphasizes individualism and equality, a low power–distance in Hofstede's terminology. "One person, one vote" exemplifies these values. Non-democratic states clearly do not subscribe to these values. In such states, power is usually vested in a few powerful people who consider those belonging to their in-group as particularly deserving. New democracies may nominally subscribe to democratic values, but seldom have these values had time to become an ingrained part of the society. Differences in political values show up in the "rule of law" in developed countries and the "rule of man" in many developing countries. The rule of law suggests that there should be a clear statement of what is right or wrong and that it should be applied equally to all people. The rule of man suggests that what is right or wrong may depend on the situation and that each situation should be interpreted by those in positions of power. Some societies believe that rules apply the same way to all people, others that rules change depending on circumstances. Democracies typically subscribe to the rule of law philosophy.

Democracy, although it often means regular changes in government, implies order and a certain amount of predictability. When elections will take place, who can be elected, and the platforms of those vying to be elected are clearly set out. Newly formed democracies aspire to the same ideals but are often unable to implement them effectively. Thus changes of government may combine democratic ideals with those in positions of power seeking to retain their power by any means, or people demonstrating en masse to change governments before the appointed time. Non-democracies are frequently stable because the people in power are expected to remain for the long term and their views are known; however, those in power can be overthrown or die, and the leadership can change suddenly and unexpectedly.

In the developed world, there is a substantial separation between government and business and, by and large, there is support for free markets and free enterprise. In developing countries, conflict of interest is not seen as a concern, and businesspeople may continue to run their businesses while serving in top government posts as minister of trade or minister of finance, for example. In many developing countries, the state is also seen as the agent of economic change, and state planning is believed to be essential for the economy as well as for a fair distribution of resources. The state is paramount in centrally planned communist countries such as the People's Republic of China, Cuba, North Korea, and Vietnam, but even where developing countries have free market economies, they are more likely to look to the state to play an important role in overcoming the failures or excesses of the free market system. For example, in the kingdoms of the Middle East (Bahrain, Kuwait, Oman, Qatar, Saudi Arabia, the United Arab Emirates) the monarchs still rule absolutely and therefore have substantial influence on how business is carried out; at the same time foreign investment can be welcomed, and some kingdoms have laws to protect these investments (Punnett et al., 2006). Of course, this can change at any time, as the events of 2011 have illustrated.

Most of the countries currently listed as developing were, until quite recently (the 1950s), colonies of the European powers. This colonial heritage is likely to influence their business practices in a number of ways:

- Colonies were traditionally producers for markets in the European countries. This means that for many colonies, the concept of marketing is largely unknown, with the focus put on production instead.

- Colonies were in subordinate positions and instructed by the "colonial masters" (as the European powers were called) in matters of government, economics and business. Decisions were made elsewhere, and in many of these countries there is still a tendency to look to others for decisions.
- A top down decision-making style was enforced and accepted. Decisions were made at the master level, with little input from the local level, and these decisions were not questioned. This remains in the management style of many companies in developing countries.

It is difficult to be certain of the influence of colonization in a postcolonial society, but one can be certain that there is an influence. Further, as countries move away from colonial times, we can expect their management practices and styles to change. Possibly they will become more like the developed world, in terms of management, but it is equally possible that they will provide their own unique approaches to management, and that these approaches will be adapted and adopted by countries that currently are considered more developed. The evolving management dynamic will be interesting for management scholars and students.

There is also apparently a link between economic freedom and income levels as well. The Fraser Institute describes economic freedom as encompassing personal choice, voluntary exchange, freedom to compete, protection of person and property, and institutions and policies as consistent with economic freedom when they provide an infrastructure for voluntary exchange, and protect individuals and their property from aggressors seeking to use violence, coercion and fraud to seize things that do not belong to them – this description includes much of what we associate with democracy (Gwartney and Larson, 2002). The Institute reported that countries in the top quintile of economic freedom have a per capita gross national income on average of U.S.$23,450, those in the next quintile drop to U.S.$12,390, then U.S.$6,235, U.S.$4,365, and U.S.$2,556 for those in the lowest quintile. As incomes increase, economic freedom also increases (Gwartney and Larson, 2002: 20). In 2008, the top ten countries in terms of economic freedom were Hong Kong (note that Hong Kong is not in fact a country) Singapore, Ireland, Australia, USA, New Zealand, Canada, Chile, Switzerland, United Kingdom; and the bottom ten were Venezuela, Bangladesh, Belarus, Iran, Turkmenistan, Burma, Libya, Zimbabwe, Cuba, North Korea (www.heritage.org accessed 28 January, 2008).

A Canadian consultant tells the following story about a project in the People's Republic of China. The Canadian consultant met with a group of Chinese managers from the Chinese automotive parts industry. The Chinese asked what they needed to do to sell their products in Canada. The consultant responded that the requirements were the right product, consistent high quality at a competitive price, with reliable, on-time delivery. The consultant expected the Chinese managers to accept this as a challenge, but something they could address. Instead, the Chinese expressed surprise. "Why?" they asked. It became clear with further discussion that because the consultant's client was the Canadian government and the consultant was accompanied by the Canadian trade commissioner, the Chinese managers had assumed that the Canadian government could simply require Canadian auto companies to buy Chinese parts. The consultant's assumption was that these business arrangements were made on a company-to-company basis; the Chinese managers' assumption was that these would be government-to-government arrangements. These different assumptions about the political environment were based on the different structures and attitudes to which each party was accustomed in its respective home location.

EVIDENCE OF CORRUPTION

International managers are also interested in the degree of corruption that exists in different countries, and there is a perception that developing countries are more corrupt than developed ones. This is supported by Transparency International's Corruption Perceptions Index (www.transparency.org accessed 18 July, 2010). This index is prepared on the basis of information provided by an array of people with experience doing business in the various countries, and it ranks countries from least corrupt (number 1) to most corrupt (number 180). The 2009 index ranks New Zealand number 1, followed by Denmark, then Sweden and Singapore, followed by Switzerland, Finland and the Netherlands, then Australia, Canada, and Iceland (the top ten). At the other end of the scale, Somalia is at the bottom, with Afghanistan, Myanmar (Burma), Sudan, Iraq, Chad, Uzbekistan, Turkmenistan, Iran and Haiti making up the bottom ten. The USA is number 19 on the list – not in the top ten but among the least corrupt. Not all developing countries rank low; for example, Barbados is number 20, is just below the USA, and Qatar and St. Lucia rank next, followed by Chile and Uruguay.

Rankings on an index such as this change, of course, from year to year, and managers should be sure to have the most up to date data when making business decisions. Interestingly, however, the changes have not been dramatic, generally the countries with better scores remain among the least corrupt, and the worst countries remain among the most corrupt. This suggests that corruption is often deeply ingrained in the fabric of a society and that it is difficult to change corrupt practices. Also, it is important to recognize that definitions of corruption differ, so what may be considered normal behavior in one location, may be considered corruption elsewhere. An example that is often given is a payment to customs officials to enhance the movement of goods through customs – in some countries, this is considered the normal way to do business, in others, it is considered highly improper.

ETHICS AND CORPORATE SOCIAL RESPONSIBILITY IN THE CONTEXT OF DEVELOPMENT

Ethics and corporate social responsibility are critical considerations for managers everywhere They may be particularly a concern in developing countries because what is considered ethical in a developed country may be considered unethical in a developing country and vice versa. For example, in the USA lobbying is considered a normal activity – companies and industries send registered lobbyists to influence government representatives, asking these government representatives to make decisions that will positively affect the company or industry, and offering information and political support in return. In other countries this is considered unethical, and the equivalent of bribing the government. Similarly, in North America it is normal to tip restaurant waiters and taxi drivers, but people from many parts of the world are mystified, or even insulted, by this practice, because the waiters and taxi drivers are simply performing an expected service…doing their job. In parts of Africa, Asia and Latin America, it is customary to tip customs officials, while North Americans see this as bribery, because it is intended to get preferential treatment.

Developing countries have often been portrayed as more corrupt than developed countries, as identified in the previous section. That is, there is more need for unreported payments and gifts in business dealings. These payments may be to civil servants, government officials, or other businesses. While this suggests that managers in developing countries may have to deal with issues of "extra payments", it is worth noting that it is often managers from the developed countries who make these payments and contribute to the continuation of the practice. The mismanagement of funds in Iraq by U.S. companies, and the scandals relating to Australian companies and the food for oil program in Iraq are two illustrations of the fact that corruption has to exist on both sides.

Other ethical issues that may arise in developing countries have to do with the laws in these countries, or sometimes the lack of laws and regulations. For example, child labor is still common in many parts of the developing world, slavery continues, harmful pesticides are allowed, environmental protection is lax, working conditions poor, and so on. In some cases, a practice such as child labor, which is seen as "unethical" not to mention illegal in a developed country, is necessary in a particular developing country for families to survive. In other situations, such as killing elephants and poaching ivory, the practice may be considered unethical in the developing country, but the country, because it is poor, lacks the resources to police existing regulations.

CONVERGENCE VERSUS DIVERGENCE AMONG COUNTRIES

The global business environment that is today's reality means that national economies are more closely linked than in the past. A variety of factors suggest that national cultures may become more similar because of globalization – these can be thought of as forces for convergence. For example:

- Increased trade means that people around the world are exposed to products from other countries (many people point to the fact that people around the world wear basically the same jeans and t-shirts).
- Increased foreign investment means that companies take their corporate cultures and practices into new locations and also learn from these new locations, taking aspects of culture and practice home (many people identify similarities in subsidiaries from Argentina to Zimbabwe).
- Increased travel and communication for business and personal purposes means that people experience and learn about different behaviors, and adopt and adapt these to suit their preferences (many people comment on the availability in every big city of restaurants serving foods from every corner of the world).
- Increased regional and global trading agreements and organizations have as their mandate the standardization of trade arrangements across countries (many people decry the loss of specialized products because of these agreements).
- The advent of the Internet and the consequent globalization of the media has meant that common awareness of events around the world is the norm (many people listen to radio stations ranging from the BBC to NPR and Al Jazeera on their computers).
- Shared global concerns, such as global warming, which are not defined by national boundaries, require global responses and lead to shared values (solutions found in one location need to be shared by all).

All of these factors suggest that we are moving towards a global culture and greater global integration, with less importance for the nation state. In addition, as developing countries' economies grow and improve, we can expect that their citizens will want many of the consumer goods currently common in the developed world. At the same time, there are other forces leading to divergence. Developing countries may want a stronger voice for their nation states – listen to the news, and this becomes obvious. There are also still major differences between developed and developing countries. Consider some of the following:

■ Terrorist attacks around the world illustrate the vast differences that some people perceive between "us" and "them."

■ Religious differences have often pitted Christianity against Islam, Hinduism against Islam, Catholic against Protestant, Shia against Sunni, and so on.

■ People are proud of their cultural uniqueness and seek to maintain their cultural values, sometimes trying to legislate these (for example, the French-language "police" are responsible for maintaining the purity of French used in France). In Canada, there was a move in 2010 to introduce Sharia law for Muslims for certain family matters.

■ Jeans and t-shirts may be popular around the world, but equally, women wear the traditional Middle-Eastern veil in London, New York, and Toronto.

■ Immigration has led to a mix of peoples around the world, but these immigrants often live in ethnic communities within cities and maintain their national and cultural characteristics within these communities.

■ Extensive exposure to foreigners and foreign media can increase awareness of home values which contrast to these, and are seen as especially "good."

There seems evidence, therefore, that there are still major differences to be found around the world, and that cultural differences are likely to persist. This is likely to remain the case for developed/developing differences, simply because of the major economic gap that continues between countries.

As noted earlier, the United Nations' (2010) World Investment Report had a focus on carbon reduction. The report said that developed countries should be encouraged to increase their financial and technical support for low carbon initiatives in developing countries. It also said that International Financial Institutions should actively support moves to low carbon options, and public-private partnerships to work on low carbon technologies. The suggestion is also put forward to establish a low carbon technical assistance center to support developing countries' formulating and implementing climate change mitigation strategies and plans. This suggests that incorporating carbon issues into discussions of levels of development will become more important in the future, and that managers will have to be aware of how countries score relative to their carbon footprint. The following section discusses an index that combines carbon use and economic well-being.

THE HAPPY PLANET INDEX

The world in 2011 was concerned about the environment. There were major conferences and publications about the need to reduce the carbon footprint of countries around the world, and the fears about the impact of global warming were real for many people. In this environmental context, managers are beginning to ask how they can succeed financially while taking the environment into account. Some managers are themselves concerned about these issues, others see them as presenting an opportunity to show what good corporate citizens their companies are. The Happy Planet Index (HPI) provides a way of viewing the success of countries, taking into account their impact on the planet. This viewpoint may become more and more relevant in the coming years.

In this section a different, newly developed index is discussed. This index is called the Happy Planet Index and it has been developed and promoted by the New Economic Forum.

As the previous sections have shown, there are many ways of looking at differences between groups of countries. A major focus for a long time has been economic; such as growth in economic size, GDP, wealth, and other similar measures. There are many people who believe that these measures are limited and do not capture the realities of the world we live in. This concern has become especially salient because of the current concern with climate change and our carbon footprints. In Chapter 2 the Human Development Index (HDI) was discussed, an alternative to economic measures that seeks to incorporate quality of life as well as economic factors when comparing countries. Several developing countries, it was pointed out, score quite highly on the HDI, even though, in general, GDP per capita is broadly correlated with HDI scores – that is, developed countries generally score higher than developing ones on the HDI.

The pursuit of economic growth, with its GDP, has not resulted in a stable and well-off world. The world is facing a situation of diminishing natural resources and unpredictable climate change. In this context, the HPI was launched in July 2006 as a radical departure from the previous focus on GDP. The report identified health and a positive experience of life as universal human goals, and the natural resources that our human systems depend upon as fundamental inputs. The HPI proposes that a successful society is one that can support good lives that "don't cost the Earth." The HPI measures progress towards this target – the ecological efficiency with which happy and healthy lives are supported.

The second Happy Planet Index (HPI 2.0) was based on improved data sets for 143 countries, covering 99 per cent of the world's population. (See the Happy Planet Index 2.0 "Why good lives don't have to cost the Earth," www.happyplanetindex.org; accessed September 20, 2010.) Scores on the index range from 0 to 100 – with high scores only achievable by meeting all three targets embodied in the index – high life expectancy, high life satisfaction, and a low ecological footprint.

The following summarizes some of the main results of HPI 2.0:

- Costa Rica has the highest HPI score (76.1 out of 100). Costa Rica also has the highest life satisfaction in the world. Costa Ricans have the second-highest average life expectancy in the New World (second only to Canada). Yet their carbon footprint is low. A footprint of 2.1 global hectares or less is considered "consuming its fair share of natural resources" (termed "one planet living"), and Costa Rica is just above this at 2.3.
- Of the ten countries following Costa Rica, all but one is in Latin America. The Latin American and Caribbean nations have the highest mean HPI score for any region (59 out of 100).
- The bottom ten HPI scores were all encountered in sub-Saharan African countries, with Zimbabwe bottom of the table with an HPI score of 16.6 out of 100.
- Developed nations are in the middle. The highest-placed Western nation is the Netherlands – 43rd out of 143. The UK is midway down the table – 74th, behind Germany, Italy, and France. It is just behind Georgia and Slovakia, but is ahead of Japan and Ireland. The USA is low on the list at 114th.

Some of the countries that score well are small islands (including the Dominican Republic, Jamaica, Cuba, and the Philippines). In contrast, the countries that are meant to represent successful development do not do very well. Unfortunately, no country successfully achieves the three goals of high life satisfaction, high life expectancy and "one-planet living".

The HPI 2.0 also looked at changes over time for countries where data was available. The results are not encouraging:

- Most of the countries have increased their HPI scores marginally between 1990 and 2005, the three largest countries in the world (China, India, and the USA) have all seen their HPI scores drop in that time.
- There are positive movements in some countries (for example, in Germany – an increase of 23 percent between 1990 and 2005, Russia – up 30 percent, and Brazil – up 13 percent). However, most OECD countries' HPI declined from the 1960s to the late 1970s. They have made some gains since, but scores were higher in 1961 than in 2005.
- In the OECD countries, life satisfaction and life expectancy combined have increased 15 percent over the forty-five-year period from 1961 to 2005, but ecological footprints per head had increased by 72 percent.

A clear message of the work done to produce the HPI is that it is possible to live long happy lives with a relatively limited carbon footprint. The contrast between Costa Rica and the USA illustrates this. Costa Ricans live slightly longer on average than Americans and report much higher levels of life satisfaction, yet have a footprint which is less than a quarter the size on a per capita basis. People in the Netherlands live on average more than a year longer than people in the USA and have similar levels of life satisfaction, yet their per capita ecological footprint is less than half the size.

The report points out that countries with the same ecological footprint support lives with differing levels of well-being and health. Vietnam and Cameroon have the same ecological footprints (1.3 global hectares), but people in Cameroon cannot expect to live more than 50 years, and reported very low life satisfaction, while the Vietnamese have a high life expectancy (73.7 years) and a higher level of life satisfaction than people in Cameroon. The Vietnamese also reported a life expectancy higher than that found in many European countries and a correspondingly higher level of life satisfaction (6.5). These examples show that life expectancy and satisfaction are not necessarily dependent on increasing economic wealth, consumption, and use of resources.

The HPI provides an interesting alternative way of looking at how well the countries of the world are "developing." Countries with the same ecological footprint support lives with differing levels of well-being and health.

If one plots the HPI against GDP/per capita adjusted for purchasing power, richer, more developed countries clearly experience a higher level of well-being and the poorest countries tend to have the lowest well-being. So, once again there appears to be a divide between the rich developed world and the poor developing world. According to the HPI report, the most important gains in terms of both life expectancy and life satisfaction occur over the first £10,000 (approximately U.S.$16,500) of GDP distribution – beyond that, there is little systematic difference between nations. The most important lesson seems to be that countries, such as Costa Rica, can achieve high levels of life satisfaction, at a relatively low level of GDP per capita, while maintaining a high ecological standard. If Costa Rica can achieve this, surely all the countries of the world can aspire to reaching these and higher goals.

SUMMARY

This chapter looked at a variety of additional factors that differ between developing and developed countries. The chapter discussed demographic differences, including population growth, population dispersion, age distribution, literacy and numeracy, and gender roles. It also considered cultural values and how these appear to differ between developed and developing countries, and political systems variations as they relate to development. The chapter examined the issue of perceptions of corruption, social responsibility, and the question of whether countries are converging or diverging in terms of the concepts previously discussed. Finally, it presented a relatively new index, the Happy Planet Index, and discussed some of the findings of this research and the implications of these findings.

LESSONS LEARNED

Having completed this chapter you should be able to examine the differences between developing and developed countries. In addition:

- You should be able to analyze sociocultural values and political systems between developing and countries and how they impact on development.
- You should be able to examine and understand the issue of ethics in international operations.
- You should be able to discuss the subtleties of legal and illegal payments and be attuned to such cultural nuances that affect these payments.
- You should be able to discuss the Happy Planet Index and the challenges managers face in balancing concerns about human well-being and the environmental while pursuing economic goals.

DISCUSSION QUESTIONS

1   As a manager, examine sociocultural values and political systems as they relate to development in developing and developed countries.
2   Discuss how the countries of the world are developing in terms of economics while maintaining high ecological standards.
3   Contemporary international managers will need to demonstrate a higher level of skill than those exhibited by traditional managers in the past. What do you think these skills are? They are also faced with ethical dilemmas not common to their domestic counterparts. How can they better prepare and equip themselves to deal with these dilemmas?

EXERCISE

Choose two countries, one developed and the other developing. Discuss and give a comparative study on the demographic differences, population growth, age distribution, literacy and numeracy, and the gender roles.

Chapter 4

Management issues and examples

OBJECTIVES

This chapter introduces a model of management and discusses the five processes of management that make up the model. The chapter also gives a comparative study of management in the People's Republic of China (PRC) and India, and helps the reader understand management practices in developing countries.

The objectives of the chapter are:

- To explain how management models in developing countries differ from those in developed countries.
- To identify management processes and how culture influences them.
- To consider how important it is for managers from developed countries to be sensitized and understand the culture of developing countries and vice versa.
- To identify and highlight the similarities, cultural differences, and differences in management approaches between the PRC and India.
- To understand the management practices found around the world.
- To help the reader understand that managers in the PRC and India face many of the same challenges and opportunities; and that they find varying ways to deal with these challenges and take advantage of the opportunities.

INTRODUCTION

As pointed out in Chapter 2, the countries that are categorized as developing cover a very wide range, with many differences in level of development, culture, politics, history, and so on. All these factors influence management, so they must be considered in any specific country. Nevertheless, pick up any book or text entitled simply "Management" and you will find these make an even greater assumption – that management can be discussed from a global perspective. In effect, these books are written for an audience in the developed world and are based on experiences of managers in these countries. In this chapter, I take the perspective of managers in developing countries and use the characteristics outlined in Chapter 2 to draw inferences regarding management practices. In addition, I draw on existing literature about management in specific countries. I look at the People's Republic of China and India, two very large countries that are growing rapidly economically, and which have been the subject of much interest in recent years.

There is relatively little research on management in developing countries. Das et al. (2009) found that research papers published in mainstream economic journals are linked to level of development. They found that countries with the lowest incomes and weakest economies received the least attention in the literature; for example, over a twenty-year period they identified four papers on Burundi and more than 37,000 on the United States. Similarly in management, Thomas commented in 1996 and Baruch in 2001 that examinations of management have focused on locations in the industrialized world, particularly North America and Western Europe, resulting in management theories that are biased. Bruton (2010) said that there was limited research on the poorer countries of the world, and identified only a small number of articles dealing with issues associated with poor countries in the past two decades. In addition, Perez-Bates et al. (2010) identified a dominance of North American-based authors (84 percent of published articles) in what they considered core management journals, with only about 9 percent from Western Europe and 7 percent from the rest of the world. This evidence makes it clear that we know little about management in "the rest of the world".

There is some literature on specific developing countries, and readers with an interest in a specific country should seek out these studies. Unfortunately, this literature is often not available outside of the country of origin, and rarely are translations done, so access can be limited. In recent years there has been a substantial interest in the People's Republic of China and some research on management has been done comparing management in the PRC to the USA and other developed countries. In India there is a substantial body of indigenous management literature. The same is true of some Latin American, African, and Middle-Eastern countries. The so-called BRIC countries – Brazil, Russia, India, China – have recently been the focus of some interest, and in 2011 a conference among representatives of these countries as well as South Africa, led to the acronym BRICS, and South Africa is one of the African countries where substantial research has been done. Overall, there appears to be a burgeoning interest in developing and emerging economies, and we can expect management literature on these countries to increase in the coming years.

Existing management theories are based on the developed countries, and it is not clear which theories apply in developing countries and which do not. Because of this, it is very difficult to make statements about management in developing countries. The best approach is to look at the factors that have been identified as defining developing countries and make informed judgments about how these are likely to affect management, necessarily using the lexicon and conceptual constructs of the available literature, which is based on management in the developed world. In the following sections we look at a typical model of management and examine how the characteristics of developing countries can interact with aspects of this model. This model is one that you will find, in some form, in most texts on management, so it is a Western-based model, even though we consider it from a developing country perspective.

MANAGEMENT AND CHARACTERISTICS OF DEVELOPING COUNTRIES

Management has traditionally been described in terms of a process, and five activities which make up the management process – planning, organizing, staffing, directing, and controlling – are

Figure 4.1 *The management process: general*

usually discussed as the bases of management (see Figure 4.1). These are often portrayed in texts as sequential and iterative. Management begins with planning which sets the strategies, objectives, and goals for an organization – planning drives the need for and style of organization and other management activities intended to help achieve plans. Organizing is the activity of dividing up the tasks that have to be undertaken to carry on the day to day work in order for the organization to be successful. This is followed by staffing, where people and associated resources are identified to carry out the necessary functions to achieve plans. Staffing is followed by leading, which ensures that staff behave in desirable ways that result in achieving plans. Leading is followed by controlling, an activity which is designed to measure progress towards plans and provide feedback to stimulate corrective action.

This model of management will be used to discuss how the management activities in developing countries may differ from that in the developed countries. First, however, it is important to look at the model itself and its Western biases. The process in the model is based on a sequential, logical, rational set of discrete activities which are typical of a Western, developed country view of the world. The model assumes control over the environment, so that making plans, designing structures, choosing people for specific jobs, and measuring outcomes, are all reasonable activities.

Non-Western countries often do not see the world in the same straight line, sequenced pattern. Time in many non-Western societies has been described as analog rather than digital and the context of communication is as important, or more important, than the content. A contrast of Saudi Arabian decision-making with that of the USA talks of the Saudis circling while the Americans move in a linear direction (from the movie, *Going International*). Many non-Western countries believe more in the role of fate and do not assume that people have significant control over their environment.

These few identified fundamental differences in world-view may mean that the very term "management" will mean something quite different in some developing countries, if it can be thought to exist at all. Nevertheless, the management model that is the norm in developed, Western countries will be used as a template for this discussion. Developing countries have generally been found to be somewhat more collective than developed countries, somewhat more accepting of power differentials, somewhat more averse to uncertainty, and more fatalistic (Hofstede, 1984). All of these attributes are likely to influence interpersonal behavior and how the processes of management are carried out, as the following illustrates.

Planning

Collectivism suggests that planning will generally be a group activity and the idea of consensus will be important. At the same time, acceptance of power differentials suggests that ultimately decisions will be made by those in positions of power (however attained), although input may be sought from subordinates. Preference for certainty/aversion to uncertainty adds to the likelihood that subordinates will look to their superiors for decisions, because this eliminates a degree of risk. In other words, subordinates will tend to try to anticipate the choices of their superiors, rather than examine alternatives not thought likely to gain acceptance by superiors. Preference for certainty may suggest a need for careful decision-making, with contingency plans; however, this is not likely to be the case where the society is fatalistic. Fatalism implies an acceptance of the will of a supreme force or set of forces without question, and this may in turn make planning in detail seem contrary to this acceptance. In practice, it may give rise to delays in implementing plans to ensure that all last-minute surprises can be accommodated. During 2010, the Indian authorities were accused of having wasted most of the seven years they had to complete the preparations for the 2010 Commonwealth Games; reportedly they constantly ignored the warnings of the Commonwealth Games governing body about not being finished in time. The Indian culture has sometimes been described a fatalistic, and perhaps we see this fatalism at work in this situation.

Organizing

Collectivism suggests that work will be organized on a group or team basis, with tasks to be accomplished by groups rather than individuals. Acceptance of power differentials likely means that clear-cut hierarchies will be established, with power residing at the top. Preference for certainty/aversion to uncertainty means that rules, policies, and procedures will be important and that employees will want a clear idea of what is expected of them. Fatalism implies acceptance of what happens without question, and this is likely to reinforce the acceptance of decisions from the top and willingness to follow the rules imposed from the top without question. It also suggests that rewards based on individual accomplishments and sanctions associated with individual accountability will have less meaning. Agboolo (2011) described a situation in Botswana where a company introduced individual performance incentives and met with substantial resistance to the change. There are likely many reasons for resistance to such a change, but certainly in a collective society, one would expect such resistance.

Staffing

Collectivism suggests that staffing decisions will be made on the basis of people being able and willing to work together. This may mean people of similar backgrounds, including the use of family members working together in groups (a practice that might be viewed negatively in North America and Europe). Acceptance of power differentials likely means that staffing decisions made by those in positions of power will be accepted and not questioned, and those in power will make decisions about staff that reinforce their power. Factors such as ethnicity, religion, age, and gender, that relate to power, will be taken into account in staffing decisions, and nepotism (favoring family members and close friends) can be expected. Preference for certainty/aversion to uncertainty reinforces acceptance of staffing decisions made by superiors. This is seen as providing security, and is reinforced by fatalism, which can mute ambition and encourage such acceptance, even where it may be unpleasant. As noted, in many developed countries "nepotism" or the favoring of one's relatives in business dealings is seen as negative, in contrast, in developing countries, family members are trusted, and therefore to be favored. Similarly, people often associate positive attributes to those who belong to the same tribe. For example, in a study in Kenya (Lituchy et al., 2009), when asked about culture, leadership and motivation, many respondents talked about their tribal origins and customs associated with their tribe. Tribal roots and loyalties were seen as an important aspect of identifying leaders; and, some respondents indicated that leaders would, of necessity, be male.

Leading

Leadership that is collective, based on power, and providing certainty may best be described as paternal or benevolent autocracy. In other words, the leader is concerned with the good of the group, and both leader and followers believe that the leader knows best, therefore an autocratic style is expected and accepted. This style of leadership provides security because the leader's power position is accepted by his (possibly her in unusual situations) subordinates. Fatalism supports this leadership style because the powerful leader cannot be wrong – bad decisions become "God's will." The question of leadership succession looms large in that leaders will tend to protect their position by elevating chosen subordinates; for example, in North Korea in 2010 the elderly leader elevated his son to a position that would likely result in his taking over the reigns of leadership, thus creating an emerging dynasty. Similarly, in Cuba, when Fidel Castro was ill and no longer able to govern effectively, he appointed his brother Raul Castro to take over the reigns of government. This is possibly the only way for the organization to stay relevant in a nondemocratic, or otherwise nonparticipative environment. Of course, this style of leadership can also end in the overthrow of the leader. The so-called "Arab Spring" of uprisings in many countries in the Middle East and North Africa in 2011 resulted in the end of a number of long-term leaders, who had been in power for more than thirty years.

Controlling

Controls in a collective society will be group rather than individual based – i.e., goals will be set for groups and teams, output will be measured at the group level, quality will be a group responsibility, and so on. Controls will be determined by those in positions of power and they will control rewards and punishments that will be meted out in response to good performance or unacceptable performance or behavior, usually to groups, rather than individual performers. Rules and policies and procedures that are clear will provide security and thus will be desired. At the same time, fatalism combined with acceptance of power differentials means that the superior may make exceptions to the rules, and this will be considered acceptable, even right. In individualist societies, it is common to hear that, "the squeaky wheel gets the grease", implying that if you want something, you should speak up, and speaking up, as an individual, is accepted and encouraged. This in turn implies that management in receptive to new ideas and possibly criticism. In collective countries, by contrast, there is an equivalent saying that, "the nail that stands up gets hammered down." This suggests that speaking out as an individual is seen as negative and not encouraged. It is best to leave decisions to those in positions of power and to avoid controversy, especially in a fatalistic world.

The management style described here as typical, based on the characteristics of developing countries is one that in North America is often called "Theory X." This management style is based on the belief that people work essentially for economic reasons and that they would prefer not to work. Employees are not trusted and communication is limited, with important information not shared. It is essentially top-down management, with tight controls. North American workers often rebel in this environment and complain that it is repressive and does not take into account their wants and needs. The difference with developing country societies is that in many cases employees accept this style, therefore it may work. In addition, there is a certain implication that, while autocratic in nature, it may be seen as a benevolent autocracy and paternalistic. The leader is expected to look after subordinates (as a father is expected to look after the family, or a chief is expected to look after his tribe) and in return for this, employees are loyal to the leader. The reverse, "Theory Y" is based on the belief that people want to work, that they can be trusted, and encourages participation and open communication. While this sounds positive in the North American context, it may actually be unsettling for employees who see power differentials as appropriate and who want structure to avoid uncertainty.

The situation is, of course, more complex than a simple Theory X Versus Theory Y framework. Punnett and Greenidge (2009) described the Anglophone Caribbean as high on uncertainty avoidance and low on power–distance. The low power–distance means that employees should react well to flatter structures, participation, open communication, and so on, which implies a certain degree of uncertainty. They also want structure in the form of clear policies and procedures to reduce the uncertainty.

Having discussed these management processes and how culture might influence them, it is appropriate to question them more generally:

1   Is planning a necessary part of management? If events are predetermined, planning may at best be a waste of time, and at worst a questioning of a higher power.
2   Should firms be formally organized? If personal influence is important in day-to-day activities, it may not be appropriate to identify formal positions within the firm.
3   Can people be assigned to fill positions within the firm? If people prefer to work at tasks as they arise, it may not be helpful to allocate them to specific slots.
4   Does management actively seek to direct and motivate subordinates? If people believe they should work hard for the good of their group, it may be counterproductive to actively lead them.
5   If people are fatalistic can they accept responsibility? They may not necessarily commit to performance, as they will react to a changing situation.
6   Are control systems necessary to achieve desired outputs? If employees are willing to act as instructed by their superiors, controls may be redundant.

It is important for managers in different cultures to be aware that their own assumptions may deserve close scrutiny. This is particularly true for managers from developed countries operating in developing ones, and vice versa. In the following sections, management practices in two specific developing countries – the People's Republic of China and India – are considered to illustrate how management may be influenced by the country environment. China and India have been selected as examples because of their rapid economic growth, the internationalization of the business environments, and the substantial interest in business and management in these countries. They have also been selected because their environments share similarities, but they are also quite different (Cappelli et al., 2010; Rowley and Cooke, 2010). Both countries have opened their economies since 1990, they have both experienced GDP growth rates in excess of 8 percent per annum, they have both received high levels of foreign direct investment, both countries have high degrees of poverty, especially in rural areas, and both have widening disparities in income and wealth, and, of course, they are the most populous countries in the world, accounting for nearly half of the world's population.

THE PEOPLE'S REPUBLIC OF CHINA: AN EXAMPLE

The People's Republic of China is one of the largest countries in the world, geographically about the same size as the USA; with a population of 1.3 billion it represents about one-fifth of the world's population. China has gone through major changes in the past century, and this makes it particularly interesting from a management perspective. Today, China is considered a developing country, but this may be misleading if we consider the historical reality. China's recorded history goes back some five thousand years; archaeological records of the sixteenth century B.C. show one of the world's oldest continuous civilizations, and in 2021 B.C., the empire was unified by Qin Shi Huang. Successive dynasties developed bureaucratic systems to control the large and diverse physical territory and people. Clearly China knows much about management. Equally, most people would agree that China's approach to management is different from what is typically practiced in most developed countries.

In the past twenty years, China's "open door policies" have shifted its economy from a highly centralized, planned one to a market economy, particularly with growth in small-scale enterprises. China has also been one of the world's largest recipients of FDI during this period. This has stimulated high rates of GDP growth, and has provided employment for millions of rural migrants. In turn, there have been increases in income and living standards, and increases in purchasing power and growth in the domestic consumer market. By contrast, there has been a marked contraction of state and semi-state sectors – in 1978, over 78 percent of the urban workforce were in the state sector and by 2007, this was less than 23 percent (Rowley and Cooke, 2010).

Smyth and Zhai (2010) noted, however that the state sector is still important, and dominates in defence, power, oil, telecommunications, coal, aviation, and shipping, where FDI and private ownership are still restricted. Smyth and Zhai found that managers in state-owned companies complained about political interference and weak and idiosyncratic governance.

Entrepreneurship has been encouraged since the 1990s, and small- and medium-sized enterprises (SMEs) have expanded rapidly according to Cunningham and Rowley (2010). In addition, they noted that China's entrance into the World Trade Organization had led to increased competition, and social and regional inequality has increased, with a "floating population" of economic migrants and a widening gap between skilled professionals and unskilled workers. Increased private enterprise and entrepreneurial ventures have resulted in the adoption of some "Western" management practices such as profit sharing and bonuses, in some companies. Nevertheless, Chinese cultural values do not fit well with many Western management concepts.

Cooke (2010) identified Confucian values that influence management in the Chinese context as:

- harmony;
- keeping good relationships, with reciprocal obligations and duties including hierarchy;
- respect for seniority and age (those of higher social rank can and should receive more respect and favors);
- collective thinking;
- behaving within accepted social norms;
- avoiding hurting others within the group;
- family as the primary unit of identity and loyalty with a sense of vertical loyalty and duty.

He noted that in China, "face" is considered critical to harmony, therefore it is important that you do not "lose face" or cause others to "lose face". This influences virtually all interactions, including those between superiors and subordinates. *Guanxi*, the Chinese term for a system of reciprocal relationships that are important in Chinese society, is necessary to maintain relationships. The Chinese expend considerable effort to maintain and reinforce social bonds, and these allow the system to function smoothly. *Guanxi* is seen as even more important in the current environment, because of competitive pressures. The ability to form alliances with those who control resources and services is seen as critical for success.

In this cultural context, many "Western" management approaches simply do not work. Employees do not want to express ideas that may be different from superiors and prefer to take orders and do what the supervisor says and they do not want to socialize with their superiors.

According to Rowley and Cooke (2010) Human Resource Management practices have evolved along with the changes in the business environment; however, traditional Chinese approaches remain important. Many managers reported that the *Guanxi* orientation requires sophisticated skills in developing interpersonal relationships, many of which may last for generations as obligations are acknowledged and reciprocity is understood as a continuing requirement. Maintaining interpersonal relationships is seen as more important than following rules and regulations. Collectivism and egalitarian approaches also affect workplace relationships and the distribution of rewards.

Poon et al. (2010) considered the relationship of rewards and performance. They found that complex, hybrid systems were emerging in reaction to market forces, autonomy, competition, and the practices in multinational companies. Performance appraisal systems in China have traditionally been based on seniority, political orientation and moral integrity, not performance, competence, and profitability (Cooke, 2008). The cultural values of harmony, face, collectivism, and so on mean that differentiation is undesirable and social outcomes are valued over individual achievement; free expression of views is difficult because of a belief in hierarchies and high acceptance of power differences. Poon et al. (2010) found that performance management is more common in the private sector, and knowledge-intensive companies. They say that it is more formalized, but they also note that performance management is essentially a Western concept which is difficult to implement in the context of Confucian traditions of familialism and authoritarianism, which incorporates norms of dependence and acceptance of hierarchy. Smyth and Zhai (2010) noted that when state-owned enterprises needed to downsize, they disguised the reductions in labor by indicating that employees were "on leave", "long term rest", had "left their posts", or taken "semi retirement."

The rapid growth and expansion of the Chinese economy over the past two decades has resulted in shortages in skilled labor, and the retention of talented skilled workers is key to business success. Interestingly, according to Cooke (2010) firms are cautious about spending on training because of turnover, and they prefer to recruit trained employees. Also, the younger generation is the product of the Chinese government's one-child policy, which limited families to one child in order to curb population growth, and they are more materialistic than the previous generation. Financial rewards have become very important for this group of employees. Profit-sharing and stock options are seen as positive but attempts at after-work social events have not been very successful, because employees prefer to work more hours and earn extra. In some companies, mentoring has been adopted, but seems to be an outgrowth of the apprentice system which was common previously and is consistent with Confucian values.

Overall, as this brief discussion indicates, it is clear that what constitutes "good management" in China may be quite different from what would be found in most developed countries. This is, of course, attributable to the Chinese culture, more than to the fact that China is considered a developing country. Nevertheless, it highlights the types of differences that managers find around the world. The next section considers India, and management in India, as another example of a developing country.

INDIA: AN EXAMPLE

India has ancient roots and is one of the most diverse countries in the world, encompassing six major ethnic groups, many smaller ones, and eighteen official languages. "For nearly a millennium, the Indian subcontinent experienced repeated conquest, political subjugation, and economic exploitation, culminating in the rule of the East India Company and the British Crown from about the mid-nineteenth century through 1947" (Cappelli et al., 2010: 44).

Indian management has been developing over centuries, but only recently has business been allowed to flourish in a relatively free economy. India's GDP has been rising by nine percent per year or more, in recent years. This is largely attributable to the decision in the early 1990s to liberalize the economy and dismantle what was known as the license raj – a system of government regulators, inspectors, and bureaucrats who essentially controlled business activities. Foreign investment rose rapidly in response to the reforms, from about 5 billion in 1996 to close to US$64 billion in 2008. The current Indian business environment has less regulation than in the past, and much more competition. This has forced Indian businesses to develop world-class competencies in order to survive and prosper. There has been a long-standing tradition of entrepreneurship among the people of India, and the economic reform has allowed these entrepreneurs to flourish in the last decade.

Cappelli et al.'s (2010) book *The India Way – How India's Top Business Leaders Are Revolutionizing Management* provides major insights into current Indian management practices, based on interviews with a broad range of Indian executives. The following discussion summarizes some of the findings.

As a striking contrast to the USA and Western Europe where business leaders in 2010 were viewed with scepticism, Cappelli et al. noted that big-business leaders in India have come to be emblematic of national achievement and fortitude, and the *New York Times* likened business executives in India to rock stars (Landler, 2009). Cappelli et al. noted that the "melding of business and national leadership is central to the Indian way of doing business. Many business leaders are deeply involved in societal issues, and they deem it appropriate – even requisite – to voice their views on subjects ranging from climate change to child nutrition" with "national purpose as much a part of the business mindset as financial results and reputational gain" (p. 3).

The authors identified the following four "pillars" of current Indian management (pp. 4–5):

- "Holistic engagement with employees" – sustaining employee morale and building company culture is seen as key to success.
- "Improvisation and adaptability" – dealing effectively with a complex, often volatile environment with few resources and much red tape requires that managers adapt to new situations and improvise where necessary
- "Creative value propositions" – inventing new product and service concepts to satisfy demanding consumers, and doing so with extreme efficiency, keeps them competitive.
- "Broad mission and purpose" – emphasizing personal values and the broader social purpose mean business leaders take pride in family, region and national success, as well as business success.

While the previous aspects of Indian management are described in positive terms, the authors also noted that there were still numerous bureaucratic delays throughout India, and that corruption and palm greasing were endemic. These aspects of doing business in India may be changing, but they were changing relatively slowly, and managers still have to deal with them on a regular basis, at least in 2010.

In terms of culture in India, the authors identify the following as important:

- Deference for authority, respect for seniority, government and traditions, and believing in hierarchy.
- Importance of family, and the dominance of personal over professional relationships.
- Reliance on intuition, indirect expression of viewpoints, and silence.
- Belief in four desirable aims, based on Hindu principles – righteousness, wealth, desire, and salvation/liberation.

There are many reasons cited for the success of Indian businesses. Among these are a strong entrepreneurial spirit and a trained and eager English-speaking workforce. According to *The India Way*, successful Indian managers have managed to use their cultural values effectively in addressing the opportunities and challenges they face. For example, the successful Indian companies treat employees as family with reciprocal obligations; however, they also find innovative ways to empower employees and get them to give meaningful feedback to their superiors. At the same time, the Indian managers, themselves, feel that they are not as performance-oriented as they should be, because of the stress on personal relationships.

A contrast identified between American and Indian managers is that American managers focus outside the organization, while Indian managers' focus is internal to the organization. American chief executive officers (CEOs) are described (Cappelli et al., 2010) as primarily concerned with investors and regulators, looking for new opportunities, businesses, mergers, and acquisitions. Their Indian counterparts are described as focused on long-term customers and employees as extended family. American CEOs do not see managing the corporate culture and engaging employees as personal responsibilities, while the Indian CEOs see themselves as role models for individual employees. Going along with this attitude, Indian CEOs and managers felt that training and development of employees was more important than their American counterparts, and they involved employees more in aspects of the business. Not surprisingly, according to Capelli et al., Indian leaders generally scored highly on transformational aspects of leadership such as "inspirational motivation", "idealised influence behaviour", and so on, and they were low on passive/avoidant aspects such as "management by exception" and "laissez-faire".

A COMPARISON OF INDIA AND THE PEOPLE'S REPUBLIC OF CHINA

The previous brief descriptions of recent accounts of management in India and the People's Republic of China identify some similarities between the two countries, as well as some interesting cultural differences and differences in management approaches.

There are some striking similarities in the structural descriptions of the two countries:

- Both are very large, physically and in terms of their economies.
- Both are described as ancient civilizations which have each gone through many changes over many centuries.

47

- Each has at some time been a major global player and a rich, dominant force in the economic and business world.
- Both have recently shifted their economies from centrally planned to a market focus.
- Both have recently received substantial international interest and they have been the recipients of substantial levels of inward foreign direct investment. At the same time, their larger organizations have also been outward looking, and outward foreign direct investment has become an important factor in their economies.
- Changes to more market economies, increased foreign investment, and increased exports have all had positive impacts on the GDP growth in both countries; however, each country continues to have large numbers of people living in poverty.
- Entrepreneurial activity is credited for economic and business growth in both countries.
- Managers in both countries complain of government interference, bureaucracy, and corruption.

There are also similarities in some of the cultural descriptions of the two countries. Harmony and keeping good relationships are important in both countries, with an emphasis on a holistic approach to employees in India. There is a respect for seniority and age in both countries, and the family is the primary unit of identity and loyalty. Both countries show deference to authority, respect for seniority and traditions, and a belief in hierarchy.

There are also differences between the two countries. Chinese organizations are described as being cautious about spending on training for employees, while this is a central focus of Indian organizations. Indian organizations also find ways to empower employees, in spite of the cultural deference to authority, while the Chinese employees are described as preferring to take orders. Business leaders are described as being the heroes of India, and the same is not the case in China. The Indian business leaders are credited with a broad mission and purpose, emphasizing the success of the country, and the same is not noted in the case of China. The Indian leaders are also seen as having an ability to improvise and adapt, while the Chinese seem to be more traditional. The cultural values of harmony, face, and collectivism in China mean that differentiation is seen as undesirable, yet, for current employees, financial rewards are very important; it is not clear to what extent this is the case in India.

The similarities identified here mean that managers in these two countries face many of the same challenges and opportunities, and these managers have to find ways to deal with these challenges and opportunities. While there are similarities in terms of their environments, it is also likely that managers will select different specific management approaches. These two examples serve to illustrate the similarities that managers face in developing countries, while illustrating, at the same time, that managers in China and India would likely see their management approaches as quite different. These two examples, thus, also serve to underscore that there will be differences among developing countries, in spite of the similarities.

Columbia FDI Perspectives (Broadman, 2011) provided interesting information on differences between companies from China and India investing in Africa. The report says that there are inherent differences in ownership and other aspects of the firms which lead to perceptions of risk being different, as set out below.

Chinese firms operating in Africa tend to be large state-owned enterprises, building new facilities; they are vertically integrated, conduct most of their business with governments, and sales are largely in Africa. Chinese companies rely on using their home government's extensive resources and outbid other companies for contracts. Chinese management and employees are not encouraged to integrate into the African socioeconomic environment.

Indian firms, in contrast to the Chinese, are private sector firms, varying in size, and they enter African markets by acquiring established businesses. They are also vertically integrated, but much less than their Chinese counterparts. Their sales are to local private entities rather than government agencies. Indian managers and employees are encouraged to integrate into the local African environment, and the companies facilitate this through informal networks and participation in local activities.

Chinese and Indian firms, as well as international firms from elsewhere in Asia are making inroads in global markets. The still face challenges however. The Economist Intelligence Unit (2010) identified an interesting challenge for emerging multinationals from Asia – branding. The article says that companies in Asia have grown into large businesses because they were in the right place at the right time. For example, in China, construction companies have benefited from the move from rural areas to urban ones; car companies have benefited from a move from bicycles to automobiles; banks have benefited from protected markets; other companies have benefited from the West's search for low-cost production. These companies have grown without the use of brands. The Economist argued that this can't continue. Rather, it argued, branding is critical to going global, and companies will need to develop branding strategies if they are to succeed in the global environment. Branding seems not to be well understood in Asia, and this is likely to be true in developing countries more generally. Developing countries have largely focused on the production side of business rather than the marketing side. This is an outgrowth of the colonial history where the colonial powers took on the marketing of products and services and expected the colonies to simply respond to production requirements. Managers in developing countries need to change this mindset and learn to have a marketing mentality and approach. Branding is one aspect of this management change. As the Economist noted, branding is more than a name or a logo; it is the complete customer experience, including less tangible components, such as quality, design and style. In order to develop a successful brand, a company needs to understand what differentiates it from the competition. Traditionally, companies from developing countries have relied on price and being low-cost producers, with a production mentality. A shift to a new management paradigm requires that managers recognize the importance of innovation, research, development, design, and marketing. This shift requires investment in intangibles, which is often difficult for managers in developing countries to accept. Investment in intangibles is particularly challenging for relatively small companies with limited resources, because the outcomes and benefits are not easy to measure, thus, the cost–benefit tradeoffs are not clear-cut and quantifiable.

SUMMARY

In this chapter we have looked at the process of management and how this process is likely to be seen in developing countries. A model of management was introduced, including planning, organizing, staffing, leading, and controlling activities. Each of these activities was briefly examined in terms of the characteristics of developing countries discussed in the previous chapter. In addition, the chapter asked the basic question of whether this Western model of management is applicable in non-Western countries, particularly developing ones. The chapter considered two examples of developing countries, from a management perspective – China and India were selected because of current interest in these countries, and their large size and importance in today's global economies. Management approaches in these two countries were described and contrasted. A number of similarities were identified, and differences were also highlighted. This chapter serves as the basis for a more in-depth consideration of the process of management.

In the next chapter, the explanations of development are examined in an effort to help the reader understand how and why countries develop economically. In the following chapters, each of the management activities introduced here will be explored in more detail.

LESSONS LEARNED

Having completed this chapter you should be able to look at a typical model of management and examine how the characteristics of developing countries can interact with aspects of this model. You should understand how management practices differ in developed countries from developing countries. You should be able to distinguish management practices in India and the PRC and identify similarities as well as differences in culture and management approaches. You should realize that managers in developing countries encounter many of the same challenges and opportunities as managers in developed countries.

DISCUSSION QUESTIONS

1   Developing countries are found to be more collective than developed countries. Discuss how the processes of management are carried out in a collective society.
2   Developing countries are generally relatively high on power–distance. Discuss how this is likely to influence interpersonal behavior.
3   Select two developing countries and compare their management practices and explain how management is influenced by the country environment.
4   Managers in developing countries have to recognize the importance of innovation, research, development, design and marketing. Explain and evaluate what is required to bring about a new shift in management paradigms to achieve this in these countries.
5   Proponents of the "divergence" perspective argue that cultural differences make it difficult for developed country theories and practices to be applied in non-Western cultures. Do you agree with this? If so, why? If not, why not?

EXERCISE

In small groups, students are asked to choose two developing countries do a comparative analysis and explain the different management processes and how culture might influence them. Each group should share their findings with the class.

Chapter 5

Explanations of Economic Development

OBJECTIVES

The purpose of this chapter is to discuss the limits of our current understanding of economic development, and to present and evaluate factors that are generally associated with economic development.

The objectives of the chapter are as follows:

- To explore ways to achieve and sustain economic growth over a certain time period and develop solutions on how to improve the standard of living for ordinary people.
- To create a better understanding of the formulation of public policies designed to bring about economic growth in developing countries.
- To examine the causes and effects of economic development and evaluate why some countries are richer or poorer than others.
- To evaluate the different arguments for and against economic development and explore how resources are used which lead either to economic growth or lack thereof.
- To demonstrate that there is no "one size fits all" theory, and show how some theories ignore factors such as culture and personal preferences and how these affect economic development.
- To highlight the idea that there is no certainty regarding which public economic policies will work and which will not, in a particular country or region.
- To examine the different policies government can put in place to encourage economic development.

INTRODUCTION

The first chapters of this book have described differences between developed, richer countries and developing, poorer nations. These chapters considered the changing environments in these countries, as well as both negative and positive recent developments. The chapters have identified a variety of terminology issues associated with development, and the last chapter, Chapter 4, looked at a model of management and how characteristics of developing countries would affect the model. It also considered, in some detail, management in the People's Republic of China and in India. Throughout this discussion, there is an underlying assumption that there are reasons why some countries are richer and more developed, while others are poorer and less developed. In this chapter, we examine the most common explanations for economic development. This chapter does not provide details of economic theories, rather it provides a simple account of the factors that generally are associated with economic growth.

There have been a wide array of approaches to economic development, and there is no agreement on what works and what does not. Some countries have adopted free market strategies and limited government involvement and been successful. Some countries have found that government planning and support of desired sectors has worked. Some countries have focused on import substitution, others on exports; some on fixed exchange rates, others on flexible rates; some have established institutional frameworks, others have been laissez-faire; and so on. There are many and varied systems, and some have worked in some places and not in others. One article says "the main players in development – governments in the developing world, as well as the World Bank and the NGOs – have tended to move from fad to fad. First it was big dams, then education, then microcredit. And now we're back to big dams" (Parker, 2010: 87). The problem is that we do not have nice experimental situations when we look at economic development. We do not know what would have happened if certain policies had or had not been implemented.

Professor Duflo, an economist at MIT, showed a graph of the billions of dollars in development aid that had been given to Africa in recent decades, along with the continent's GDP per capita over the same period. The graph showed that aid had risen sharply, but GDP had not (Parker, 2010). On the surface it seems that aid does not lead to economic development. Duflo warned, however, that we cannot draw causal conclusions. She noted that without aid, Africa's economy might have turned out better, the same, or worse – without a control that did not receive aid, there is no way to know. In terms of economic development, it is often virtually impossible to have such a comparison. Interestingly, Duflo, co-founder of the Abdul Latif Jameel Poverty Action Lab at MIT, is subjecting economic development policies to what she describes as randomized control trials. She is randomly assigning groups to different experimental situations to compare the results. She argues that this is the only way to actually test the results of any intervention. An example of Duflo's approach involves 120 schools in India. The question was whether a particular approach would decrease teacher absenteeism. In sixty schools, teachers were asked to have a photo taken with their students at the start and end of the day. Pay was then adjusted according to attendance. Compared with the control group of the same size, the photographed teachers were half as likely to be absent.

This is an interesting approach, but difficult to implement in broad economic terms. Consequently, most of our real life experience is based on the experience of a small number of countries, or perhaps only one country. Singapore, for example, is often held up as a good example of how a small country can expand its economy. Singapore and Jamaica are approximately the same size and were at the same economic level fifty years ago. Since then, Singapore's economy has grown substantially and Jamaica's has not. But, does this mean that Jamaica's would have grown similarly if it had followed the same policies as Singapore? We do not know, and we cannot know. In the following section a number of explanations of economic development are considered and the reality for poor countries is examined in this context.

TRADITIONAL ECONOMIC EXPLANATIONS VERSUS DEVELOPMENT ECONOMISTS

Broadly, one can say that traditional Western economics is concerned with the allocation of resources and with the optimal growth of those resources over time. This view of economics holds that countries develop economically, through market forces. In a market economy, economic benefits flow to participants, individuals or countries, from self-interested and voluntary acts. This is considered efficient and leading to the greatest overall economic growth. This view considers free trade as beneficial to all trading partners, and holds that a country will benefit by concentrating on producing those products and services that it produces efficiently (because of relatively abundant factors of production), and exporting these, while importing those that it produces relatively inefficiently. These economists see problems with economic growth and development as attributable to forces that restrict the free market, such as government-created barriers, tariffs, and so on. In order for countries to develop economically, according to this view, barriers need to be removed. In effect, traditional economic arguments are in favor of free trade, as benefiting all trading partners, and against government intervention, which is seen as increasing costs and leading to inefficiencies. These arguments are based on assumptions which are believed to be reasonable across countries, and valid in the real world.

Development economics goes beyond this approach and argues that country-specific characteristics have to be taken into account. Development economists believe that the situation is more complex, and that simply relying on market forces, with no government interference, does not guarantee benefits to all partners, or economic growth. These economists argue that the situation in poorer countries is very different from that in richer countries, and that the assumptions on which free trade benefits are based do not necessarily hold, when a country is poor. The very fact that a country is economically less developed means that it is not in a position to compete effectively and take advantage of the benefits of free trade. For example, if we consider the 'characteristics' of poor countries, outlined in chapter two, the following suggests some of the results relative to trade (expanding on the discussion earlier):

- *People are concerned with basic needs or, in the "better-off" of these countries, with achieving economic stability.* This means that their concerns are their immediate needs rather than things like quality and service, but quality and service may be the cornerstone to effective exporting. Immediate needs take precedence over longer-term strategies, which may be the key to developing ongoing successful exports.
- *Infrastructure is limited. Roads, railways, ports, and other physical facilities are nonexistent in some locations and only adequate in the "better-off" developing countries.* Infrastructure is critical to effective exports. Inadequate roads, railways, ports, and so on mean additional costs for products and services, delays in getting them to markets, and a variety of problems that can make exports uncompetitive.
- *Social services are limited. Education, health, and other social services are nonexistent in some locations and only adequate in the "better-off" developing countries.* Where education, health and social services are limited, it is difficult to find employees with the skills needed to export, and employees are more likely to be absent or their productivity low for health reasons.
- *Economic Resources are scarce, and projects need to be clearly justified to warrant governmental or nongovernmental support.* Scarce resources mean that only the most relevant projects can be undertaken and these may not be products or services that are exportable. Limited resources are often devoted to projects which perpetuate those in power rather than the more general good of the country.

Beyond these factors, there are other considerations:

■ Poor countries often cannot afford to invest in "value added" activities; for example, canning fresh fruit and vegetables or manufacturing products from basic materials. The result is that poor countries often export commodities; these commodities are processed in richer countries, and the poor countries import the higher priced products that result. Sugar production in a country such as Barbados is a typical example – sugar cane is grown in Barbados and a basic level of processing done there, the sugar product is then shipped to the United Kingdom for more significant processing, and the resulting white sugar is imported back into Barbados. The value of the exported sugar product is substantially less than the value of the imported white sugar, and some would argue that there is no net benefit to Barbados.

■ Poor countries are not in a position to negotiate beneficial terms of trade with their richer trade partners. In conventional free trade economics, all countries benefit from moving from no trade to free trade, but they do not benefit equally. The benefits that accrue to each trading partner depend on their ability to negotiate the terms of trade. Poor countries are often obliged to accept the terms offered by richer partners because their negotiating position is weak. The poorer country is anxious to find an export market, it may not have many options, it may have limited international experience and expertise, and so on – this puts it at a disadvantage in negotiations. Thus, even if we accept that all trading partners benefit from trade, it seems clear that rich countries will, in many cases, benefit more than poorer ones.

In addition, the benefits of free trade are usually described as long term, while there are significant costs and adjustments in the short term. These costs and adjustments may be too great for poor countries with already fragile economies; if unemployment, poverty, and trade deficits are worsened in the short term, a poor economy may simply collapse. At the same time, foreign direct investment benefits foreign investors and the local elite, rather than the "ordinary" people, so that the result is greater disparities in income, justice, and quality of life. The result can be economic and/or political chaos and collapse, and, in effect, the long-term benefits never come.

Sir Arthur Lewis, a Saint Lucian economist, is well known for his contributions in the field of economic development. In 1979 he won the Nobel Memorial Prize in Economics, becoming the first black person to win a Nobel Prize in a category other than peace. Lewis (1955) believed that neoclassical economics does not accurately describe the condition of economically less-developed countries (LDCs) because it assumes that labor is in short supply. The Lewis model is based on two sectors in the economy in a developing country – the modern and the traditional. The modern sector is small and uses considerable amounts of capital, and the traditional sector is large and not capital intensive. Very little capital accumulation occurs in the traditional sector, and a large amount of excess labor exists there and the marginal product of labor in the traditional sector is zero. As an incentive to get people to leave the traditional sector and work in the modern sector, wages in the modern sector are somewhat higher than in the traditional sector. An increase in the amount of capital in the modern sector would therefore increase the marginal product of labor in the modern sector and total output, without affecting the traditional sector. Capital accumulation in the modern sector is therefore the method for growing a less developed economy without doing any real damage to the traditional sector. According to this model, capital accumulation in the modern sector will lead to rising incomes as well as rising income inequality. Eventually, capital accumulation will reach a level at which the marginal product of labor in the modern sector will equal the marginal product of labor in the traditional sector and the two sectors will become integrated.

The main issue addressed in development economics is how to achieve and sustain economic growth over time and improve the standard of living for the ordinary people, and the formulation of public policies designed to bring about economic growth. A challenge for poor countries is that they lack the resources needed to carry out the research necessary to underpin economic decisions. Decisions are often made by a powerful few, who may make decisions that are to their own benefit rather than for the good of the country. Even when the powerful make decisions that they believe will benefit the country as a whole and the ordinary people, they may not be in a position to evaluate the situation effectively and objectively. Many developing countries have found themselves in a position where economic decisions are made for them by donor/lender countries and agencies whose role is to encourage development. These decisions have not always had the desired economic effect and many people now also question this approach.

Over time, a variety of views have developed regarding the best way to achieve sustained growth, and the policies that will help achieve this. The following discussion outlines the major views. Some economists have argued that the most important consideration in economic development are internal to the developing country, others have argued that external considerations are equally important.

INSTITUTIONS, POLICIES, AND ECONOMIC DEVELOPMENT

One approach to economic development focuses on the role of institutions in achieving economic growth Lewis (1955). According to this approach, richer countries have laws that provide the environment for firms to engage effectively in business activities. These countries have property rights that facilitate investment, government power is restricted by an independent judiciary, and contracts are enforced. Henry and Miller (2009) said that research has shown this to be a causal relationship, "countries whose colonizers established strong property rights hundreds of years ago have, on average, much higher levels of income today than countries whose colonizers did not" (p. 261). This sets the stage for the findings of LaPorta and Schleifer (2008) that countries who use English common law provide investors with better protection and less government ownership than others; these common law countries have better financial development, less corruption, smaller informal economies, and lower unemployment.

Henry and Miller (2009) gave the following example to illustrate the impact of institutional choices:

> In 1953, when Korea broke into two separate nations, they had similar levels of income and ethnic and cultural makeups, but very different institutional arrangements. North Korea concentrated on central planning, while South Korea relied on property rights and markets. Fifty plus years later, South Korea's per capita income is ten times that of the North's.
>
> (p. 261)

Henry and Miller go on to note that macroeconomic policies may have as much influence as the broader institutional framework. In an examination of Barbados and Jamaica, in the Caribbean, they reach some interesting conclusions. Barbados and Jamaica, in many ways, present an interesting "natural experiment" that allow one to look at the impact of different policies, while keeping other factors constant. These two small Caribbean countries are both former

British colonies, with descendants of Africans brought to the Caribbean as slaves as their main population. Following independence, these two countries had very similar political, economic, legal institutions, and their social systems had common roots. The analysis of these countries from 1960 to 2002 shows an average growth rate of 2.2 percent in Barbados and only 0.8 percent in Jamaica. In 1960, real GDP per capita was $3,395 in Barbados and $2,208 in Jamaica; by 2002, it was $8,434 in Barbados and $3,165 in Jamaica – the gap had widened from $1,187 in 1960 to $5,269 forty years later. The interesting question is what accounts for the difference. Henry and Miller believe that governmental decisions at critical times account for the difference. Jamaica responded to rising unemployment, income inequality and social tensions with extensive state intervention in the economy – nationalization of companies, import barriers, strict exchange controls, job creation, housing development, and subsidies on basic food items. Barbados, in contrast, kept government spending under control – it avoided nationalization, kept state ownership to a minimum and adopted outward-looking growth strategies. These authors attribute Barbados' superior economic performance to "monetary restraint, fiscal discipline, openness to trade, and ultimately wage cuts to restore competitive unit labor costs – that had the side effect of enabling the monetary authority to maintain the exchange-rate parity without losing external competitiveness" (p. 206).

The example of Barbados and Jamaica presented here provides a good example of the complexity of understanding the causes of economic development. Economic development is likely a combination of forces that depend very much on the environment at a particular point in time. In other words, institutions are undoubtedly important, and so are government policies, as illustrated by Barbados and Jamaica, but the results in Barbados and Jamaica might have been different under different circumstances. One aspect of the Barbados–Jamaica comparison is that Barbados maintained a fixed exchange rate of 2:1 relative to the U.S. dollar while Jamaica allowed its currency to float and devalue. Some people argue that this stability in the Barbados financial environment encouraged investment, both local investment and FDI. In the recession of 2008, Berkmen et al. (2010) analyzed the reasons that some countries were more affected than others by the global recession, and they concluded that countries with more flexible exchange rates fared better than those with fixed exchange rates. Berkmen et al. concluded, in terms of policy lessons for developing countries, that rapid credit growth and high leverage, aggravated by fixed exchange rates, were largely responsible for negative economic performance in the recession of 2008. Note that this seems to be the reverse of the Barbados–Jamaica example, where a fixed exchange rate seemed to have a positive effect on the Barbados economy. We can learn from these results how some countries react to particular events, but we cannot necessarily generalize from them. Each developing country faces a particular situation and decisions and policies will be effective or ineffective in the context of this situation. Nevertheless, a number of theories of economic development have been promulgated over the past century. In the next section, we give a brief overview of these.

OVERVIEW OF SOME THEORIES OF ECONOMIC DEVELOPMENT

There have been a variety of theories of economic development which have been suggested over the past century, and undoubtedly before (see Contreras, 2010; Ray, 2008 for a full discussion of competing theories of economic development). These theories all have something to contribute to our understanding of economic development. At the same time, none of these theories has been accepted as definitively explaining why some countries develop more quickly than others. As the previous section argued, development is a complex process that is affected by many forces, so each theory can be seen as one piece of a puzzle. Contreras (2010) summarized thinking on economic development as set out in the following sections.

LINEAR STAGES OF GROWTH

The Marshall Plan for economic reconstruction made possible an amazing and rapid revival of industrial Europe. Europe's success in rapid reindustrialization was to be very influential in how policymakers in industrialized countries approached the economic problems of developing countries. The key to development was simple; implementation of a program providing for a massive injection of capital coupled with public sector intervention designed to accelerate the pace of economic development. This would compensate for the lack of internal savings and investment in developing countries.

Rostow (1960) argued that advanced countries had all passed through a series of stages. He designated the stages as follows: (1) the traditional society; (2) the preconditions to take-off; (3) the take-off; (4) the drive to maturity; (5) the age of high mass consumption. Rostow argued that advanced countries had all passed the stage of take-off and had achieved self-sustaining growth. The developing economies were either in the "preconditions" or "traditional" stage. All that these societies had to do in order to take-off (to reach self-sustaining growth) was to follow a certain set of rules of development. The take-off stage could only be reached if three criteria were satisfied – the country had to increase its investment rate, with investment amounting to no less than 10 percent of the national income (either through investment of the country's own savings or through foreign aid or foreign investment); the country had to develop one or more substantial manufacturing sectors with a high rate of growth; a political, social, and institutional framework had to exist or be created to promote the expansion of the new modern sector.

Rostow equated economic growth with economic development. To stimulate growth, the country had to increase savings and investment. Given the low savings rates in developing countries, the government was responsible for creating a class of people with a propensity to save. The government also had to ensure that people who saved more would obtain a greater share of the national income. Otherwise, national income would be consumed rather than invested.

Despite its appeal, the Rostow model proved to have problems. The linear-stages-of-growth model blamed developing countries' stagnation on internal factors, namely a lack of internal savings and investment. The model assumed that foreign investment or aid could replace internal savings and investment, and would result in economic growth. This assumption was based, in part, on the success of the Marshall Plan in Europe. Thus, the model assumed that but for the low savings and investment rates, developing countries and Europe were the same for purposes of development.

Post-World War II Europe had lost its infrastructure and industrial base, but social structures remained intact – skilled labor and a competent managerial sector, a stable civil and criminal legal framework, while in developing countries, the levels of human resources could not compare. Consequently, economic aid and foreign investment were not enough to industrialize developing countries. If sustained growth was to be achieved in developing countries, the society itself had to be restructured. The linear-stages-of-growth model focused only on the symptoms of an ailing economic society, it did not determine what factors led to a society that saved very little and invested even less.

57

NEO-MARXIST DEVELOPMENT THEORY

Neo-Marxists broadened the scope of orthodox Marxist doctrine by looking at exploitation among nations. Marx's doctrine stated that the worker was being robbed by the capitalist class. The worker received only a fraction of the value of the product which his labor produced, and the difference was expropriated by the capitalists – the private owners of the factories and the machines. The neo-Marxists gave this theory an international dimension based on the behavior of nations. They concluded that industrialized countries historically extracted surplus value from developing countries. Specifically, they argued that developed countries paid very low prices for the primary products imported from developing countries, transformed them into finished products and sold them back to developing countries at very high prices. This resulted in chronic poverty and misery in developing countries.

These economists argued that the path to industrialization was difficult and even impossible to follow because developing countries were brought into the capitalist international economy as producers of cheap raw materials; thus, foreign capital flowed to and modernized only one sector of developing economies – the primary products sector. These factors contributed to static economies in developing countries, which meant that capitalism could not be achieved. Many countries still accept this view.

STRUCTURALISTS

Structuralists see the goal of development as movement from a traditional rural, subsistence agricultural economy, to an urban economy with manufacturing and services as its major focus. The question for these economists is how to expand into the modern economy while contracting the indigenous traditional economy. The focus is on eliminating reliance on foreign demand for its primary exports (raw materials) while encouraging expansion of the internal industrial sector. Many developing countries subscribe to this belief, and are downplaying their agricultural and traditional sectors while encouraging manufacturing and services.

In the latter part of the nineteenth century and the beginning of the twentieth century, Latin American countries were exporters of raw materials. Classical economics held that the region had a comparative advantage in raw materials, meaning they could produce raw materials more efficiently than other regions. As such, they should concentrate on expanding such exports. Latin American economists disagreed. They believed that exports of raw materials was not a feasible path to economic development. Given the low price for exports of primary products, developing countries were unable to make enough money to pay for all of the imports they needed, including high-priced manufactured products.

Structuralists argued that the fruits of those advances were being retained by the industrialized nations in the form of increased profits for the manufacturer and higher wages for the workers. Given these "structural" impediments in the world economy, the structuralists argued that economic development had to be pursued through an expansion of the domestic industrial sector. They also believed that development had to include the expansion of new technology and methods of production; thus, structuralists also measured development by the number of economic sectors using the most advanced levels of technology.

Structuralists argued that the changes needed to bring about economic development could only be achieved by state intervention; for example, government-imposed tariffs on imports which were designed to encourage infant industries and stimulate the internal market by protecting new industries within the country. Tariffs were seen as 'evening the playing field' between a manufacturer in an industrialized country (with better access to capital and technology, and more productive workers) and one in a developing nation. Structuralists believed that the underdeveloped capital markets in developing countries meant that only the state could generate and manage the sizeable investments needed to industrialize. This meant that state ownership was often seen as the best option for governments. Overall, policies known collectively as "import substitution," were geared to encouraging the country to industrialize. Structuralists accepted the idea that capitalism was positive, did not believe that the market alone could achieve the capitalism that industrialized countries were enjoying. Rather, these economists believed that governments of developing countries had to actively promote industrialization through government regulation of the economy.

This approach to development continues to be used in use in many developing locations, with an emphasis today on exports, and often the export of services. Government-led initiatives have not, however, always effectively created the necessary investment for industrialization, and involvement of the state has created inefficiencies. Countries are still seeking alternatives to development.

Current thinking also emphasizes the positive role of foreign direct investment and many countries actively seek foreign investment, and have policies in place to promote inward flows of foreign direct investment. It is often argued that foreign investment is particularly important for developing countries because they do not have an abundance of local capital for investment. Given that investment seems to be one of the potential drivers of economic growth and development, it may make sense for countries to seek investment from abroad, especially where the domestic capacity for investment is limited.

This thinking was not always "in vogue", and in the middle of the twentieth century many governments feared foreign investment as a new form of colonialism. Substantial investment from abroad was seen as dominating the domestic economy and making developing countries ever more dependent on the developing ones. Many countries that today seek to attract foreign investors still have concerns about the influence and impact this has on the country that receives the investment. In order to benefit from foreign investment, while avoiding some of the potential risks, countries have regulatory policies and procedures in place to evaluate and control investors. Of course, this in turn introduces more bureaucracy and government intervention, both of which may have negative consequences, and can discourage FDI.

PRIVATE MARKETS/NOT GOVERNMENT INTERVENTION

Neoclassical theory experienced a resurgence in the 1980s. It is not coincidental that, during this same period, the governments of most of the industrialized nations were governed by conservative political parties. Neoclassical economic theory dismissed neo-Marxist theory as flawed and unrealistic. It also rejected structuralists' claims that developing countries' problems were due to structural impediments in the international economy and that domestic structural flaws required significant state intervention in the economy.

Neoclassical economists believed that economic stagnation in developing countries was a by-product of poorly designed economic policies and excessive state interference in the economy. They argued that in order to stimulate the domestic economy and promote the creation of an efficient market, developing country governments had to eliminate market restrictions and limit government intervention. This was to be accomplished through the privatization of state-owned enterprises, promotion of free trade, reduction or elimination of restrictions on foreign investment, and a reduction or elimination of government regulations affecting the market.

Modern economic theory of development has built on the theories presented previously, but it sees a variety of factors influencing development. The following section summarizes information presented by Hoff and Stiglitz (2010).

CURRENT THINKING ON DEVELOPMENT

Hoff and Stiglitz (2001) note that development may be both easier and harder than was previously thought. They say that the older theories suggested that all a country had to do to ensure development was transfer enough capital and remove government-imposed distortions. Under newer theories, the situation is seen as more complex. A country needs to induce a movement out of the old equilibrium, sufficiently far and in the right direction that the economy will be attracted to a new, superior equilibrium. This may require fewer resources but it may take more skill, and could lead the economy to a worse equilibrium – as they noted, some would argue has been the case in certain economies in transition. Hoff and Stiglitz refer to Darwin's insights in *The Origin of Species*, that the plants and animals of the Galapagos differed in spite of the similar physical conditions. Darwin concluded that the physical conditions of a country were not the most important element of success, rather it was the nature of the other inhabitants, with which each has to compete (Darwin [1859] 1993: 540). Hoff and Stiglitz say that the economy is like an ecosystem, with multiple equilibria – more important to the evolution of the system than the fundamentals, such as weather and geography, are variables such as luck and accidents of history, which can play a role in determining that environment, and thus in the selection of the development equilibrium. They stress the importance of democracy as a check on government, and say that the ability of government to act as an agent of development may depend on the strength of democratic forces and on the extent to which voters are divided along class or ethnic lines. They note that many developing countries are polarized by class or ethnic differences, which makes it difficult for the state to act as a "developmental state" in decisions about public goods or redistribution. They also note that in Africa civil disturbances have proved to be an important impediment to development.

Hoff and Stiglitz say that modern development economics rejects the idea of "equilibrium" that underlies traditional neoclassical analysis. In earlier theories, knowledge of the fundamentals and the initial conditions enables one to predict the course of the evolution of the economy. Modern development economics tends to be influenced more by biological than physical models. Traditional accounts emphasize the forces pulling toward equilibrium, and with similar forces working in all economies, all should be pulled toward the same equilibrium. More recent thought focuses more on evolutionary processes, complex systems, and chance events that may cause systems to diverge.

Hoff and Stiglitz make an interesting case for the role of history in economic development, and say that history influences a society's technology, skill base, and institutions. As an example, they note that the loss of life from the Black Death resulted in a shortage of labor which in turn resulted in labor-saving innovations in Europe, with profound implications for the historical evolution of the continent. They also note that history affects outcomes by affecting beliefs. An outbreak of corruption, or the revelation that some firms in an industry passed off shoddy goods as high-quality goods, can tarnish the reputation of the whole industry. They refer to Tirole (1996) who said that the revelation that any member of a group was dishonest in the past will increase the time it takes for any given agent to establish a reputation for honesty; this will actually lower the individual's incentives to be honest and create a cycle of corruption, where "the new members of an organization may suffer from the original sin of their elders long after the latter are gone (p. 1)". They also argue that history matters because of exposure to cultural values, which shape preferences. Changes in the ways that members of one generation earn their living may influence the next generation through changes in childrearing, schooling, informal learning rules such as conformism, role models, and social norms. They say that the market itself is a social institution that shapes preferences and can foster or deter characteristics of openness, competitiveness, and self-interestedness.

They also say that institutions may be part of an equilibrium, and yet be dysfunctional. They cite Arnott and Stiglitz (1991) who showed that informal social insurance could crowd out market insurance and decrease social welfare. They conclude that developing countries may be caught in a vicious cycle where low levels of market development result in high levels of information imperfections, and these information imperfections themselves give rise to institutions, for example, informal, personalized networks of relationships, which actually impede the development of markets.

SOME CONCLUSIONS ON ECONOMIC DEVELOPMENT

It seems clear from this discussion that we do not fully understand the causes of economic development. We do not know why some countries are richer and others poorer. We cannot say with certainty what policies will work and what policies will not. In general, there seems to be a fair amount of agreement that democracy and a free market economy provide a positive environment for economic development. There is some agreement that government intervention should be limited if possible, and used in targeted ways. There is some agreement that trade is positive, and that countries benefit from trade. In contrast, it is also clear that developing countries need to develop their internal capacities in order to benefit more fully from trade, and this may mean, in some cases, that they support local industries and encourage import substitution. Today, most people would agree that development is more than simply economic development, although economic measures are the easiest and most convenient ones to use to measure development, and these measures correlate with other measures that attempt to incorporate the quality of life.

In spite of the apparent agreement on certain issues identified in the previous paragraph, it is interesting to note some facts about a variety of countries:

- Japan's ministry of industry and trade played a major role in guiding Japan's development in the 1950s.
- European and Japanese development in the second half of the twentieth century have often been attributed to the massive spending by the USA on reconstruction in Europe and Japan.
- China was a communist country with central government spending when its economic boom started. It remains a communist country, with no democracy, although it has allowed a substantial degree of free market activity in recent years, and its economy continues to grow and thrive.
- Singapore achieved its high level of economic development and GDP per capita under a system which was nominally a democracy, but which for many years was described as a "benign dictatorship".
- Russia has been growing economically since the fall of communism, but its political forces are in a state of change, and no one seems to know for sure how to describe the political situation there; in spite of this instability it is lauded as one of stars among the BRIC countries.

61

- India's economic growth and development continues in spite of the government bureaucracy and red tape, both of which are reportedly substantial.
- Africa, as a region, was reported to have grown much faster than Western countries in 2009, but its record on democracy had deteriorated.
- Virtually all countries have governmental offices responsible for development, and these seek investors, encourage local producers, and promote exports, even as they may decry government involvement.

These examples serve to underscore the idea that there is no "one size fits all" as far as economic development goes. One reason for this is likely that economic theories largely ignore factors such as culture and personal preferences. Earlier in the chapter, Singapore's growth was compared to Jamaica's relative economic stagnation. The two countries started off economically in a similar situation and can be compared economically over time. The two countries are, however, culturally very different, and it is questionable whether the Jamaican people would accept the type of policies that were implemented in Singapore. Economists will continue to identify a variety of policies and investigate them. It is hoped that, as this continues, we will develop a better understanding of development, so that we can ensure that development takes place for all the people of the world, and we find ways of eliminating poverty.

Sala-i-Martin (1997) formulated a list of variables most consistently associated with economic growth. The list included the following:

Savings – Studies have consistently found a positive relationship between savings rates and economic growth rates. Some studies have shown government savings (budget surpluses) to be related to growth, although one could argue that government expenditures on education, health, infrastructure and the like is necessary to provide the basis for economic growth.

Investment – Studies have also shown a consistent positive relationship between investment and economic growth rates. According to Perkins et al. (2001) investment in equipment has the largest and strongest positive relationship, but all investment has a positive relationship.

Life expectancy – longer life expectancy appears to be related to more rapid economic growth. Presumably this relationship exists because life expectancy is related to a generally healthier population and in turn a more productive labor force. In addition, life expectancy may encourage saving and capital accumulation over a longer time, and perhaps people invest more in skill and education if they expect to live a long time (Perkins et al., 2001).

Level of education – increased levels of education are related to greater economic growth. An educated workforce is more skilled and likely to be more productive. Consequently the labor force will be more highly paid. This in turn may also encourage savings and capital formation.

Exchange rate policies – Sala-i-Martin (1997) found that distortions in exchange rates have a negative relationship with levels of economic growth. The situation of the People's Republic of China in the first decade of the twenty first century seems contrary to this, as the PRC's exchange rate was reported to be substantially lower than the "real" market rate, and yet economic growth in the PRC was consistently high during this time. The earlier comparison of Barbados and Jamaica also noted that some people believe that Barbados' fixed exchange rate may contribute to its better economic performance.

Trade policies – in addition to exchange rate policies, studies have consistently found that countries which are open to global trade have higher rates of economic growth.

There are good arguments that policies that limit trade and are protectionist in nature distort trade patterns and mean that developing countries do not use their resources efficiently. At the same time, as noted earlier in the chapter, developing countries are often at a disadvantage when negotiating terms of trade.

Natural resource endowments – historically, countries with abundant natural resources have experienced relatively high rates of economic growth. Perkins et al. (2001) noted that more recently countries that are resource rich have actually fared poorly. It is perhaps the case that it is how the resources are used that leads either to economic growth or the lack thereof.

Finally, Perkins et al. (2001) noted that "a striking fact is that there are no rich economies in the tropics other than Singapore, the Hong Kong territory of China, and a few, small, oil rich countries" (p. 71). They noted that tropical countries have more virulent diseases, more erratic rainfall and generally poor quality soil for agriculture. Sala-i-Martin (1997) had also included geography in his list of factors related to economic development. From a more positive development perspective, I would argue that this may simply be an accident of time, and hope that development is possible for those of us living in the tropics. Perhaps Singapore and Hong Kong can serve as examples of what is possible in the tropics.

Considering the previous list, there is not much that a country can do about its geographic location or resource endowment in order to encourage development. At the same time, the list does suggest that governments can put into place policies to encourage savings and investment; they can invest in education and health to increase life expectancy; they can monitor the use of their natural resources; they can provide a trading environment that is conducive to global trade, while ensuring that they negotiate a fair deal with trading partners. Governments can also evaluate the benefits of a flexible exchange rate system that allows the currency to float freely; however, for some developing countries there may be advantages to the certainty associated with a fixed exchange rate system.

SUMMARY

In many ways the discussion in this chapter underscores the limits to our current understanding of economic development. It is much like the story of the blind men and the elephant – each describes only what he feels – the tail is like a snake, the leg like a pillar, and so on. Each of the explanations of development is a part of the puzzle, but we do not see the whole picture. We also do not know, in many cases, what is cause, and what is effect. For example, political stability may lead to economic development, but equally it may be that development leads to political stability.

This chapter has explored a number of explanations of economic development. All of these explanations probably have some validity, but none provides a complete explanation of development. It is important to continue to investigate the causes of development, and, it is hoped, we will eventually understand the linkages among various factors that may contribute to development.

Managers must manage in a world that includes both richer and poorer countries. In the next chapters we turn attention to management issues in developing countries. We examine these issues from two perspectives, indigenous managers and expatriate managers; expatriate managers are both those from developing countries going abroad and those from developed countries going to developing ones. There is not a lot of literature dealing with how management takes place in developing countries, so, in the following chapters, we rely substantially on logical linking of characteristics of development to management issues. This, in itself, is a "Western" approach and may introduce its own biases, and wherever possible we draw on research from developing countries to illustrate the points being discussed.

The upcoming chapters follow the model of management outlined in Chapter 4. The next chapter will address issues associated with planning, including international strategic planning. Then we will look at organizational issues, including international operations. This will be followed by chapters on staffing and international human resource management. We then consider leadership and motivation in a developing country context. Lastly, we will address issues of control from an international and developing country point of view. In the final chapter we will review the issues addressed throughout the book and conclude with a look to the future.

LESSONS LEARNED

After completing this chapter you should have a better understanding of traditional economic explanations of economic development, as well as the special concerns of development economists and the role of institutions in achieving economic growth. You should be able to define and describe various economic theories and give examples of their success or lack thereof. You should also be able to discuss how resources can be used for economic growth. You should have a broader view of various countries in terms of their economic situations, and be able to compare and contrast these countries. You should be aware that development is more than simply economic development, and you should be able to explain the factors that are important to achieving a better life as well as economic well-being.

DISCUSSION QUESTIONS

1   Examine the sources of economic growth in developing countries and the extent to which they can be affected by government intervention.
2   Discuss the differences between economic growth and development.
3   Identify two measures of economic development and discuss the pros and cons of these measures.
4   What characteristics are typically associated with economic growth? Discuss features that in your view might distinguish an economically developing country from one that is not.
5   Compare the growth rates of two developing countries of your choice. What factors might explain the differences in their growth rates?
6   Compare the growth rates of the People's Republic of China and a developed country. What factors might explain the differences in their growth rates?

EXERCISE

Theorists believe that uncovering the drivers of economic growth will allow us to tackle the global poverty problem. In small groups, discuss this belief. What type of data do you feel you need to translate theoretical predictions into concrete policy lessons? Each group will share its views with the class as a short presentation.

Chapter 6

Planning and strategic management in developing countries

OBJECTIVES

This chapter focuses on the first process of management – planning – and provides concepts and models of strategic planning. It examines these concepts and models from a developing country perspective.

The objectives of the chapter are as follows:

- To highlight how little information there is on how management takes place in developing countries.
- To introduce and discuss a variety of strategic concepts and models.
- To examine how these concepts and models are likely to be work in a developing country context.
- To introduce a model of international strategy, including various international entry options.
- To demonstrate the different entry strategies that a company can consider as it internationalizes.
- To draw attention to the fact that different companies follow different internationalization paths, and they do not necessarily follow a particular model.
- To address issues of international strategic planning, organization and international operations.

INTRODUCTION

In Chapter 4, a model of management was introduced. This model begins with the management process or activity of planning. Planning is described as the activity which sets the strategies, objectives, and goals for an organization. It drives the need for and style of organization and other management activities intended to help achieve plans. The planning activity is clearly pivotal to everything that an organization does. It determines where the organization intends to go and what needs to be done to get there.

Planning is an interesting concept because it encompasses the longer-term and strategic decisions that deal with the overall organization, its vision and its mission. It also guides decision makers as they address the shorter-term and daily decisions that keep the organization running. Strategy is often seen as the responsibility of the chief executive officer (CEO), who may be called president, or managing director, or sometimes general manager. The CEO is the person leading the organization, along with her/his executive team and top managers, while daily or operational planning is usually seen as the responsibility of middle managers and supervisors.

Plans and the planning process can be thought of as a hierarchy of time horizons, with the longest, strategic planning, being primarily a responsibility of the CEO and the executive team, and the shorter-term plans (the tactical or business plans, and the operating or day-to-day plans) being delegated to successively lower levels within the organization. In the developed country view, effective organizations have plans which are harmonized within the context of the strategies and medium-term operating goals and objectives.

In developed countries, it is generally accepted that employees throughout an organization must accept and buy into an organization's strategy if it is to work, and the day-to-day, small decisions can be made such that that the organization follows its strategic course and reaches its goals and serves its mission. Clearly, the longer-term and shorter-term activities are intertwined. In this chapter, we deal with strategy first, then we address issues associated with short-term planning. Once again, the issues and terms are those that are typically found in the developed country literature; however, we examine how the characteristics of developing countries can impact on these ideas. The following section outlines the elements of strategy and defines some of the terms commonly found in the literature.

THE ELEMENTS OF STRATEGY[1]

Although there is general agreement in the literature on the concepts involved in strategy formulation, sometimes terminology can vary. For our purposes, we will try to use the terms as they are most commonly accepted. First, the terms are defined. Typically, and simply, in the literature, the elements of strategy are usually described in the following terms:

Vision – a statement of what the organization can be in the future and where it wants to be; an image of a possible and desirable future for the organization; a realistic and attractive future. The following is an example of a vision statement which was developed for a university in a developing country:

We are a model of excellence in management education, research, strategic partnerships, operating in a physically and technologically world class environment, where faculty and staff produce high-quality graduates and advance knowledge in the management disciplines.

Mission – a statement of what the organization does; a statement of its purpose; a description of the reason the organization exists and how it intends to serve its various stakeholders. The following is an example of a mission statement which was developed for a university in a developing country:

We develop the management capabilities of the people of the Caribbean through the creation and dissemination of world class knowledge and quality teaching informed by our stakeholders.

1 This section is based on a presentation given by Donald Wood at a strategic retreat for the Department of Management Studies, the University of the West Indies, Cave Hill Campus, June, 2006.

Note that both the vision and mission statements are short, but contain key elements of the organization's purpose and view of the future. These are intended to be statements which guide the organization. Some organizations like to display these statements so that stakeholders are aware of them, and employees are reminded of them on a regular basis.

> *Values* – the beliefs that are important in the organization; a set of statements to guide corporate behavior; the constraints and conditions by which the organization will formulate its strategy.
> *Strategy* – the overall direction for the organization; how the organization will achieve its vision and mission, given its values.
> *Tactics* – the specific operational means by which the organization's strategy can be achieved.

These terms are often difficult to delineate and differentiate. Figure 6.1 illustrates how these concepts interact. In the picture, circle A represents the organization. The organization is portrayed as being on one shore, and wanting to get to another shore, and there is a barrier islet between the two. The organization's *vision* is of itself enjoying the advantages of being on shore number 2, and its *mission* is to get there. The question is how best to achieve this *mission* and realize the *vision*. Its *values* will determine the *strategy* that the organization chooses, and the *tactics* required that are appropriate to the selected *strategy*.

In Figure 6.1, the organization is pursuing its *vision* of being on the other shore, with all the desirable attributes and results of being there. The *vision* is critical to progress and provides the driving force, or corporate passion to succeed. Indeed, the *vision* can be said to define success for the organization.

Once having achieved agreement on this *vision* on the part of stakeholders, the organization can then articulate its *mission*. In our simplified example, the *mission* is clear – to take the organization to the other shore. In reality, *mission* statements are more complex and reflect the often competing demands of various stakeholder groups, while maintaining a common *vision*. Most organizations find these consensus elements, the *vision* and the corresponding *mission*, need to be revisited and reconfirmed or adjusted every several years to reflect changing internal and external realities.

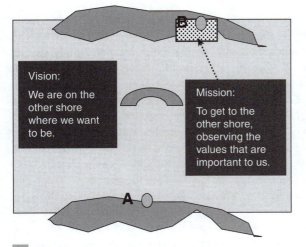

Figure 6.1 *Illustration of strategic elements*
Note: used with permission from Eureka Management Consultants

The *mission*, then, is to get to the other shore. The next question is: how should we proceed in a way that will serve the consensus elements? The conditions and constraints on the *strategy* choice reflect the beliefs and requirements underlying the needs of the stakeholders. These are the *values*. These *values* determine the methods the organization believes are acceptable in pursuing the *vision*.

Values tend to change as an organization evolves and as conditions change and the composition of the various stakeholder groups change over time. The executive team has, as part of its responsibility, the task of tracking and understanding these *values* and navigating the organization in response to them. In this example, the organization has chosen to get to the other shore as fast as possible, and it is not particularly concerned with the cost – its values reflect speed as important and cost less so. Its strategy will reflect these values – likely, a selection of travel by air will be the *strategy*. The organization *strategy* is to fly to the other shore. Then its *tactics* (operational plan) will be to go in a straight line at a high speed by airplane.

If the organization's *values* were different – for example, if speed is important, but cost is also important, the *strategy* might be to get to the other shore by sea. This *strategy* will require different *tactics*. Instead of a pilot and airplane, it may now choose to go to the other shore using a motor launch, which is fast but not as costly as air travel. It will encounter different environmental factors, such as the currents in the water that need to be taken into account, given this option. This defines the operating nature of the organization and the skills and resources to be brought to bear on the tactical challenge of navigating past the barrier islet to the other shore in a way that reflects the organization's *values*. Note that in changing the *values*, the organization has had to change the way it operates, but this change in operations has not affected the longer-term *mission* or *vision* – these remain the same – to get to the other shore and enjoy the envisioned result. When the *values* changed, the *strategy* and resulting *tactics* and associated expertise needed to change.

If the organization were to reflect other values, for example, if it wanted to show concern for the environment and was willing to trade off speed while keeping costs low, it might find that a *strategy* of using a sailboat was more appropriate. Again it would need to adjust its operations or *tactics* to accommodate the different resource requirements and skill set to manage the voyage, taking into account a different set of environmental factors (wind speed and direction, for example). Note once more that the *mission* and *vision* are not affected, only the *strategy* and *tactics* change reflecting the *values*.

The strategic elements described here sound formal and well defined. This is often the case for larger organizations, but is less likely in small organizations. Many companies in developing countries may not have given much thought to their strategy and may simply operate on a day-to-day basis, taking advantage of whatever opportunities arise. Nevertheless, small organizations can benefit from thinking about the elements of their strategy as this can help them understand themselves and their environment. Strategy is usually seen as a top management responsibility, even though input is sought from all levels of the organization and stakeholders outside of the organization. In developing countries, as they have been described here, this is especially likely to be the case. Top management, especially in family-owned firms, may feel that it is entirely up to them to decide where the company goes and how it achieves its goals and objectives. Even in small companies, however, it seems appropriate to share the company's vision and mission with all employees, so that they can feel that they are contributing to achieving these.

In order to develop an appropriate strategy, managers need to understand what their organizations can and cannot achieve given the environments in which they operate. There are several models in the strategic literature,[2] which are used for analyzing the organization and

2 The ideas presented in this section are based on Hill and Jones (2007).

its environment. Two popular conceptualizations are SWOT and PEST. SWOT refers to the Strengths and Weaknesses of the organization and the Opportunities and Threats in the environment. PEST refers to the Political, Economic, Social and Technological aspects of the environment which need to be understood to identify the appropriate opportunities and threats.

The SWOT and PEST analyses need to be done in the context of the organization's mission. They are not absolutes, but are related to the mission – in other words, strengths are strengths in the context of the corporate mission; a strength in one context may be a weakness in another. For example, a pool of unskilled labor is a strength in a labor-intensive company making large volumes of simple, inexpensive products and it may be a weakness in a company that is serving a high technology market. Similarly, an opportunity for one company will not be an opportunity for another. For example, Africa's lack of electrification is an opportunity for companies making solar powered products but not for companies selling traditional electrical products.

In a SWOT analysis, the organization's strengths and weaknesses are analyzed to identify what the organization can and cannot do effectively, and the environment is analyzed to find opportunities for the organization as well as to be aware of, and perhaps prepare for the threats that it faces. A SWOT analysis looks for the fit between the organization and its environment to find the most appropriate strategy, consistent with its vision and mission. Strengths and weaknesses are internal to the organization and opportunities and threats are external to it. The organization wants to capitalize on, and use, its strengths to take advantage of opportunities, while limiting the negatives associated with its weaknesses, and avoiding threats. The PEST analysis is essentially an extension of the external analysis, and it identifies the specific aspects of the environment that need to be assessed.

STRATEGY IN DEVELOPING COUNTRIES

These are what might be called generic models that relate to strategy. They are intended to apply to any company and to be used by managers in all organizations. From this perspective, the models should be applicable in developing countries as they are in developed countries. It would seem that all companies need to have a vision of where they are going and what their primary purpose is (mission), and to develop a roadmap for getting there (strategy and tactics) that fits in with their values. Equally, it would seem that any company needs to understand its own capabilities (strengths and weaknesses) and how these relate to the environment in which it operates (opportunities and threats) and in order to understand this environment, it needs to analyze political, economic, social, and technological factors. While this is likely generally correct, there are a number of factors in developing countries that may make the models less applicable. Some of these are:

- In developing countries, small- and medium-sized firms dominate the corporate landscape. Strategic management literature from developed countries has been developed mainly with larger companies in mind. Smaller companies may be less likely to address strategic issues in a formal sense. They may feel that a longer-term strategy is actually a constraint, as they need to be able to move quickly. For example, a small firm may unexpectedly encounter a joint venture possibility that takes it in a new and unexpected direction.
- In developing countries, a large number of firms are family owned/controlled, or owned/ controlled by a small group of closely knit people. In such firms, strategy may be determined by the personal values and objectives of the owners rather than by a systematic analysis of the firm and its environment. For example, if a family member develops an

interest in solar energy, the family owned firm might move in this direction, even though it does not logically fit its strengths.

- In developing countries, the environment is generally more unstable that that found in developed countries. Firms have to be able to react to the unexpected rather than be constrained by a plan. If these firms are to succeed, they need to be flexible and responsive, and this may make strategic planning seem less relevant. For example, an unexpected change in government can change a company's strengths and weaknesses, and open up new opportunities and threats.

- In developing countries, relationships between firms and those in political power are often closer than in developed countries. This means that firms are often expected to act in ways that the political system dictates. This means that the normal SWOT analysis may not be relevant. For example, if the people in political power decide that a certain type of investment is desirable or undesirable, the firms may find it necessary to make this kind of investment, in spite of the business merits of the investment.

- Certain aspects of the environment may be especially important in developing countries and others less so, likely changing the focus of the environmental analysis, so the traditional PEST may not be as relevant. For example, many developing countries have a relatively poor infrastructure, thus environmental issues associated with moving products or services, from production site to consumers, may be especially important.

- Cultural values in different countries may influence attitudes towards the long-term and strategy. In some places a long-term orientation may encourage the idea of looking to, and planning for the future. In contrast, a fatalistic orientation may suggest that making plans is contrary to God's will and that the firm's success is in God's hands. Rational, thinking cultures may find strategic analysis and planning attractive, but, emotional cultures may prefer decisions made on the basis of what feels right or what is emotionally comfortable.

- In countries where power–distance is high, those at the top may feel that it is solely their responsibility to decide how the company is operated. Lower-level employees may be content to simply carry out orders, and may have little concern with the company's 'strategy', and may not want to have input into strategic choices. In fact, lower-level employees may find it somewhat frightening to be involved in these choices, and may not be interested in knowing about them.

Although there are reasons why companies in developing companies may find the development of strategy less attractive than their developed country counterparts, there is likely value to the strategic process in both situations. The process of identifying a vision, mission, values, strategies, and tactics, as well as the SWOT and PEST analyses are helpful to almost all organizations in developing a better understanding of the organization and its relationship to its environment.

The strategic models designed in developed countries have value for companies in developing countries, although the details of the models may have to be adapted for the specifics of the local environment. While the elements of strategy development may be universal, the processes used to develop strategies and strategic plans can be expected to differ among countries of differing levels of enterprise development and differing methods and values reflecting their cultures. For example, in the previous outline it was suggested that a family member with an interest in solar energy could well influence the company's direction. In a SWOT analysis in this situation, the family member's interest would be considered a strength. Similarly, if the political powers are supporting a particular investment, this would be considered an opportunity. The generic models may be useful in developing countries, but the specifics may be somewhat different from what they would be in a developed country.

When one combines the internal strengths and weaknesses of the firm with the external opportunities and threats, the resulting understanding is often called the firm's competitive advantage. The next section considers the concept of competitive advantage.

THE BASIS FOR COMPETITIVE ADVANTAGE

A firm's competitive advantage comes from the firm's capabilities relative to the market's needs and wants. A competitive advantage can come from a wide variety of sources. Consider Wikipedia – an innovative idea that has become a standard way of providing information in the Internet world of the early twenty-first century; Facebook is a similar phenomenon that arose out of an individual's desire to link his classmates electronically. In both of these cases, an innovative idea matched a market need and provided an organization with the competitive advantage of being unique and therefore the first of its type. In contrast, China's economic success is largely based on the country's ability to dominate manufacturing over the last several decades, because of its large and cheap labor force and therefore low-cost structure. These examples illustrate a common distinction in terms of competitive advantage. Some companies compete and succeed on the basis of low cost; others compete and succeed on the basis of differentiation. This is a simplistic dichotomy because cost advantages can come from many sources, and differentiation can also come from many sources.

Cost advantages can come from access to abundant resources, such as the abundant labor in China, or it can come from technological advances, such as Internet developments and robotics, or innovative management practices, such as goal setting that increases output, or any variety of other resources that lead to lower costs. Differential advantages can come from new products or services, such as Facebook, alternative uses for existing products or services, such as used materials to build reefs, different means of addressing current challenges, such as mini solar panels for use in Africa, or any variety of innovative ways of serving markets. A subset of the differential advantage is a competitive advantage based on serving a small niche market, such as high-priced designer children's clothes.

A competitive advantage based on cost and price relies on the ability to produce at a relatively low cost, and usually involves establishing economies of scale. A cost-based competitive advantage is often focused on production. A competitive advantage based on differentiation generally relies on the ability to understand and communicate with specific markets and market to them effectively.

Of course, both production and marketing are important in any organization and they have to complement each other. Facebook has to have a sound production basis (websites, webmasters, web designers, technicians, and so on) to keep its millions of users happy so that they continue to use it. Walmart may rely on low-cost production in sites around the world, but it also needs the market's recognition of the Walmart name and methods of serving its customers. It needs these market strengths in order to ensure that it can achieve the volume of transactions it needs to sustain its low cost buying advantage. This has resulted in Walmart being successful in almost all markets where it opens a store.

Developing countries have, for many years, relied on providing commodities, locally and internationally. These commodities, such as bananas, sugar, and natural resources, are sold based on cost and price. As discussed in an earlier chapter, the colonial heritage that many developing countries share has probably encouraged this focus. Colonial economies were established and developed to provide commodities for the colonizers, and the focus in the colonies was on efficiency of production. Insofar as marketing was considered, it was done by the colonizing country. The former colonies are often described as plantation economies (or, as they develop, post-plantation economies) and one of the hallmarks of plantation economies is a lack of marketing expertise, and ability to appreciate the importance of marketing.

The low-price leader in any market gains competitive advantage from being able to produce at the lowest cost. This will undoubtedly continue to be an important strategy for companies in developing countries. Many developing countries have low wages and a large labor force that is willing to work for little pay. Many also have natural resources that are abundant and relatively cheap. Companies will continue to exploit these cost advantages through a price leader strategy and a focus on production. In spite of this, marketing is still important for these companies, and companies from developing countries need to develop their marketing abilities if they are to succeed globally.

As the world has changed over the past several decades, former colonies have been required to become more globally competitive, as subsidies and preferential treatment for their products and services have been phased out by the developed world (for example, Europe has reduced the levels of protection it provides for the ACP – Africa, Caribbean, Pacific – countries). Globalization has also meant increased competition for many commodities and many developing countries have found that labor costs are rising. Even in China, known for its low-cost advantage, companies are moving into newer value added products and services. For example the Chinese government has set a goal to become the number one producer of electric cars by 2012, a Shenzhen-based company is about to become the world's largest DNA sequencing laboratory, and China is planning to launch an all-Chinese manned space station (*Economist*, 2010). Many developing countries are currently realizing that they need to understand and focus on differentiation and finding specialized niche markets, where their products and services are considered valuable. This implies a shift to a marketing orientation rather than a production orientation, and a focus on global niche products and markets.

Differentiated goods and services satisfy the special needs and wants of particular groups of customers and this provides a competitive advantage. Companies focus on value that allows them to charge a comparatively higher price and obtain a better margin. The higher price and better margin allows these companies to be profitable with lower levels of sales. A relatively small market is thus of interest to a company selling a differentiated product or service.

A differentiation strategy means that the company needs to ensure that customers see and recognize what is special about its products and/or services, and therefore differentiates it from competitors and alternatives. This often involves additional investment costs, such as market research, creating a brand and brand awareness, advertising, and public relations as well as research and development, and design of new product offerings. These additional costs must be offset by the increase in revenue from higher profit margins. Small companies, with limited resources, often find it difficult to make the decision to invest in these intangible areas. Investment is needed for tangible aspects of the business, such as buildings and machinery, people and resources, and so on, and these, naturally come first. The other investments are often as important, however, as the following excerpts from an article on branding illustrates.

An *Economist*, article entitled "Brand and deliver – Emerging Asia's new corporate imperative" noted the need for brand development in Asian countries. The same is true throughout the developing world. The *Economist* article says that cost advantages are eroding, markets are opening and competition for customers is intensifying. Many of these competitors will be Western companies that have honed their branding skills over many years. At least one interviewee for the report estimated that Chinese companies have less than ten years in which to change their business models.

The article notes that branding isn't only about succeeding in local markets, it's critical to going global. Businesses in emerging Asia (and the rest of the developing world) are ambitious, as illustrated by the volume of outbound FDI and merger and acquisition deals from India and China. The article comments that these companies will find it difficult to succeed in "going global" without a strong brand.

Organizations that cannot afford either a wide scope cost leadership or a wide scope differentiation strategy can identify a competitive advantage through a niche strategy. A niche strategy focuses effort and resources on a narrow, well-defined segment of a market. A niche strategy is often used by smaller firms. A niche approach is appropriate for many companies in developing countries because of their relatively small size and limited resources.

Niche markets are often contrasted with mass markets. Niche products have a special, differentiated appeal to a limited number of purchasers. Mass products have a broad appeal to the undifferentiated mass of consumers. Mass products for mass markets usually rely on economies of scale and cost efficiencies, and compete largely on the basis of price. Niche products rely on differentiated features, and compete on the basis of these special features, meeting special and even unique consumers' needs where the price of the product is of secondary concern. Niche markets, by definition, are relatively small, but they are also associated with relatively high margins; therefore, niche markets can be as profitable as mass markets (LeDuc, 2005).

There have always been mass markets and specialized niche markets. In recent years, this division appears to have intensified, at least in the developed world (Punnett, 2004c). If you go into many shopping areas in Europe and North America, you find WalMart, the king of mass merchandising, but nearby you also find specialty stores with high-priced, unusual merchandise. Consumers will tell you that they go to WalMart for much of their regular day-to-day purchases, but that they go to the specialty stores "to get something unusual," "to feel good," "to pamper myself," "to get a special gift." In other words, shopping at specialty stores provides a different experience from shopping at a mass merchandiser. Specialty stores often offer opportunities for niche marketers, who are seeking limited markets they can serve in keeping with their limited supply capabilities.

Good business opportunities are available in both mass markets and niche markets. The following section outlines some of the attractions of a niche strategy for companies in developing countries.

Niche strategies for companies in developing countries

A niche product or service can be considered as an item whose primary value lies in differentiation and its particular attractiveness to a relatively small number of purchasers. A niche market is a relatively small, specialty market, which is relatively price inelastic, and where its primary demand is for differentiation or uniqueness. Typically, niche products and services are perceived by purchasers as high value and differentiated, and are priced accordingly.

The word niche comes from the root 'nest' and is defined in the *American Heritage Dictionary* as "a suitable situation or activity" and a "recess for a statue." The root of the word, as well as the definitions, is helpful in understanding what we mean when we talk of a specialized niche market. A niche market is a place where a product or service finds its nest, it is a suitable situation or activity for the product or service, and the product or service fits like a statue into its special recess or niche. Niche products or services are particularly attractive for smaller companies, partly because their profitability does not rely on economies of scale, and partly because they are often too small to be attractive to large-scale marketers (Kaufman and Punnett, 2009). In addition, development of a global brand is not necessary for these markets, at least not initially.

Companies can succeed in niche markets by identifying a small number of customers, and providing these customers with the products and/or services that they want. The important aspect of serving a niche market is provision of appropriate quality in a consistent and timely manner, so that the customer is highly satisfied.

High-value niche markets are subject to sudden shifts in consumer tastes and patterns. In a study of North American niche markets, Punnett (2004c) identified a number of niche products as having potential for Caribbean companies. These included high-priced children's clothes (such as dresses for weddings and christening robes), products for pets (such as personalized blankets and leashes), hand painted drawer knobs, and exotic tropical condiments (such as passion pepper jelly and guava–mango jam). These products are all subject to sudden shifts. A downturn in the economy can affect the likelihood of sales of high-priced christening robes or dog blankets; a change in fashion tastes can make a brightly painted drawer pull or an exotic jelly yesterday's or tomorrow's (not today's) product. This means that companies that have a niche market strategy must be flexible and able to change product details relatively easily. Smaller producers have an advantage over larger ones in that there is inherent flexibility in smallness. Larger producers find it much more difficult to shift production than do small producers, often due to investments in automatic equipment or other means of large-scale production. This means that small companies can capitalize on their size and flexibility to meet the potentially cyclical nature of high-value niche markets (Punnett and Morrison, 2006).

Borrowing an economic concept, niche markets can be thought of as the points of tangency between production possibilities and consumption preferences; that is, where production possibilities fit with consumer preferences. In Figure 6.2, line A–A1 represents what a particular company can produce given a set of resources and constraints (production possibilities), lines B–B1 and C–C1 represent two different sets of consumers and their preferences given product costs and features (consumption preferences). Where the lines are tangent (X and Y) can be thought of as representing niche markets. At X or Y, the producer is maximizing the use of resources, within constraints, and meeting the specific needs of a specific set of consumers.

For companies in developing countries, the link between the producer and the market is the most difficult to manage effectively. How does the company learn about potential markets and assess potential markets effectively? Small producers, by definition, have limited resources to invest in market analysis. One reason that niche markets have become more attractive for companies in developing countries in recent years is the advent of the Internet and the increased

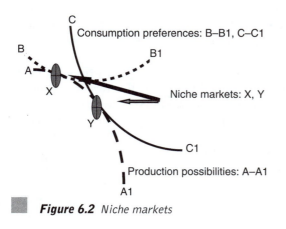

Figure 6.2 Niche markets

ease of communication around the world. Companies following a niche strategy can now do a substantial amount of market research without having to undertake the costs and time associated with travelling to potential markets. In addition, access to friends and family in potential markets is much easier today, and many companies are using their country's diaspora as effective conduits between markets of interest and their production possibilities at home.

As discussed, the appropriate strategy for a company is a function of its internal capabilities and the external environment in which it operates. An important aspect of the environment is the industry in which the company operates, and how competitive the industry is. Michael Porter (1980, 1998) proposed that understanding the competitive nature of the industry was critical to making the right strategic choices. Porter's five forces model is outlined in the following section.

PORTER'S FIVE FORCES MODEL

Porter's model consists of the following five forces:

> *Competition within the industry* – this considers existing firms in the industry and the degree to which they compete with each other.
> *Threat of new entrants* – this considers how many potential new entrants there are and how likely it is that new entrants will become a reality in the industry.
> *Bargaining power of suppliers* – this considers the strength of suppliers to the industry and how powerful they are relative to the companies in the industry.
> *Bargaining power of buyers* – this considers the strength of buyers in the industry and how powerful they are relative to the companies in the industry.
> *Availability of substitutes* – this considers if there are substitute products or services and how acceptable these substitutes are.

These forces are certainly of interest and relevant to establishing an effective strategy and will be considered by many companies as part of their strategic analysis. They do, however, imply a well-organized industry, and this may not be the case for many industries in many developing countries.

Typically, economic activity in developing countries tends to centre on principal firms, not industries. Often these firms are mini-conglomerates operating in a number of sometimes unrelated industries. Their target markets domestically and internationally tend to be small relative to the industries of which they are a part. Consequently, the characteristics of those industries, in Porter's model, are often too macro to be relevant to small players. There are many other reasons why it may be difficult to use this model in developing countries. For example:

- It may be difficult to ascertain the level of competition among firms where these are family firms and there may be agreements among families regarding when and where they compete.
- It may be difficult to assess the likelihood of new entrants when the new entrants may come from other countries, and the markets are small niches.
- It may be difficult to know the bargaining power of suppliers if they can be curtailed or otherwise affected by government policies.

- It may be difficult to judge the bargaining power of buyers because they may be foreign but represented by a local entity.
- It may be difficult to identify substitutes because they may not currently be available locally, but could become available at short notice.

Companies in developing countries will, nevertheless, want to assess the industry in which they operate and the degree of competition they face, both locally and internationally. Essentially, the less competitive the industry is, the greater the opportunity for profits, and the more competitive it is the lower profits will be. Using Porter's model, if companies compete a lot, this will drive prices down. If new entrants are likely, prices will be kept low. If suppliers have a strong bargaining position, costs will be higher. If buyers have a strong bargaining position, prices will be low. If substitutes are readily available, prices will have to match the prices of the substitutes. A very competitive industry implies higher costs and lower prices. Of course, this is an extreme situation.

Models such as Porter's go beyond the apparent simplicity and subjectivity of a SWOT analysis. They provide a more structured approach to the analysis of the environment. The primary reason for this analysis is to identify those aspects of the industry that provide opportunities and those that are threats. If the industry generally competes on a price basis, your company's strategy may be to improve quality and service and maintain price, striving for differentiation to strengthen your price where possible. If there is a threat of new entrants, your strategy could be to form a joint venture with one of these new entrants. If substitutes are seen as a threat, your strategy could be to provide evidence of the superiority of your company's product or service. If suppliers are strong, your strategy might be backward integration to become your own supplier. If buyers are strong, your strategy may be to offer better prices in return for longer-term contracts.

From the perspective of a company in a developing country, particularly a small company, any industry looked at globally, may seem very competitive, and the company may feel it has little bargaining power on any front. There are a number of things for managers in this situation to keep in mind. First, small does generally mean less power, but power can be increased by joining with others. Small also means you may be overlooked and you can use this to your advantage by making strategic moves when no one is looking. Small also means flexible, so you need to be open to the opportunities that a larger company would not find interesting. Small companies often feel that they cannot address global markets, because they do not have the capacity. In the next section, a model of internationalization is presented and this serves as a means to identify the various international forms of entry available to firms.

INTERNATIONAL STRATEGY AND INTERNATIONAL BUSINESS DEVELOPMENT

Figure 6.3 illustrates a typical pattern of internationalization. Many companies do not follow this pattern and there is no necessity to follow this pattern. This is particularly true today when 'born global' companies are becoming more common, and there is no reason that an idea for a product or service conceived in Nepal cannot have global applications. Global communications have made it more likely today that investment for a product or service can be found, market research conducted, and production and sales undertaken without ever leaving Nepal, or any other developing country. The reality still remains, however, that most products and services develop for the local market and grow from there. Figure 6.3 illustrates such a growth strategy.

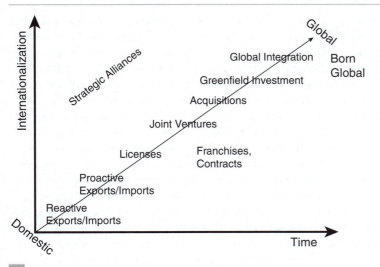

Figure 6.3 *International business development*

The following discussion briefly explains each stage of development identified in the model in Figure 6.3:

Domestic – A purely domestic company is one that does not rely on international linkages in any way. Such companies are unusual today, because most companies either obtain supplies (ingredients, bottles, packaging, and so on) from outside sources, or sell some of their products to neighboring countries or to tourists. Such companies may be more likely in developing countries where there are micro companies that produce for a limited local market. At the same time, because of relatively limited resources, it may be the case that they are less likely. For example, farmers raising goats and bottling goat's milk may be using imported bottles even though they may not realize it. Many small companies in developing countries would be considered domestic in any case, because they see themselves as domestic, and they are not conscious of their international linkages, and do not have to manage these linkages.

Reactive exports – Reactive exports occur when a company does not seek out export markets, but, rather, reacts to something in the export market. Usually this occurs when firms are approached by foreign buyers and given the opportunity to export relatively small quantities of their products. Most firms see this type of exporting as relatively risk free, as the new market is essentially guaranteed by the foreign buyer, and terms are usually relatively favorable to the seller, because the buyer has an interest in the product. Also, such transactions often "feel" domestic, because the seller does not need to understand a foreign market and the transactions take place as if they are domestic sales. Nevertheless, exporting leads the producer into new and unknown challenges, including export and import requirements, packaging, labeling, tariffs, and so on. For companies in developing countries, the export requirements may be onerous, especially because many of these companies are small. Exporting, even on a small scale can require substantial time and effort, and for a small operation, this may be difficult, and can divert attention from the main, local business. Exporting is clearly an opportunity for most companies, but the reality should be explored before saying yes to any export offer.

Proactive exports – Proactive exports occur when a company sees foreign markets as a major opportunity. Such a company seeks out foreign markets and actively looks for ways to export. This is a significant change from the reactive exporter and may occur after a company has had some experience exporting on a reactive basis. It will have built know-how and expertise on the exporting process, through reactive exports, and may thus feel that it can address more markets more aggressively. Proactive exporting implies a change in strategy where exporting is seen as an important component of the company's revenues and profits, possibly as important as its domestic component. This means that a proactive exporter has to be active about the export process, and needs to devote substantial resources to successfully exporting to a variety of different markets. This attention to exports can have a negative impact on domestic operations and sales, so companies need to be prepared for the impact of exports. In developing countries, where companies are relatively small, with limited resources, the diversion of resources to exports requires careful thought and preparation.

Licenses – Licenses are a way to expand internationally without substantial investment in foreign markets. Licenses involve an agreement between a licensee and a licensor; the licensee owns the rights to a product or service and wants another company, the licensor, to produce the product/service on its behalf. For some companies, licensing agreements provide a way to get local production in a foreign market, with its attendant benefits, without the costs of investment. Local production can mean lower costs, because it avoids some brokerage, transportation and distribution costs, and tariffs and taxes that may be imposed on foreign products.

For companies from developing countries, licenses can be a viable way of getting into foreign markets. The downside of licenses is the reliance on a foreign producer for quality and availability, so licensing partners have to be carefully researched and agreements written to cover a variety of possible problems. A particular concern with licenses is the possibility that the licensee will "steal" the licensor's special competitive advantage, and companies need to pay particular attention to protecting those components that make their products or services special. These issues can be especially concerning for companies from developing countries working with counterparts from developed countries, because the developed country counterpart may have more resources and be able to negotiate from a position of greater power. This means that developing country companies have to be particularly vigilant and careful in developing a licensing agreement.

Joint ventures – Joint ventures involve working with others as partners. Joint ventures provide a good opportunity for developing country companies to use their limited resources efficiently and effectively. These companies can seek partners who provide complementary strengths. That is, if the developing country company lacks management expertise, it can seek a partner who is strong in this area; if it lacks financial resources, it can look for a partner with strong finances; if it needs marketing know-how, it can seek a partner who has this ability, and so on. Partnerships are not without their challenges, however, and the choice of partner and structure of agreements are critical to the success of a joint venture. This is particularly true for smaller companies from developing countries, because there can be a mismatch when a small company partners with a larger one from a developed country. The larger company is likely to be in the power position and the smaller may find that it has to go along with the goals and policies of the larger one, and these may not be best for the smaller company. This means that it is critical for the smaller company to take the time to examine a variety of potential partners to find the right partner, and to structure the partnership agreements so that they are beneficial to both sides, and provide "win-win" outcomes. Companies entering into joint venture agreements should consider what happens if there are conflicts, and if the partnership does not go as planned; in other words, they should plan for the possibility of a breakdown of the partnership.

Acquisitions and greenfield investments – For companies that have the resources, acquiring foreign companies or investing in new, "greenfield", 100 percent wholly owned, properties is a possibility. These are seen as attractive because the investor controls the entire project through ownership. Companies from developing countries, which are often relatively small and have limited resources, may often not be in a position to acquire foreign companies or invest in new properties. It is generally the large, well-established companies from developing countries that are involved in acquisitions and greenfield investment. For smaller companies, acquisitions and greenfield investments or establishing 100 percent wholly owned subsidiaries, require careful consideration, because they generally require substantial levels of investment and resources; this means financial, managerial, supplies, marketing, and so on.

Strategic alliances – Strategic alliances are arrangements where companies cooperate without necessarily sharing ownership, as in a joint venture. They are alliances for strategic purposes. Many of the arrangements described previously could be considered strategic alliances, because they involve cooperation for strategic reasons. There are other arrangements that can be considered as strategic alliances as well. For example, companies may cooperate on research that is expensive (say, for cancer cures) but compete in terms of development of new products; companies may cooperate on advertising and promotion (say, American Express and the Olympic Games) even though they have no other relationship; companies may share a distribution channel to achieve economies of scale in distribution (say, books and videos) even if the products are sold separately. Another example involves Adidas and Coty. The Adidas brand is well known in athletic products, and Coty is well known in cosmetics and personal products; these companies have cooperated through an agreement where Coty produces an Adidas brand deodorant. Strategic alliances, carefully selected, are a good way for companies from developing countries to expand their reach. Especially for smaller companies, such alliances can provide substantial benefits. The challenge is to identify appropriate partners who will be interested in an alliance. There has to be benefit to all sides in an alliance, and the small, developing country company may not be able to demonstrate that it can provide these benefits, particularly if their potential partner is too large to see a significant benefit from a linkage with a small partner. These companies will need to identify benefits and find a way to persuade potential allies of these benefits, possibly seeking out smaller, more eager partners.

Global Integration – Global integration means that companies look at the world as a whole and decide where it is best to obtain the inputs for their products and services, where it is best to produce them, what is the best means of distribution for different markets, and so on. Global integration is relatively unusual even among large companies from developed countries. The large resource based companies, such as steel makers and oil companies, and the global auto makers, might be considered globally integrated, but for most companies integration is on a smaller scale, perhaps regional. Most companies from developing countries may not be in a position to consider global integration; however, the concept of maximizing efficiency by looking at operations holistically makes a lot of sense, because small companies with limited resources need to ensure that these limited resources are used as effectively as possible.

The previous discussion has focused on outward-looking strategies. Inward-looking strategies are equally possible. Companies can be approached to import (reactive importing), they can seek out supplies and resources from foreign locations (proactive importing), they can act as licensees, establish joint ventures with foreign companies to develop local products and services, serve as the outsourcing arm of a global company, become a subsidiary of a globally integrated company, and so on. Many companies in developing countries begin their international operations in this way. Because of their relatively small size and limited resources, they may not have considered international activities, but they may need to import product inputs, and they may be well positioned to serve as a local producer, through a licensing agreement, for a foreign company, or act as the local partner for a foreign investor, and so on.

There are also several international expansion possibilities that were not included in this discussion. These include contracts, franchises, turnkey operations, and outsourcing. Briefly, the following examines these options.

Contracting – Contracting is usually a relatively short-term agreement to undertake a specific project and complete identified goals and objectives, within a specified time frame, for a stated fee. International contracts are sometimes undertaken by individuals – for example, a retired professor may agree to teach a course in a foreign location. International contracts are common for many professional firms, such as management consultants, IT specialists, legal services, construction companies, and so on. Typically, contracts are awarded through a bidding process, where companies prepare a proposal and the proposals are reviewed by the contracting organization in terms of the work content, outcomes, and charges, and so on. Sometimes, contracts are awarded on the basis of an individual or company's well-known expertise. For example, an individual, Red Adair, and his expert group of fire-fighters, was known globally as *the* person to call to put out oil fires, including those of the Gulf War of the 1990s, even when he was in his seventies. Contracts are a good way for smaller companies to gain international experience, because of their clear objectives and limited timeframe. It is important, however, that companies (and individuals) ensure that their understanding of the details of the contract is the same as that of the contracting organization; especially with regard to how and when costs will be reimbursed and fees paid. Details, such as the withholding and payment of taxes need to be considered, or the contractor may be in for unpleasant surprises. This is critical for small companies which cannot afford to incur large expenses or losses of any kind.

Franchising – Franchising is usually seen as appropriate for a company (the franchisor) that has the ability to "sell" its entire operation and image to various operators (the franchisees). McDonald's is often held up as the epitome of a franchise. A strong franchise such as McDonald's can command a good price for others to operate McDonald's restaurants, and the franchisees are willing to buy into the McDonald's concepts – menu, look, service, and so on – because these are well known and accepted around the world. In order to franchise successfully internationally, a company needs to have developed a strong brand and presence in its local environment. There are some companies from developing countries that have successfully moved abroad through franchises, but it is a relatively unusual expansion strategy. In order to successfully franchise, the company needs to have absolute control of some key aspect of the business that prohibits its franchisees from simply running the business under their own name.

Turnkey operations – Turnkey operations usually involve large infrastructure projects with specialized expertise. The provider completes a large project, such as a dam, highway or a railroad, then turns this over to local operators. These projects are often dominated by companies, and groups of companies from developed countries, because of their access to the substantial resources and experience needed to complete these large projects. In developing countries, companies are most likely to be involved in turnkey projects on a regional basis; however, more and more, local companies are partnering with foreign companies to be involved in projects that they could not take on, on their own, and this is a strategy for companies that have developed the specialized expertise associated with large infrastructure projects.

Outsourcing – Outsourcing refers to the use of unrelated companies to provide specialized services. Often, these have been companies that provide specialist support on the use of specific products or services – such as laptop computers or software programs. Outsourcing has been used for a wide variety of services, ranging from janitorial and cleaning services to legal and medical services. Developing countries have often been the source of outsourcing services. The lower labor costs in most developing countries have made them a target for establishing outsourcing operations for companies from developed countries.

The previous discussion illustrates the many ways that a company can internationalize. For many developing country companies, because of their limited resources, exports may be the only degree of international operations that are feasible. For others, more international expansion will be attractive, and for some, global diversification or integration will be possible. For many companies, a mix of international approaches is most appropriate; for example, some exports combined with licenses and joint ventures. As illustrated in earlier chapters, some companies from developing countries have grown to be global giants. There are many others that have developed a small number of products or services which they sell in selected international markets.

SUMMARY

This chapter discussed the concepts associated with strategic planning and introduced a variety of models for identifying an effective corporate strategy, and considered these from a developing country perspective. It also discussed strategy from an international perspective. It introduced an internationalization model and discussed various international entry options from a developing country perspective. Companies do not always internationalize along a path from local to global, nor do they want to internationalize to the degree of global integration; many companies become exporters and go no further, others move quickly from local to foreign investment, still others reach a certain stage and sell out. And, most companies pragmatically employ a mix of these strategies and entry forms. Further, as noted initially, some companies are "born global" and their operations are international from inception. The model presented in this chapter is intended to illustrate the different entry strategies that a company can consider as it internationalizes. The next chapter will expand on these strategies and their operationalization, using a fictional example.

LESSONS LEARNED

After completing this chapter, the reader should understand the elements of strategy and planning, and be able to discuss these from a developing country perspective. You should be familiar with various ways to internationalize, and be able to describe various entry models. You should also be able to explain a "typical" process of internationalization over time. You should be aware that many developing countries are currently realizing the need to focus on global niche products and markets, and you should be able to explain why this suggests a shift of emphasis to a marketing orientation instead of a production orientation. You should also be able to explain outward and inward strategies and why they are equally viable for companies in developing countries.

DISCUSSION QUESTIONS

1   The appropriate strategy for a company is a function of its internal capabilities and the external environment in which it operates. Discuss the pros and cons of this statement.
2   As a manager, discuss what you understand to be the difference between strategic planning and short-term operational planning.
3   Explain whether you think Western-based theories of strategic management can be applied in developing countries.
4   Select a particular developing country and an industry within that country, and discuss the competitive environment.

EXERCISE

You are a manager of the leading solar water heating company in _____ (country). Your company is planning to internationalize and establish a solar water heating business in _____. Discuss the following:

■   What factors will you use to assess the internal situation?
■   What strategic planning tools and approaches will you use to establish the company?

Chapter 7

Organizing and operating an international company

OBJECTIVES

This chapter examines the various steps in the internationalization process, using a fictional company, and the model presented in the previous chapter. It also discusses the way companies are organized, and how this changes in response to an international strategy.

The objectives of the chapter are as follows:

- To consider and understand the realities of organizing and operating from a developing country base.
- To consider how international expansion might take place.
- To recognize the challenges of internationalization and how companies in developing countries deal with these challenges.
- To illustrate how firms in developing countries encounter the same challenges as those in developed countries but with different priorities, emphases and capabilities.
- To explain how companies are organized, and highlight small company structures, that are typically based around the major functions that have to be carried out to operate the business.

INTRODUCTION

In this chapter we look at the various possible steps in the internationalization process, or the international modes of entry. We also consider the reality of organizing and operating an international company from a developing country base. The challenges of operating from such a base are explored as well as ways of overcoming these challenges. We conclude with a brief consideration of organizational structures and how they are likely to develop.

A fictional product is used to track the reader through the internationalization process. Drawing on the internationalization model from the previous chapter, a product called "Tanty Goodluck's Sauce" develops from a purely domestic base into a global company. The fictional Tanty Goodluck is seen as starting by making the sauce at home in a small developing country (perhaps in the Caribbean), using a recipe from her grandmother. The sauce was very popular with family and friends who found it quite different from the sauces available at the supermarket. Gradually, Tanty started bottling her sauce and selling it at local stores. Again it was very popular, and Tanty had to expand in order to produce her sauce on a commercial basis. She opened a small production facility and employed a couple of people to help her. This created a variety of issues as she had to ensure she could supply the supermarkets and this meant complying with sanitary regulations, bottling and labeling her product, ensuring the supply of ingredients, distributing and marketing the product, and managing her employees. Tanty enjoyed dealing with these issues and developed a substantial expertise in commercially producing Tanty Goodluck's Sauce. From this base, Tanty expanded her enterprise until it became global. The company is Goodluck Enterprises and the product is "Tanty Goodluck's Sauce".

THE INTERNATIONALIZATION PROCESS

In this section the various internationalization options are considered for "Tanty Goodluck's Sauce". Each option has its own set of challenges and requires Tanty Goodluck to adjust her strategies and plan carefully for the next stage of internationalization. Her focus moves beyond the strategic level to the tactical levels which include operational considerations. The first level of internationalization considered is reactive exports.

> *Reactive exports* – Tanty is approached by a visitor from Canada who has tried the sauce and
> wants to import a few cases to see if the clientele at her specialty shop in Canada likes
> the product. Tanty is delighted and says of course she will send the five cases that they
> agree on. Tanty soon discovers this is not as simple as she imagined. She has to arrange
> for an export license, ensure her label conforms to Canadian laws, get a customs broker,
> arrange for air shipment and insurance, make sure her Canadian customer is ready to
> receive the product, and a host of other things, along with finding a way to get paid and
> translate Canadian currency into local currency.

As soon as a company moves to exporting, even on a small scale, the company has to change its thinking. Exporting and importing may seem relatively simple compared to other forms of international expansion, but as Robinson (1978: 69) noted more than thirty years ago: "It should be clearly understood that export requires a set of highly specialized skills having to do with packaging, marking, documentation, selection of carriers, insurance, foreign import regulations, foreign export finance, and the selection of overseas commission houses, representatives, and/or agents." In other words, companies cannot enter into exports, even reactive exports, without thinking through the process. Among the issues that have to be addressed to move products and services from one location to another are:

- Export documentation requirements on the part of the home country. Countries have specific requirements that have to be met before products or services can be exported. If the appropriate paperwork is not completed, the product/service will simply not be allowed out of the country
- Import documentation requirements on the part of the foreign country. Countries also have specific requirements that have to be met before products/services are allowed into the country. Again, if the paperwork is incomplete, the products or services will simply remain at the "dock" or "port", where it will incur various charges associated with warehousing and demurrage and/or be returned to the home location (at the exporter's expense).

- Appropriate packaging and labeling. Packaging and labeling is required for two reasons. First, packages and labels protect products or services ensuring that they can be safely transported by air, rail, ship, truck, and so on. Second, packages and labels must meet home and foreign country requirements.
- Use of intermediaries. There are export brokers on the home side and import brokers on the foreign country side. These intermediaries are experts in exporting and importing and they can make the process much easier for the exporter and importer; however, intermediaries add to the cost of the export/import process and should be chosen carefully.
- Choice of transportation. There are usually many transportation options available to the exporter/importer. There are tradeoffs in terms of costs, speed, safety, reliability and convenience. The usual physical transport means are by air, rail, ship, truck, or some combination.
- Payment methods. Exporters/importers must agree on what currency will be used and how payments will be made. Potential changes in currency values mean that any transaction which involves spending or receiving foreign currency implies risk. In addition, transferring currency across national borders is often subject to government regulations and taxes.
- Payment of tariffs and taxes. There are still a variety of export and import tariffs and taxes that may be required when products/services leave or enter a country. These can add substantially to the cost/price of products and services and must be considered as part of the exporting decision.

The issues identified are issues faced by any exporter or importer. For companies exporting from developing countries, these issues can be particularly challenging. The documentation required at home can be complex and unclear, where export requirements may have not been well developed. Expectations on the other side in the foreign, developed country may have been written for other developed countries, and may make assumptions that the developing country exporter has difficulty complying with. The appropriate packaging and labeling may be difficult to find in some developing countries. Intermediaries may be less available in developing countries and have less expertise. Banks and financial organizations may have a relatively limited set of options available. The exporter from a developing country dealing with clients in developed countries will generally find that they are not in a power position when negotiating terms of export, thus they will usually accept the terms that their trading partner prefers. This means that, by and large, they will accept more of the risks, such as the financial exchange risks. In addition to exporting some of the product, the Goodluck company might well be involved in importing as well. As the company grows, it may need to get some of its key ingredients from neighboring countries, it may look for a source of bottles and containers outside its home country, it may find better labels that are foreign made, and so on. This involves another set of skills as managers seek out information on cost, availability and so on of inputs from foreign sources. Where foreign sources are attractive, deals have to be negotiated and relationships developed; legal agreements have to be signed and financial arrangements made. At the same time, moving to foreign suppliers may affect domestic suppliers negatively, so consideration has to be given to the domestic impact as well. Companies from developing countries may be seen as small and relatively unimportant to a large foreign supplier, and this can put the developing country company in a vulnerable position should the foreign supplier decide not to make a shipment.

Tanty Goodluck soon found that the company needed additional staff to address the new set of administrative issues associated with their venture as it internationalized. The additional revenues and profit prospects more than justified hiring some specialist staff, but it also requires Tanty to build up her own management abilities. The needed specialists were not easy to find in the developing country in which the Goodluck company was based, and the new personnel needed some additional training.

Proactive exports – To continue with Tanty Goodluck's story, Tanty enjoys the initial exporting process and gets through it successfully. She has now become an exporter, albeit a reactive exporter, reacting to an invitation from the marketplace, and she has developed an appreciation of the complexities of exporting.

After successfully exporting to her customer in Canada for some time, Tanty begins to think that there might be other specialty shops in Canada that might be interested in her product. She enlists some friends in various parts of Canada to do some market development on her behalf. She sends them samples which they take to various country fairs and city food markets to get a general reaction; the reaction is positive so they approach a number of specialty shops on her behalf. Soon Tanty has orders from across Canada. She had planned for this possibility, and is able to move to a larger facility, hire more people, and increase production to meet the demand.

She has also had to develop a more formalized management structure, because exporting has become a major part of her business and she needs someone knowledgeable, who can focus on exports and export marketing and finance, while she continues to focus on the local market. Over time, Tanty and her team explore additional markets in the USA and Europe. They continue to rely on friends in these countries to do the initial market research, although the Goodluck Company now has a substantial staff to manage the export division, and they visit their foreign markets on a regular basis.

When a company moves to proactively exporting, it means that the strategy has fundamentally changed. Domestic sales are no longer the only focus, but attention has to be given to the export aspect of the business. This means that, in addition to the issues previously identified as important to succeed in exporting, the company now needs to develop an expertise in finding and evaluating potential export markets. It also becomes very important that the company considers how exports affect the company's domestic business. This is particularly relevant for companies in developing countries. Many of these companies are relatively small, lacking in resources, and family owned. These conditions mean that there are usually not a lot of excess resources to invest in expansion, so the decision to export proactively has to be carefully considered. Family members may not have the expertise or interest required to export successfully, and it can be difficult for family-owned firms to bring in non-family members to manage the export operations. Moving from a domestic company to exporting has benefits and can potentially improve revenues and profits, but it also entails additional risks, and the exporter has to manage these risks if exporting is to be worthwhile.

The exporting company needs to understand the domestic exporting requirements, and the foreign standards, restrictions, regulations, and tariffs and taxes. The exporter has to evaluate the pros and cons of different shipping methods and ensure that packaging and labeling is appropriate. The exporter needs to work out the details of collecting payment from abroad, banking requirements, and dealing with foreign exchange translation. There may be legal issues, liabilities, insurances, and dispute settlement mechanisms that have to be understood. The exporter also has to be aware that new markets means new cultures, new tastes, new preferences and these may require adapting one's product or service. New markets may also entail unfamiliar logistics, distribution systems, sales methods, promotion, and so on. On the domestic side, governments often have export support systems, including trade missions, financial assistance for export promotion, credit guarantees, and all of these can and should be utilized by exporters.

www.export911.com (accessed May 2, 2011) identified a variety of steps and costs in the exporting process including: materials/labor/overhead, custom packaging/inspection/freight, buying agent fees/mark-ups/commissions, bank charges/interest/insurance/certification/licenses, handling/theft/pilferage, brokerage/loading/wharfage/demurrage/overtime, import duties/road/ rail transport/mark-ups/advertising. This illustrates the need to assess the export process carefully and to include all of the costs in considering the viability of an export product or service in a foreign location.

A small company in a developing country was encouraged to export by a Food and Agricultural Organization project. The owner complied with the requirements, including the labeling requirements, and procured the necessary labels with the required information. Some months later, the owner received an order which was larger than the labels she had available. She decided to use some of her old labels in order to make up the order in a timely manner. The old labels did not contain the information required by the USA. Unfortunately, the U.S. authorities decided to inspect her order and refused the entire order. Further, they singled out her orders for inspection in the future. This real incident illustrates the need to ensure that all export requirements can and are met before attempting to export.

Licenses — Continuing with Tanty's story, on a visit to Canada, Goodluck's most established market, a client suggests that a substantial part of the price of Tanty's sauce is the cost of getting the product from where it is produced to Canada. The Goodluck Company produces and bottles the product at home and ships it to its foreign customers. After much discussion in Canada and back at home, a decision is made to identify a company in Canada who can produce and bottle Tanty Goodluck's Sauce under license. This is a major step for the Goodluck Company and requires substantial legal advice to structure the licensing agreement. The Company is particularly concerned that the licensee maintains the quality and consistency that has become their hallmark; and, most importantly, that they do not lose control of their now recognized brand. A key aspect of the licensing agreement is that Goodluck supplies the critical herbs and spices for the sauce from home, where they are grown, ground and mixed to Tanty's specifications. In addition, a member of the company visits at regular intervals to check the facility and the quality and consistency of the product.

Licensing is an option for companies that want to expand beyond exporting, but do not feel that they have the resources or expertise to invest abroad. Essentially a licensing agreement involves granting of certain rights by the licensor, who owns the rights, to the licensee, to use those rights, in return for payment for the use. A shift from exporting to licensing often takes place because there are advantages to producing in the foreign market. The costs associated with exporting can be avoided through licensing, and this can provide cost advantages. Licensing has both benefits and risks, however. On the downside, the licensor places substantial trust and reliance on the licensee for quality and reliability of production, and protection of the licensed assets. This means that the choice of licensee is critical and time should be taken to ensure that the licensee is trustworthy. Protection of assets is vital and the licensor needs to ensure that these are protected legally, as well as through other control mechanisms. Finally, payment agreements should provide benefits to both parties, and it is not always clear at the outset what appropriate financial terms are. Many licensing agreements therefore call for renegotiation once both parties can evaluate the potential of the licensing agreement.

Companies from developing countries need to be particularly careful when entering into licensing agreements. They may not have the resources needed to protect their competitive advantage, and they may be reliant on only one or a small number of products/services, so loss of any advantage is really critical for these firms. Developing country firms may also be in relatively weak negotiating positions, as they may have only a few licensees to select from, and the licensees may have many licensors. This lack of negotiating power can lead companies to accept less than advantageous agreements. Developing country firms should therefore approach licensing agreements with caution. There are advantages to licensing, but only if the agreement provides real benefits to both parties, so the cost–benefit analysis is particularly important.

Many food and drink products have "secret ingredients" which only the licensor has access to, and by keeping control of these, the licensor does not risk losing this competitive advantage. An example of such a product from a developing country is Angostura Bitters, a Trinidad and Tobago based company, which boasts of its secret recipe which is kept locked in a bank vault. In the case of a product such as Tanty's sauce, if a licensing agreement was reached in a foreign location, Tanty could supply the special secret mix of seasoning from her home base, and thus keep control of an aspect of her sauce which makes it special. Of course, companies should also use all available means, such as patents and copyright to protect their intellectual property. In addition, Tanty may retain marketing control over her products, licensing only the manufacturing of the sauce.

> *Joint ventures* – Tanty Goodluck wants to expand further. The licensing arrangement has
> worked well, but management at the Goodluck Company wanted to go further in a
> variety of markets and they are unsure about setting up too many licensees and
> monitoring them effectively. They believe that a joint venture arrangement will give
> them better control, at a level of investment that the company can manage. Because
> they have substantial experience in Canada, they decide to look for a joint venture
> partner there. They have developed a network of contacts in Canada and through this
> network they look for potential partners and evaluate them against a list of criteria
> that they had decided on. They again seek legal advice on how to set up the joint
> venture and have a consultant help them with the necessary agreements to ensure
> that the joint venture works, and that they have in place the necessary protocols for
> dealing with conflicts and possible termination of the venture. This move to foreign
> ownership is exciting for the Goodluck Company and its management, especially
> Mrs. Goodluck, but it means a major increase in complexity of operations and
> management.

Joint Ventures have often been likened to marriages, and like marriage partners, joint venture partners need to be compatible. Selecting the right joint venture partner is key to success. The partners should have similar objectives and goals, and their strengths should be complementary; that is, if one partner lacks financial resources, the other partner should be strong in this area. The literature suggests that a company should not enter into a joint venture without careful examination of a variety of partners, looking closely at these issues of objectives, goals, and complementarity. The literature also suggests that partners should be of similar size. For companies from developing countries, available partners from developed countries may often be larger and more experienced. The developing country firm may initially see this as positive, because it gives them access to more resources and expertise. The reality, however, may be that it puts them in a less powerful position, where they have to accept the terms dictated by their larger partner. A joint venture works best when each side needs the other side to be successful. Joint ventures often fail, usually because the parties find they have different objectives, conflict arises over meeting objectives, or if one side is unwilling to provide needed resources in a particular situation. A small company in a failing situation may have to accept less than preferred terms to dissolve the partnership. This means that it is particularly important for these firms to work out details for dealing with conflicts, and in the worst case, dissolving the partnership. Such agreements are often likened to prenuptial agreements, where marriage partners agree to the outcomes if they divorce. Partners in a joint venture should ask "what happens if we disagree?" before finalizing a partnership agreement. This can be critical for small firms, and those from developing countries, because of their likely low power position and heavy reliance on personal relationships. A joint venture is only successful if it lasts and if all partners feel that they benefit appropriately from working with their partners.

Joint ventures can be structured in many ways, in terms of ownership, management and control. In terms of ownership, partners may have equal shares, or one partner may have a majority of the shares and other partners are minority shareholders. In terms of management, all partners may provide management, or managers may be hired separately for the venture. Partnership agreements can specify which partner provides the chief executive officer, managing director, financial controller, and so on. Specific voting rights can be identified for certain types of decisions to ensure that all partners vote on specified issues. The legal details of a joint venture agreement are very important and should be developed by a knowledgeable, arm's length lawyer. It is tempting for smaller firms, if they feel they have developed a good personal relationship with a partner, to want to avoid some of these costs and to go along with the partner's suggestions. Investing time and money at the beginning will more than pay for itself by giving the partnership the proper framework to succeed.

> *Acquisitions and greenfield investments* – Once the Goodluck Company has had some experience with foreign ownership through a joint venture and they want to expand more in Canada and elsewhere, they examine opportunities through the acquisition of existing, possibly competitor facilities that they may own outright or where they can have a majority ownership. If appropriate facilities are not available, they may consider a greenfield investment where they build their own custom-designed facility. Of course, at that stage the investment becomes substantial, and Mrs. Goodluck may have to consider inviting other financial partners in, taking the company public, or seeking venture capital, if she has not done so already.

The advantage of 100 percent ownership is that one is totally in control, there are no partners to disagree with, no licensee to worry about. Similarly, the advantage of a greenfield investment is that one gets exactly the kind of operation that is desirable for a particular product or service. The downside is that there is no partner with whom to share the risks and the company has to have access to adequate resources to undertake such a major move. There are financial risks, and if the venture fails, the company will bear all of the loss. There may also be political risks, as a foreign company with 100 percent ownership is often closely scrutinized by the government. If governments see "foreignness" as negative, there may be government audits, regulations on how you can operate, restrictions on profit repatriation, and various other government interventions. There may also be human resource concerns, as the company will likely have some people from its home country working in the foreign country. This will entail issues of dealing with different local conditions, understanding the new culture, moving expatriates and their families, and so forth. Clearly, this is not a likely move for a small company or one that has little international experience.

Strategic alliances – Along the road from reactive exports to an international company, Mrs. Goodluck will have had to expand in many directions, particularly in terms of supplies for her special sauce, which she may now have to obtain in a variety of locations. She may have formed strategic alliances with a variety of growers and farmers cooperatives to ensure a consistent supply of quality ingredients. She may also have formed alliances with other producers of jams, jellies, condiments, and so on, to work together; for example, to market and distribute their products jointly or to exhibit at trade fairs together. She may have joined regional associations to lobby governments for special provisions for products such as hers. Strategic alliances are essentially any alliance for strategic purposes. A special form of strategic alliance sometimes occurs among competitors who agree to work together for a period of time, say, to do basic research or even cooperate in using some capital facilities, such as packaging or bottling, then they expect to go their separate ways as they develop products and compete for market share. Small companies can use strategic alliances to good advantage to extend their reach, without making a major commitment to a partnership. For example, Tanty could develop an "umbrella brand" and market selected additional products as "Tanty" products, while not actually producing them.

Global integration – Moving from local to global, Mrs. Goodluck and her executives will have learned a lot about the international make-up of her industry. Among other things, they will know where financing is available, they will know how to obtain supplies at the best price, they will understand the differences in various markets and how to adapt their marketing to take these into account, they will have employed people from different parts of the world and learned about various cultures. At this stage they may be in a position to evaluate their worldwide operations and consider global integration. This means that they will look at the world as a whole and decide where it is best to obtain the inputs for their product, where it is best to produce the product, what is the best means of distribution, and so on. For example, they may find it is advantageous to buy land in Guyana and Bangladesh and grow the necessary ingredients there, have the raw ingredients shipped to India and Trinidad and Tobago for processing into the sauce, then ship the sauce in bulk to markets around the world where it is bottled close to the major markets. Mrs. Goodluck, of course, still keeps the secret of her special mix of herbs and spices, which means that no other company has been able to copy her sauce. And she spends considerable effort in marketing and building the Goodluck brand to diminish the possibility of look-alike competitors.

This Goodluck story ends with global integration. Mrs. Goodluck has stuck to one specialty item and built a global market for the specialty niche product. She sells essentially the same product around the world and has created a competitive advantage through niche development and worldwide integration. This can be a good strategy for small companies from developing countries, because they do not have to invest substantial resources in research and product development. With limited resources, it is important to use those resources as wisely as possible.

Mrs. Goodluck could have gone in other directions. She could have expanded her line of products to provide a greater range of similar products, she could have developed other, quite different niche products (such as banana leaf dolls) to take advantage of her growing marketing capabilities, and she could have adapted her sauce to respond to different tastes in different locations.

For many products and services adaptation is a necessity, and many companies create their competitive advantage through national responsiveness rather than global integration. Where local tastes vary a lot and product preferences are nationally differentiated, local flexibility is often the best choice. This is often the case with food products such as Mrs. Goodluck's sauce; however, globalization has also demonstrated that such products can find small markets around the world.

The Goodluck story is, of course, a good luck story. It pictures each of the international moves succeeding, so that the company can proceed to the next stage. This is not always the case, nor do companies always want to internationalize to this degree. Many companies become exporters and go no further. Others move quickly from local to foreign investment. Still others reach a certain stage and sell out, possibly using their experience to repeat the process with another venture. And, as noted earlier, some are "born global" and their operations are international from inception. The story illustrates how it is possible for a small company from a developing country to go from local to global with a specialized product. It also illustrates the different entry strategies that a company can consider as it internationalizes and the management challenges presented along the way.

Perhaps most importantly, this story illustrates how firms in developing countries encounter the same challenges as those from more developed countries, but with different priorities, emphases and capabilities. The textbook approach suitable for firms in the developed world may play out differently in the reality of small scale, chronically underfinanced and supply limited enterprises.

The Goodluck story is also outward looking and many firms may develop their international experience from the other direction. That is, foreign firms moving into the home market may be seeking licensees, joint venture partners and so on, and many companies become international by responding to these foreign firms.

As a company internationalizes over time, the way it is structured is also likely to change. The following section briefly looks at some typical organization structures.

ORGANIZATION STRUCTURES

Most small companies are organized functionally; that is they are organized around the major functions that have to be carried out to run the business. In the case of a manufactured product, such as Tanty's sauce, the inputs have to be sourced and purchased, the product has to be made and it has to be marketed and sold; in order to do this, money is needed and people have to work; so a functional organization might be made up of: purchasing, production, marketing and sales, finance, and human resources. Each of these might be a unit with the people in the unit focusing on the issues associated with their particular function. The heads of each unit would meet regularly to ensure that the work was coordinated among the units. In the case of family-owned and run businesses, the heads of various units will often be family members, so that the coordination likely takes place on an informal, ongoing basis.

Family-owned businesses quite often diversify into unrelated areas, because a family member has a particular interest or expertise. So, potentially, Goodluck Enterprises could have a factory manufacturing its sauce, a daughter running a real estate business, a son running a computer software development business, and a daughter-in-law running a retail children's clothing store, all wanting to develop and possibly go international. These businesses are all quite different and require different functions and little coordination. In such a case a divisional structure makes more sense. The divisional organization would be made up of something like: Tanty's Sauce, Goodluck Real Estate, Goodluck Software, Goodluck's Kids Klothes.

These divisions will each have its own costs and revenues, thus they can each be run as profit centers. It is possible, also, to have cost centers rather than profit centers. This would be the case if, for example, the manufacturing arm of Tanty's Sauce were separated from the sales arm (Tanty's Manufacturing and Tanty's Sales). Profit centers allow for comparisons among divisions relative to various profit measures. Cost centers rely on budgets and various cost measures for control.

As a company internationalizes and international aspects become more important, there is a need to identify some people who deal with the international aspects of the company. In the reactive export stage, this is likely to be identified with production, because the main concern is ensuring that capacity is there to serve the export market. In the proactive export stage, the concern switches to developing export markets, and it may be identified as part of the marketing and sales function. As international aspects become even more important, many companies identify a specific unit to deal with international operations. In a divisional structure, such a unit would likely manage international aspects for all divisions. Eventually, as international aspects of the business become more important than domestic aspects, companies move to a global structure of some kind. A company like Tanty Goodluck's, with a limited product line will likely identify regions of the world and organize around these – for example, North America, Latin America and the Caribbean, the Middle East, and so on. The idea is to identify groups of countries where there are similarities in terms of culture, distribution, marketing, sales, regulations, and so on, so that decisions can be made for the region as a whole.

Companies with widely different product lines will organize around the product lines. The Tata company, named after the Tata family of India, identifies Tata Motors, Tata Consultancy, and Tata Steel as its major areas of worldwide focus (www.theofficialboard.com, accessed March 28, 2011). The Chairman of the Board of each is Ratan Tata, indicating the continuing family nature of the company.

Most family-owned firms continue to be strongly influenced by family members, even when they grow into super large global firms, but clearly there is a need fairly early on, to move from family managed to professionally managed, once international aspects of a business become its major focus. The complexities of managing an international company require specialized expertise that may not be available within a family; thus, it makes sense to hire professional managers with the needed expertise, possibly geographic in nature, even though the family remains instrumental in guiding the strategic direction. Along with strategic issues, companies have to identify control systems to ensure that they monitor their progress and achieve their goals. The following section looks at control systems, and some of the challenges to implementing effective controls in developing countries.

CONTROL SYSTEMS

As a company expands and internationalizes, controls become increasingly important. Controls are intended to provide a framework to ensure that strategies are carried out; they provide the mechanisms that allow management to ensure that strategies are appropriate and that they are accomplished. In Chapter 3, the model of management presented, identified the management process starting with planning and ending with controlling, with controlling feeding back into planning. Controls, thus, provide a means for evaluating progress relative to plans, and a means to evaluate the appropriateness of the plans themselves.

Controls in a domestic company, such as the early stages of Goodluck's, can usually be relatively simple and informal. Mrs. Goodluck is in touch with the day-to-day operations of her company, on a personal basis, and other family members are likely employed in the company and are intimately concerned with ensuring success. The company at this stage may not have formal plans or controls; rather the family is interested in making enough money to continue the business. As the company grows, more formal control systems become necessary.

As an organization becomes more complex and responsibility and authority are delegated beyond family members, there are opportunities for individuals or groups to act in ways that are not consistent with the organization's strategies and goals. An effective control system limits the likelihood of this, by measuring performance and identifying deviations from planned performance. Controls are designed to identify deviations in a timely manner, so that corrective action can be taken, or if appropriate, strategies changed. This allows the company to deal with a complex and changing environment.

Particularly when a company operates in many countries around the world, a good control system is essential. A good control system has been described as accurate, objective, acceptable to employees, understandable, timely, and cost-effective. Accuracy is critical, because inaccurate information can lead to a false sense of security. Objectivity is necessary, because personal opinions are often biased. Acceptability is important, because employees will not maintain systems that they do not accept. Being understandable is vital, because it will only be used if it is understood. Being timely is key, because controls are intended to lead to corrective action. Finally, cost-effectiveness is essential, because the benefits of the system must outweigh the costs of implementing and maintaining the system, otherwise the system is not warranted.

In developing countries, many people may not be familiar with formal control systems. Typically, managers and employees may have employed personal supervision as the main means of control. Personal supervision can be effective in small operations, but this approach is not always accurate or objective, it can be unacceptable to some employees, may not be understood, and may not necessarily be timely, as it relies on individual, personal decisions. Relatively low levels of education may make it difficult for some employees to understand and maintain control systems. The situation in developing countries means that introducing formal control systems may be challenging. Companies seeking to design and implement control systems will often need to provide substantial training and development to ensure that managers and employees understand the need for the systems and are able to comply with them.

In many developing countries, standard, routine collection of data is not characteristic, and this can make the implementation of control systems complicated. Many control systems, designed in the more developed world, rely on comparisons with standards to evaluate performance. This may simply not be possible in some developing countries. For example, developed countries often have industry wide data on financial ratios, and companies compare their performance on these ratios to industry averages. This data does not exist in most developing countries. Controls in these countries often have to be designed internally, relying on internal patterns rather than comparisons with others.

Cultural differences can also affect the type of control system that is appropriate in different locations; for example, if you require objective evidence to corroborate personal statements, it may imply that someone is dishonest, or an employee may lose face if her/his beliefs are questioned. This means that control systems have to take cultural differences into account, in addition to a variety of other factors.

Control systems often include: policies and procedures; accounting, financial and auditing reports; and information on operations (sales, costs, transactions, and so on). These systems tend to be relatively well developed and well accepted in more developed countries, but they may be less accepted in developing countries, making the concept of "control" less common. This means that international companies operating in developing countries may encounter obstacles in implementing these systems. Companies headquartered in these countries and operating internationally may have to develop new, and perhaps unfamiliar, systems to control their international operations.

STRATEGIES THAT FIT DEVELOPING COUNTRIES

Emerging markets, as we have emphasized throughout this book, can provide many opportunities for companies from developed countries; and, at the same time, their companies are expanding to take advantage of opportunities in other developing countries, as well as in the developed countries. Khanna et al. (2005) noted the importance of finding the right strategies for developing countries. In particular, they identified the lack of so-called soft infrastructure in developing countries as affecting appropriate strategies in these countries. Specifically these authors identified the lack of skilled market research firms to help understand consumer preferences, the lack of logistics firms to provide a system for moving raw materials and finished goods, and a lack of search firms to help provide access to needed employees.

Their article stressed the need to adapt strategies to fit the environment in each developing country. Particularly, it outlined a process for assessing political and social systems, openness, labor markets and capital markets. The authors apply their model to the BRIC countries and reached some interesting conclusions; for example:

- Multinationals face different kinds of competition in each country – in China state-owned enterprises control about half of the economy but China encourages foreign investment, in India, state-owned enterprises are not as important and India is wary of foreign investment, Brazil and Russia are a mix of the features of China and India.
- Financial markets are different in each country – in Brazil and India, indigenous entrepreneurs are the main rivals of multinational companies, and they rely on local capital markets, in China the state-owned enterprises are funded by public sector banks.
- Corporate governance differs across the countries – Brazil and India follow practices of the developed countries, while in China and Russia, companies cannot rely on their local partners' internal systems to protect their interests and assets, especially intellectual property.

This article draws attention to an area that is often overlooked in developing countries – the 'soft' infrastructure. The fact that this infrastructure is lacking in many developing countries may provide an opportunity within these countries. Local service providers can develop services for local companies as well as foreign investors.

SUMMARY

This chapter began by continuing to review ways in which companies internationalize, and introduced a fictional enterprise and product to illustrate the challenges of internationalization.

This fictional company, Goodluck Enterprises, was used to explore some of the realities of moving from a domestic company to a global company. The chapter then examined the structural and organizational changes that accompany internationalization, and concluded with a brief discussion on organizational controls and challenges to developing effective controls in developing countries. Finally, the chapter reviewed the idea of soft infrastructure and the impact of a lack of this type of infrastructure on operations in developing countries.

LESSONS LEARNED

Having completed this chapter, you should be able to understand and identify issues faced by companies importing and exporting in the developing world. You should also be aware of the issues faced in other entry strategies, and be able to explain how companies deal with these. You should be able to discuss control systems and challenges encountered in implementing effective controls in developing countries. You should recognize what organizing and operating an international company or firm entails.

DISCUSSION QUESTIONS

1   Select a company from your home country and discuss how this company can internationalize.
2   As a manager from a developing country, you have the task of opening your business in a radically different environment. Discuss some of the strategic and organizational challenges you would face.
3   The company you are working for as an international manager operates in several countries around the world. Explain why you think a good control system is essential. Explain what you would consider to be a good control system. Explain how you would introduce control systems for the companies.

EXERCISE

In small groups, identify a local company to use as an example. Describe and explore some of the realities for this company, of moving from a domestic company to a global one. Identify the organization structures you will use in you expansion, and explain why you will use these structures. Be prepared to share the group's findings with the class.

Chapter 8

Human resource management

OBJECTIVES

This chapter gives a brief overview of the development in the field of human resources management (HRM), managing people in organizations and how this function takes place in developing countries.

The objectives are as follows:

■ To examine the function and development of HRM.
■ To recognize the vital and valuable nature of those who work in the organization.
■ To explore the HR function in developing countries using three variations PM, HRM and SHRM.
■ To consider various aspects of HRM in developing countries.
■ To discuss the brain drain phenomenon and the negatives and positives affecting developing countries.
■ To understand the role of the diaspora in HRM.
■ To identify some of the key skills required for contemporary strategic HRM practices.

INTRODUCTION

This chapter addresses the issue of managing people in organizations and how this function takes place in developing countries. In the model of management presented in Chapter 4, the third management function was called staffing. Staffing involves filling positions in an organization and making sure that the people in those positions can and do carry out the work that is required for the organization to continue over time. This is essentially what human resource management (HRM) is; however, it can be either a very simple process of filling positions and making sure that policies are followed, or it can be a complex process of integrating the organization's human resources with the organization's strategic direction for maximum efficiency and effectiveness. HRM in a formal sense is often largely nonexistent in developing countries, and for many companies, this probably works quite well. Nevertheless, it is a good idea for managers in these companies to understand the fundamentals of HRM and use those approaches that may help them manage their human resources more effectively.

 96

In the more developed countries, up to the 1950s, what is now called HRM was often called personnel management (PM), and was seen as a relatively simple administrative function of formally hiring, training, implementing management's instructions on the firing of employees, and keeping records of personnel, including attendance, vacations, pay, bonuses, and so on – essentially PM departments were responsible for the paperwork associated with having employees.

After the 1950s, in many of the more developed countries, there was an argument that the responsibility for "managing personnel" really involved a lot more, and PM was expanded to include issues such as motivation, leadership, performance, employee/management development, and career management – these departments were seen as being responsible for ensuring the overall effective management of people in the organization, built on the idea that people are the organization's most valuable resource; this was called HRM. Today, many people argue that HRM should be strategic in nature and that the function should be called strategic human resource management (SHRM). In this view, the HRM function should be closely tied into the strategic thrust of the organization because of the vital and valuable nature of those who work in the organization. In this scenario, decisions about human resource issues are made on the basis of the organization's strategic direction, and the strategic direction is influenced by human resource issues. Human Resources of the enterprise are thus planned for in terms of numbers, skills and other attributes whose need is forecast and costed.

Over the past fifty years the nature of managing human resources has changed in many developed countries – there has been a general recognition of the value of human resources as an asset, and the HRM function has become more important in organizations. This is not by any means true in all organizations – there are many where the function remains largely a low-level paperwork function and there are others where lip-service is given to the idea of SHRM, and the reality is that the function has little strategic input or influence in these companies. Nevertheless, the importance of HRM has grown substantially in many organizations in developed countries over the past half a century. The same has not been the case in developing countries.

In the next section of this chapter, the nature of the human resource function in developing countries will be examined, first, using these three variations: personnel management (PM), human resource management (HRM), and strategic human resource management (SHRM). Following that discussion, various aspects of HRM in developing countries will be considered, such as hiring, training, firing, career management, retirement, and so on. In the final sections of this chapter, we look at the impact of the brain drain on developing countries and companies, and the potential role of the diaspora for local and international companies.

THE NATURE OF HUMAN RESOURCE MANAGEMENT IN DEVELOPING COUNTRIES

Budhwar and Debrah (2001) suggested that HRM was influenced by three sets of factors: national factors including (1) national culture, institutions, business sectors, and the dynamic business environment; (2) contingent factors including age, size, nature, ownership, life-cycle stage, trade unions, HR strategies, and stakeholder interests; and (3) organizational strategies and policies related to primary HR functions and internal labor markets. Although they identify this multifaceted model for assessing HRM in developing countries, they also noted that

"HRM in developing countries is in its infancy" (p. 6) and they focus their assessments on culture, institutions, the dynamic business environment, and the industrial sector. Using these four components, they also identify sub-components as determining HRM in developing countries (p. 8): Their listing can provide a basis for any HRM researcher or practitioner regarding the factors that need to be understood in order to develop an effective HRM function. Budhwar and Debrah's contention that HRM in developing countries is in its infancy suggests that insofar as HRM exists, it is at the PM stage (or possibly it is still contained within the office of the CEO and not distinguished as a separate function at all). This is borne out by other authors in their edited book. Some examples:

- Branine (2001) says of Algeria "the management of employees in Algeria can best be described as personnel administration rather than human resource management as understood in Western industrial countries. There is no clear evidence of personnel managers' involvement in strategic decision-making or in policy formulations" (p. 165).
- Warner (2001) says of the People's Republic of China that "the reality is that the older form of PM practice is still more common in Chinese enterprises" and "PM is largely the norm even in many JVs" (p. 30).
- Khiji (2001) says that "HRM in Pakistan is passing through an embryonic stage" (p. 104).
- Tayeb (2001) says that in Iran "HRM in this country is really the 'old' personnel management" (p. 128).
- Mellahi and Wood (2001) say of Saudi Arabia "the HRM context is itself evolving and the Saudi HRM model is still in the early stages of evolution" (p. 146).

In their conclusion, Budhwar and Debrah say that "in almost all of the countries, personnel management (PM) and HRM are used interchangeably but often implying a bureaucratic PM system" (p. 249). It would seem likely that this is the case in most of the developing world. This is hardly surprising, given that the richer world has only moved to a more proactive human resource approach in the past fifty years, and that the concept of SHRM is still in essence in its infancy. Budhwar and Debrah in their conclusions also note that globalization, and the instability and uncertainty that developing countries face, make it imperative that they establish appropriate approaches for managing human resources.

This is an area where the developing countries can learn from the experience of the more developed and possibly make a major move forward by adopting HRM and SHRM practices and also by developing their own. Budhwar and Debrah say "Developing countries, then, must transform their PM into HRM" (p. 251). This, of course, is easy to say, but perhaps difficult to do. Budhwar and Debrah note the major influence of religion and traditional cultural beliefs on HRM practices in the countries discussed in their book. They conclude that these factors can have a negative influence on organizational performance; but these factors are deeply entrenched in societies so they are difficult to change. Nevertheless, companies from developing countries *can* learn from the best practices already established by their counterparts in the developed world, although these may need to be adapted to suit the local environment.

In the following section, various HRM activities are examined in terms of how they are likely to be practiced in developing countries.

HRM ACTIVITIES IN DEVELOPING COUNTRIES

In this section, we look at basic HRM activities such as recruiting, hiring, training, and career planning, and consider how the conditions in developing countries may affect these activities. It seems that companies everywhere, whether in developed or developing countries, have to carry out similar activities in order to ensure that the company has a complement of staff, and that the staff perform in such a way that the company functions reasonably well, so that it can continue to operate. At the same time, it seems that the way companies carry out these activities may differ because of conditions in developing countries. There are a number of characteristics of companies in developing countries that are likely to be important to HRM – most companies will be small- to medium-sized, with a substantial number of micro-enterprises; most companies will be family owned or owned by a small group of close associates; many companies will be engaged in basic agricultural processing, assembly work, or relatively simple manufacturing, requiring relatively low-skill employees.

It is believed that the overwhelming majority of SMEs do not engage in formal HR practices, and most companies in developing countries are small or medium sized. In a study in Sierra Leone, however, he found that there was a significant positive relationship between HRM practices and SME performance, including sales. He noted that SMEs are at a disadvantage relative to larger companies in terms of their staffing, and that more formal HR practices could help them become more competitive. In the following sections, various HR activities are examined. These sections explain what HR practices are likely to be in developing countries. We also suggest that developing countries may be able to learn from developed countries and adopt some of the activities that have been identified as HR best practice.

Some countries, with substantial investment from multinationals from developed countries may be influenced by their practices. For example, Warner (2001) noted that there were significant differences in HRM practice in firms in the PRC, depending on ownership, with foreign multinationals introducing sophisticated systems, while state-owned enterprises were essentially rooted in the past, and Park noted that South Korean firms were likely to adopt an American-style HR approach. The inverse is also true, as multinational companies (MNCs) from the developing countries invest in developed countries and elsewhere, and introduce their own HRM practices in these countries. Horwitz (2010), in a keynote speech noted that South Korean Hyundai plants in the United States and Indian Tata's steel operations in South Africa were examples where this had occurred. This situation is likely to result in hybrid HRM systems that bring together existing systems from different locations.

Recruiting

In order to staff an organization, one has to find appropriate people for positions that need to be filled. There are many ways to recruit people for jobs that need to be filled. These can range from very informal to formal. At the informal extreme, a company can use word of mouth and networking – just letting people know that a job is available and needs to be filled, or ask current employees, relatives or neighbors to suggest someone for the job. At the formal extreme, a company can hire a professional search firm to advertise the position to be filled, identify and screen potential candidates, check references and provide recommendations on suitable candidates. In-between, companies can advertise positions in various media, review applicants for other positions, go to job fairs at schools and universities, and get lists of applicants from employment agencies.

The recruitment process that is used will depend on the characteristics of the position to be filled, the characteristics of the company and industry, and the characteristics of the country in which the position exists:

- By and large, the more important the position and the larger the company, the more extensive and formal the search will be. Top-level positions such as chief executive officer or chairman of the board are not usually publicized and there are firms that specialize in finding candidates for these positions, often based on knowledge about individuals who may consider changing positions.
- The characteristics of the industry will influence the nature of the search because of the specialized skills and experience that may be required in a particular industry. The more specialized the skills needed the more extensive and formal the search is likely to be.
- The norms and expectations in a particular country will influence the degree of formality as well as the nature of the medium used for recruitment. Where formality is the norm, then most companies will be relatively formal, and vice versa. If job fairs are held regularly, they will be used, if newspapers are read regularly they will be used, and so on.

The nature of business in many developing countries suggests that it is very likely that companies will use informal methods for recruiting new employees, very often simply word of mouth. The majority of companies are small and medium sized, with a substantial proportion of micro enterprises, and many firms are family owned or closely controlled, so informal methods are generally preferred. Family members are likely to be recruited for any jobs of importance, as they are seen as more trustworthy than outsiders, and their skills and abilities are well known, so there is no need for a formal recruitment process. For lower-level positions, family "retainers" (that is, people who have worked with the family in various roles for many years) and their families are often preferred. They are known and expected to be loyal, and it is expected that the owners should look after them by providing employment. Alternatively, the friends and family of current employees are seen as preferable to strangers, even where the strangers may be more educated or skilled.

Recruitment in developing countries can be expected to be relatively informal for many positions, and companies will often recruit largely among people who are well known. In developed countries hiring close relatives and friends, or nepotism, is often seen as negative, and in some companies close relatives are not allowed to work in the same department. The common belief is that one cannot be objective about family and friends and will favor them. The reverse is true in many developing countries, where the belief is that family and friends will work hard and they can be trusted, so hiring them is seen as positive. Of course, it is also the case in small, family-run firms in developed countries that family members are usually in key positions.

The HR literature suggests that a key evolution, if family firms are to grow, is the transition from family management to management based on skills, experience and expertise. Companies in developing countries should consider the more formal options available for the selection process, particularly as they grow. A more formal process is likely to give the company access to a wider range of candidates, and candidates with better skills and experience for a particular position. In reality, family members and friends do not necessarily have the needed skills, they may not be interested in a particular job, and they may not always be trustworthy or hard working. Simply because word of mouth is the norm for recruiting does not mean it is always the best method.

Hiring

Hiring processes can also range from informal to formal. At the informal end, decision makers discuss possible candidates and make a decision, then offer the person a job, and acceptance is likely, because wages and benefits do not vary a lot, and good jobs may be scarce. At the formal end, candidates are evaluated using a variety of assessment instruments, including assessments of skills and psychological attributes; candidates may go through a rigorous interviewing and reference checking process; each candidate is assessed on merit and against other candidates. Offers are made to desirable candidates and salary and benefits negotiated before a final hiring decision is made.

If the selection process is informal, the hiring process is also likely to be informal. The candidates being considered are likely to be well known, so rigorous assessment is not likely. In addition, a formal hiring process can take time and may be seen as costly. In smaller, family-run firms, where a position needs to be filled there may be some time pressure, and additional costs have to be clearly justified. Owners and managers may not be familiar with more formal techniques if they are not commonly used, so they may not even consider a more formal approach. How well someone will fit into the existing organization is probably seen as more important than specific skills or psychological attributes. Interviewing is also likely to be informal, and may not even take place in many situations.

While the norm in hiring may be informal, this does not mean that it is always the best approach. For jobs that require particular skills and attributes, it may be more appropriate to move to more formal approaches. Testing potential employees, in-depth interviews with a variety of managers and employees, and reference checking can go a long way to ensuring that the fit between the person hired and the position and company is a good one. A challenge for developing country companies is that many of the assessment instruments have been designed in the developed countries, and it is not clear that they work as well in developing countries. The HR function may need to test a variety of instruments to identify those that seem to be effective for their needs. More formal approaches to hiring may seem time consuming and costly, on the surface, but they can save the time and costs associated with training, they help to ensure that the new employee is productive quickly, and they should alleviate the likelihood of turnover or the need to terminate a newly hired employee.

It is important to recognize that specific HR "best practices" may need to be adjusted because of local values. For example, Cunningham and Rowley (2007) found that interviews are not seen favorably in China, where personal networks are very important. Akorsu (2010) argued that typical HR practices from developed countries are not needed, and do not work in the informal economy of Ghana. Of course, the informal economy is a particular sector that is quite different from the formal economy – in the informal economy workers work at low-paying jobs without contracts, on a day-to-day basis. Under these conditions, she found that recruitment and selection was on the basis of personal contacts and on humanitarian grounds, performance was not formally evaluated, and benefits were not offered – this seemed to work well, because apprenticeships were common, and the relationship between employer and apprentice is close so these other practices are not necessary.

Training

Training, anywhere in the world, is sometimes seen as a "frill" – that is, nice to have, but not a necessity. This is often because the costs of training are immediate and obvious, while the benefits are longer term and not easily quantifiable. This is particularly the case for nontechnical training and development. Technical training, or training that is required to perform a specific job, may be seen as a necessity. Nontechnical training, such as communication, conflict resolution, team building, and so on is often not seen as providing real cost–benefit advantages.

In developing countries, this approach to training may be even more evident. In developing country companies, financial resources are limited and it may be especially difficult to make the decision to devote limited resources to training. Training that is necessary to do a particular job may be seen as relevant, but because jobs are of a relatively low skill level, it is likely that the training will take place on the job, and co-workers will be responsible for ensuring that newly hired employees learn how to perform their required functions. For example, the study cited earlier showed that, in the informal sector in Ghana, training was done through the apprenticeship system. This approach minimizes expenditure associated with training of new employees. In these countries, the more developmental aspects of training are likely to be seen as a waste of financial resources.

Although it is understandable that companies from developing countries devote relatively little of their limited financial resources to training, this may be a short-sighted approach. As companies from developing countries compete more and more with their counterparts from developed countries, both at home and in foreign markets, training and development of human resources may provide the competitive advantage to succeed in a global business environment.

It seems that investment in training and development may be necessary for firms in developing countries to compete effectively in the future. It may be important for firms to evaluate the true costs and benefits of both training and development. It is also important for companies in developing countries to identify the training and development needs that are specific to them, and build programs that are appropriate to these specific needs. Training is one area where cultural differences are likely to have an impact on effectiveness; therefore developing country training programs may be quite different from those in more developed countries. For example:

■ in more collective cultures, training will likely need to be done for groups or teams working closely together;
■ in cultures high on uncertainty avoidance, training will likely need to be structured, with correct responses clearly identified;
■ in cultures high on power–distance, training that is introduced and supported by those at higher levels are likely to be accepted, and trainers should be in positions of power.

Performance evaluation

Evaluating performance, in Western literature, is considered a critical aspect of managing people. The idea being that evaluating performance allows employees to understand the areas where they perform well, and those areas where they need to improve. This understanding is intended to help employees improve their performance and ensure that the organization is performing at a high level.

In developing countries, performance evaluation may be seen as unimportant for a number of reasons. Some examples:

■ Many employees may be at low levels, therefore evaluation is at a rather basic level – for example, did the employee produce the required number of units? Did the employee visit the required number of sites? And so on. In this case, there is little consideration of how performance affects progression through the organization. Evaluation is done more in terms of continuation with the organization.

- Many employees may be employed on a "day laborer" basis; that is, they are employed only when there is work available. This means that performance and possibly rehiring is on a basis of day-to-day performance rather than a longer-term system.
- Many employees may be family members, and the formal evaluation of family members does not work effectively. Family members are expected to participate in the organization, so evaluation seems to be irrelevant, because these family members will likely be employed regardless of their performance.
- Performance evaluation requires specification of targets and monitoring of actual performance relative to these targets. Many small companies do not collect data on a regular basis, and have only an informal idea of what levels of performance are possible or desirable.

While performance evaluation can seem unimportant in many companies in developing countries, it is likely that evaluation can have a positive effect on performance in all companies. Having a clear understanding of what is expected in terms of performance, and actual performance relative to this standard allows employees to reach for the expected levels, and adjust their work habits if they are not reaching expected levels. In many developing countries, because people may be working for basic levels of pay, and because they may want to avoid uncertainty, knowing clearly what is expected of them, and how well they are performing relative to expectations, provides a degree of certainty that can be motivating.

The way performance evaluation is carried out needs to fit the cultural characteristics of the particular country. Some examples of culturally contingent evaluation follow:

- If the country is relatively high on collectivism, then performance targets as well as evaluation will probably work best when they are group based. Singling out an individual, even for good performance, is likely to have negative consequences in collective countries. In contrast, in individualistic countries, performance targets that are individually determined seem to be effective, and evaluation is done on a person-by-person basis, and individuals are often singled out publicly for good performance.
- If a country is high on power–distance, then the performance targets can be set by the supervisors and managers for those at lower levels, and this will probably be more acceptable than participative setting of performance levels. In contrast, in low power–distance countries, participation in setting of performance targets is often considered critical to the acceptance of these targets by employees; in these countries, managers and employees usually review actual performance together and mutually agree on how well employees have performed, and if remedial action is needed.
- In more masculine countries (societies that hold traditional male values), performance is likely to be tied to tangible rewards, including pay increases and prizes, such as holidays, household goods, cars, and so on, and competition for these rewards can be an effective inducement to perform at a high level. In more feminine countries (societies that hold traditional female values), cooperation is likely to be favored over competition, and rewards are more likely to be time off, or social events that encourage interaction among group members.
- In countries where uncertainty avoidance is high, performance targets need to be specific and as concrete as possible, so that it is clear to employees exactly what is expected of them. Evaluation can then be clearly related to the expected performance, with evaluation criteria that do not leave room for questions about performance levels. Performance levels in turn should be clearly related to outcomes such as bonuses or other rewards. Where improvements in performance are needed, these should also be clearly specified to avoid

any uncertainty. In countries where uncertainty avoidance is low, people may be comfortable with relatively open-ended performance targets and measures, as they feel that this gives them more leeway to adjust to a changing environment and still perform well.

■ In countries with a longer time horizon, performance evaluation may be done at relatively long intervals, based on long-term goals. In countries with a shorter time horizon, performance targets will need to be shorter term, and long-term goals need to be broken down into near-term objectives, so that performance can be monitored and evaluated at frequent intervals.

A small, family-owned company can keep performance evaluation relatively informal. There may be no need to design and implement complex systems, in fact, these can do more harm than good, if employees do not see the need for them. Some performance evaluation, nevertheless, is needed to ensure that both managers and employees know what performance is expected and how well people are performing relative to expectations.

Career planning

The concept of career planning in organizations appears to be virtually nonexistent in many developing countries. In fact, the concept of a career is often meaningless as many people simply work in order to make enough money to live, and in some countries employees work until they have enough money "for the time being" then don't come to work for a while. The distinction between management and employees is clear-cut and there is little expectation that employees will move to management, and the concept of career planning is not meaningful in this context. Many companies are small, and often family owned. Management is usually made up of family members, friends, and perhaps a few carefully selected, trusted outsiders who bring needed skills to the organization. If career planning is considered, it is often in the context of the expected progression of family members. Family members may be expected to start at the bottom of the organization in order to learn about all aspects of operations, but they are also expected to progress through the organization relatively quickly to the management level. Particular family members may be identified to eventually become the president/chief executive officer/managing director and these family members will be singled out for special training and development to ensure that they can take on this role. For example, they may attend one of the prestigious executive education programs, at well-known universities, such as Harvard in the USA.

Career planning, insofar as it exists in developing countries, is likely to be informal. The typical small, family-owned company, likely relies on individualized assessment of performance to decide on how a particular person should progress in the organization. Trusted individuals who perform well at lower levels may be identified as having management potential, and these individuals will then receive special treatment and encouragement to help them achieve this potential. The issue of trust tends to be as important as ability and potential. The nature of small firms, especially family-owned ones, is that being able to trust people in management positions is seen as essential. Trust may be based on relationships beyond the enterprise and extend to personal, intra-family relationships as well and may have little to do with management abilities or performance.

At the same time, career planning may contribute positively to performance, in companies in developing countries. Pacek and Thorniley (2004) suggested that career planning was an important aspect of job satisfaction, and job satisfaction has been shown to relate to positive job results such as performance and productivity, as well as negative results, such as absenteeism, tardiness and turnover. Companies in developing countries should consider instituting some formal career planning to allow employees to see their jobs as more than simply a series of days of going to work. Of course, issues of culture again have to be considered, so in collective cultures career planning may be for a team or group of employees.

In addition, as companies from developing countries are growing, and increasingly becoming international, career planning becomes a necessity. These companies will find that they cannot continue to rely only on family members and close associates. Rather, they find they need to develop a professional management group. Once a company moves to a professional management approach, issues of ability become particularly relevant. These companies will find that formal career planning is essential to identifying and developing managers.

At the same time, corporate growth implies more levels within the organization, and more specialization of functions. Within such an organization, there is opportunity for employees to progress, even when they are unlikely to become managers, or even supervisors. Identifying career paths for all levels of employees can provide incentives for involvement and high performance.

Termination

Where employees do not perform at acceptable levels, or where their behavior is unacceptable (for example, they are frequently late or absent, they do not work well with others, they are abusive to colleagues, and so on), it becomes necessary to terminate their employment. In more developed countries, labor laws tend to be well established, and they specify the actions that are necessary to terminate employees. These usually include giving verbal and written warnings to employees, keeping written documentation of performance and any incidents that may lead to termination, as well as the timeframe that is required for termination to take effect, and the monetary settlement that is required. Individual companies often have their own policies as well. While these must comply with the law, they often go further, especially where strong unions are present.

In many developing countries, labor laws are less well established, and sometimes essentially nonexistent. Termination in some of these countries is relatively easy. It may be possible to terminate someone on the spot for a perceived infraction or lack of performance, or even without any specific reason. As noted previously, many employees may not be employed on a continuing basis, but on a daily basis, and they are paid on a daily basis; in this case, termination is simply a matter of telling the employee that they will not be needed in the future, and paying them whatever is owed to them at that point in time. Of course, where unions are present, and relatively strong, they may seek redress, even where employees are employed in a daily basis, so unions will be a factor in termination decisions (the following section discusses unions and labor relations). Redress is often unavailable where the rule of law is also weak.

In some cultures employers are seen as having obligations to their employees and their families, and these obligations continue even when an employee is not performing at expected levels. In these countries, employers may continue to employ people even when they are not contributing, and they may "make" work for these employees where there really is no work. In Japan it has been typical for employees to have a job for life, so once hired, it was highly unlikely that you would be made redundant or terminated. In China the communist tradition in state-owned enterprises, was known as the "Iron Rice Bowl", where employees were guaranteed a job, a place to live, and so on, as well as a certain wage, regardless of the organization's needs or the person's performance. This tradition is changing as China modernizes and moves toward more private ownership of enterprises, but it could nevertheless make termination more difficult, and keeping people on may seem easier, especially when pay is low.

A particular aspect of HRM that has not yet been discussed is that of labor relations. In most countries, employees can be organized into groupings of various kinds, usually labor unions or employee associations. The HR function has responsibility for relationships with these groups. In the following section labor relations are briefly discussed.

LABOR RELATIONS

Labor relations seem to vary substantially across the developing world. In some locations, the concept of labor unions, and labor–management negotiations and agreements, seems still in the early formation stages. Akorsu (2010) asked workers in the informal sector in Ghana about trade unions, and got the answer essentially "what are trade unions?" At the other extreme, in some developing countries, labor–management relations are antagonistic and the labor movement very adversarial, with a union activist labor environment that is very influential in governmental policy and decision-making. Unions in the developing world have often developed because of the power of the collectivism of trade unions, and the leaders of the unions became the political leaders during the struggles for independence and afterwards.

 Several brief descriptions of labor–management relations follow, to illustrate the diversity among developing countries.

Algeria (Branine, 2001) – the right to belong to a union was recognized in the mid-1960s, but the right to strike was described as an economic crime against the nation. Following liberalization of the economy in 1988, many new and active unions were created and strikes and demonstrations increased, but remain somewhat limited because of factors such as high unemployment.

Ghana (Debrah and Budhwar, 2001) – a long tradition of trade unionism, but many employees still treat trade unions with suspicion, and in the private sector management believes that they impinge on managerial prerogatives. Workers have the right to form a union and it is obligatory for the employer to meet with union representatives for collective bargaining purposes.

India (Budhwar and Debrah, 2001) – the influence of trade unions is significant. Indian unions play a more cooperative role than formerly and are less militant; however, they have a major role in terms of HR practices and policies. Indian national labor laws are substantial, and management is described as pro-labor, believing that adherence to the laws is good for industrial relations and therefore for their companies.

Nepal (Adhikari and Muller, 2001) – the state exerts a direct influence on the management of organizations, and in contrast to the state, labor unions are not very powerful. They were banned at one stage, and subsequently, once allowed, membership was very low. The benefits of collective bargaining are not widely known or recognized. The existing trade unions are split along political party lines.

Nigeria (Ovadje and Ankomah, 2001) – the trade union movement has had a significant impact on HRM practice and policies, and has resulted in legislation governing HRM. Decisions regarding wages and conditions of employment are made in consultation with unions at the industry level, but powerful unions have forced some companies to go beyond the collective agreement.

Pakistan (Khiji, 2001) – the labor history of Pakistan is described as a mix of labor repression and concessions, depending on how the political power has shifted. For example, in the late 1990s, the government introduced a policy to free the work environment from the influence of unions and unions were deprived of the power they had previously enjoyed; thus, their power was reduced to an insignificant level.

South Korea (Park, 2001) – labor unions are formed at the enterprise level, and all employees, regardless of job category are in the same union, and, by law, collective bargaining is carried out at the enterprise level. Firm specific issues are negotiated at the local level. The unions in the same industry establish an industrial federation. Since the early 1990s, the government has apparently introduced measures to discourage workers' attempts to organize for collective bargaining, and union membership has decreased.

Taiwan (Huang, 2001) – has been famous for harmonious industrial relations, which has been credited for successful economic development. Government intervention, cultural traditions, Confucian tenets, social networks and a patriarchal orientation have been credited with leading to peaceful labor–management relations.

These brief descriptions of labor relations in a variety of developing countries show that we cannot generalize about labor–management relations in developing countries. Each country has to be understood in its own context. The strength of the union movement, and unions, likely varies with a country's commitment to the supremacy of law in the society. Debrah and Budhwar (2001) do conclude that in almost all developing countries legal structures have been developed to safeguard the interests of employees, but that they are not enforced, and many countries do not promote equal opportunities based on factors such as ethnicity, gender and age. They also note that unions developed confrontational attitudes which served them well during independence struggles, but that these may do more harm than good in today's world. They suggested that where there is a cooperative labor–management environment, and the role of governments in unions is curtailed, this will be beneficial for developing countries. In the next section, a particular phenomenon, known as the brain drain, which affects developing countries disproportionately, is discussed.

THE BRAIN DRAIN PHENOMENON: NEGATIVES AND POSITIVES

For a long time, a concern for developing countries has been what is termed the brain drain. The brain drain refers to bright and well-educated younger people from developing countries choosing to leave their home country and move to a developed country to work and live. While the brain drain is often seen as a developing country phenomenon, it occurs elsewhere as well. For example, Canada often complains that its best and brightest can easily go to the USA and some do. Nevertheless, the brain drain affects developing countries to a disproportionate degree because of the relative shortage of skilled and educated young people and the relatively high need for advanced knowledge and experience.

The brain drain is often seen as negative, but there are also some positive aspects to the brain drain. In particular the brain drain results in a diaspora living abroad (for example, people of Caribbean descent living in New York) who maintain ties with their home country/region and provide substantial and varied positive inputs to the home country. The negatives and positives of the brain drain, as well as the role of the diaspora is outlined in the following discussion.

The negative side to the brain drain

In many cases, young people receive a good education, including a university education, in their home country or abroad, but they find that they cannot get the kind of job they would like at home, so they seek employment elsewhere, usually in a developed country. In addition, compensation and benefits at home may be substantially less than in a developed country, so this

107

is an added incentive to move away. Developed countries are often seen as providing greater opportunities for growth and better career paths, as well as a better lifestyle and conditions for one's family; thus, moving away from a developing country to a developed one can seem like a good decision for many reasons.

The developing country loses the "brains" of the entire family that moves away, and their experience and expertise. The loss is even greater because the developing country has had at least the main share of the expense of educating those who leave. The developed country, in contrast, benefits from the incoming brains without this expense. Developed countries have even been accused of taking advantage of this situation by targeting certain educated groups in developing countries, using marketing campaigns to attract well-trained nurses, teachers, and other needed personnel often willing to work for less pay than domestic personnel of comparable skills.

In some cases, bright young people choose to go to foreign universities. There are many reasons for such a choice: foreign universities may offer programs which are not available at home, foreign universities may be considered better or more prestigious, they may be accredited by desired bodies and therefore are more likely to be credible to employers, they may have well-known, globally recognized scholars, they may provide access to better resources, including technological and scientific requirements. Going to a foreign university is also seen as providing the opportunity to meet people from a wider array of countries than would be likely in the home environment, and thus to build a network of contacts for the future.

Where someone from a developing country goes to a foreign university, there are fees to be paid, and the fees for foreign students are often significantly greater than those charged for nationals. Over the past several decades, universities in developed countries have been actively recruiting students from developing countries, and relying on the income these students bring in to subsidize their own domestic students. In this case the developing country is losing foreign exchange as well as potentially the brains of the student. In many cases, students who go abroad to study do not return. They find good jobs in the foreign country, they meet people from around the world and make friends, they get married, have families; in short, the foreign country becomes home and there is little incentive to return to their developing country home. There is often great sadness among parents, siblings and other family and friends left behind when they bid goodbye to the young people going abroad to "seek their fortunes."

The positive side of the brain drain

Normally the brain drain is described as a negative phenomenon from the point of view of the developing home country. Fortunately, the phenomenon is not entirely negative. On the positive side, the people who leave to live and work abroad do not forget about their home country. They send money home (remittances) to help family and friends left at home. These remittances are often one of the most important sources of foreign exchange for many developing countries. They become ambassadors for the home country, telling their colleagues and friends about the home country and often encouraging foreign investors to consider their home country as a good place to invest or do business. They return home as visitors and spend money and they encourage others to visit. Some return home when they retire and build homes and bring back their pensions. Others return home to work on projects for their foreign companies. Still others choose to return at mid-career and continue their working life in their developing home country, thereby providing important senior level skills and experience.

The author was part of the brain drain and illustrates the positives and negatives. She was born in St. Vincent and the Grenadines (SVG) and received her university education in Canada and the USA. After she received her MBA, she worked for a New York-based company, and when the company was seeking an offshore location for an electronic assembly plant, she suggested St. Vincent as the location. A plant was successfully established in her home country and continued to operate for thirty years. Following her Ph.D. studies she taught at a Canadian university and married a Canadian, but maintained close ties with her family and friends in the Caribbean, and focused much of her research around development issues. At mid-career, a post came up at the University of the West Indies and she and her husband moved to the Caribbean so that she could take up the post, and concentrate her research efforts in the Caribbean. They have built a house in St. Vincent and spend time there as well as in Barbados. They expect to retire in St. Vincent. During her time overseas, the author always encouraged friends and colleagues to visit St. Vincent and to consider her home country as a place to do business, and she worked on projects for businesses in SVG who were interested in doing business in Canada and the USA. Her children now make up part of the SVG diaspora and continue to live in Canada and maintain a close connection and interest in SVG.

Multinational companies in developed countries have recognized the value of these well-educated people from developing countries and have sought them as employees and managers. Not only are they well educated and desirable employees because of this, but they also often speak several languages, are familiar with the culture and practices in their home country, and have contacts at home. Often, as employees and managers, these people promote their home country as a place to do business, and help develop business opportunities in their other home. Recent growth patterns have stimulated investors to look for opportunities in the developing world. As the developing world transitions from a source of commodities and cheap labor to more sophisticated industries, the need for and desirability of employees familiar with other cultures and countries is increasing rapidly.

The role of the diaspora

There are large groups of diaspora (people living and working abroad with roots in their country of origin) in countries around the world, and developing countries have recognized the value of these groups. Many developing countries are actively seeking to establish close links with their diasporas. People in the diaspora are able to provide substantial positive input to their home country – ranging from charitable giving, to investment, to providing specific skills. Companies based in developing countries are increasingly seeing the diaspora as a viable and valuable addition to their human resource base. Companies can seek employees with particular skills and expertise among the diaspora, either to work in the foreign location or to come home to work. They can partner with counterparts in the diaspora for specific projects, such as site identification, market research, licensing, franchising, and so on. Many countries are establishing lists of members of the diaspora who are interested in collaborating with counterparts at home, and this facilitates the process for companies seeking partners or other assistance. Some diaspora groups have established investment funds specifically for investment in viable business start-ups in their home countries; they also have formed advisory groups to assist with business start-ups and expansion, and various other business initiatives.

In today's global world, with the ease of travel and communication, the brain drain is unlikely to decrease. What seems more important, from a developing country perspective, is to accept the likelihood that some bright and talented young people will move to other countries, and to seek to capitalize on the positive side of this movement.

Developing countries can also seek to attract people with specific skills and expertise from developed countries. Many bright and talented young people from developed countries are looking for opportunities to travel to what seem like exotic locations. Many are also motivated by the opportunity to do something that they believe can make a positive contribution to a developing country, and the world. Older people at mid-career stage are also interested in expanding their horizons, and seeing new parts of the world, while also making a valuable contribution. These people can take periods of time away from their regular career and undertake short-term projects that require specific skills that may be in short supply in a developing country. After retirement, many people are very interested in putting their lifetime's experience to good use and they seek out opportunities in developing countries. Many people from developed countries who seek opportunities to contribute in developing countries do it because they see it as interesting, rather than because of the money or benefits, so they can be a relatively inexpensive experienced human resource choice. Many developed country governments have programs in place to support the export of their senior talent to assist developing countries in this way.

SUMMARY

This chapter has examined various aspects of HRM. HRM approaches and procedures have been relatively well accepted in developed countries, where they are widely used. The same is not the case in developing countries. The HRM field seems to be essentially in its infancy in these countries. There are some good reasons for this, and the characteristics of companies in developing countries may argue against formal HRM. Nevertheless, companies can also learn from the practices that have been found effective in developed countries. This chapter explored these issues as well as the need to take culture into account when adapting HRM practices in use in developed countries. The chapter also briefly explored issues associated with the brain drain, a particular concern for many developing countries, as well as the potential of the diaspora for contributing to these countries.

The chapter did not examine international HR; an important consideration for many companies in today's global world. The next chapter considers HRM issues from an international company perspective. That chapter draws on the more general literature on international HRM (IHRM), which has been developed from a developed country perspective. International companies from developing countries face essentially the same issues as they seek to make effective IHRM decisions, but may face different constraints, and these issues and constraints will be considered there.

LESSONS LEARNED

After finishing this chapter, readers should be able to consider and understand issues associated with managing people in organizations. You should be able to analyze the main issues regarding HRM in the developing country context. You should be able to discuss why developing countries may offer very different challenges for foreign firms as they implement HRM practices. You should also appreciate why it is important for companies in developing countries to begin focusing on HRM issues and be able to identify potentially interesting and useful HRM approaches for these companies.

DISCUSSION QUESTIONS

1   Discuss what you believe are the most important HRM challenges facing developing countries.
2   Discuss the most important issues relating to HRM in your country from a global perspective?

3   "In a small, developing country, HR systems are unnecessary." Discuss the pros and cons of this statement.

4   Identify the main cultural characteristics of developing countries, and discuss how these characteristics are likely to impact on HRM practices.

EXERCISE

As a group, select an organization, in your country, and evaluate its HR systems. What do you think is positive about the system? What needs to be changed and in what way? How has this company, firm, or organization aligned its HRM practices with its strategy?

Chapter 9

Managing an international workforce

OBJECTIVES

This chapter considers human resource management (HRM) issues from an international company perspective.

The objectives are as follows:

- To examine issues associated with HRM for international companies.
- To provide an understanding of international human resource management (IHRM) so that companies in developing countries can learn from the experience of international companies and avoid costly mistakes.
- To give an overview of the issues, processes, challenges and opportunities associated with IHRM. To examine various groups of employees in international companies, and the benefits and drawbacks of each group.
- To discuss HRM issues, such as selection, training, compensation, and so on, for companies that are international.
- To highlight the importance of being culturally sensitive when internationalizing, especially for companies from developing countries.
- To reinforce that companies that are insensitive to cross-cultural issues can face difficulties in new and unfamiliar environments.
- To consider issues associated with expatriates, their families and the culture shock they face, and the potential for failure that arises because of this.
- To recognize the critical nature or human resource challenges and opportunities for international managers.

INTRODUCTION

Firms from developing countries face many similar challenges to their developed country counterparts as they internationalize. This is particularly true in terms of human resource (HR) management. In this chapter, we examine issues associated with HR management for international companies. This is an area where newly internationalizing companies can learn from the experiences of international companies who have gone before, and avoid some of their costly mistakes. In particular, North American companies have reported high failure rates and a high cost of failure among international assignees. The information presented here can help firms from developing countries avoid this failure problem. Developed countries have also sometimes had an "ugly" image in foreign locations because of their lack of cultural competency. This image can cause business difficulties, and at the extreme, failure. Companies from developing countries can learn from this and seek to be more culturally sensitive as they internationalize.

In the following section, a simple classification is used to identify groups of employees available to an international firm.

GROUPS OF EMPLOYEES IN INTERNATIONAL FIRMS[1]

In order to identify the main groups of employees among which an international firm can choose for staffing, consider the following example:

An Indian firm, IndiaInc., with headquarters in India, has a wholly owned manufacturing subsidiary in the United States (INUSA), a sales office in Canada (INCan), and a joint venture with a Mexican company (INMex) for Mexican production of its products. IndiaInc. has to staff its operations in India, the United States, Canada, and Mexico, and it has employees available from all these locations who can be used in its staffing. At least theoretically, it also has access to persons anywhere else in the world. For simplicity, we can divide current and potential employees into three groups:

- Parent country nationals (PCNs). These are persons from the parent country and usually persons who are employed with the parent firm in the parent country. In our example, PCNs would be Indian nationals, usually employed with IndiaInc.
- Host country nationals (HCNs). These are persons from one of the host countries, working in the host country operations. In our example, American nationals working in INUSA, Canadian nationals working in INCan, or Mexican nationals working in INMex.
- Third country nationals (TCNs). These are neither PCNs nor HCNs. They are usually from one of the countries where operations are located, but they are not working in their country of origin. In our example, they are American nationals working in INCan or INMex, Canadian nationals working in INUSA or INMex, or Mexican nationals working in INUSA or INCan, or any of them working at the headquarters IndiaInc.

These three categories cover the majority of employees, although in reality things may not be this straightforward. For example, some people carry more than one citizenship, and do not fit neatly into one category or another (is an Indian Canadian working in India a PCN?). Others carry one citizenship but most of their education was in another country (is an Indian citizen educated in the United States and working in the United States a PCN or HCN?). Still others have substantial experience in a given country or region (is a Sri Lankan who has worked throughout North America really a TCN if she takes a job in the Canada or the USA?). These subtle variations are important, and international firms may seek employees because of their special mix of nationality and experience. This may be particularly important for companies from developing countries as they internationalize. These companies may have relatively limited

---

[1] This material is drawn from Punnett (2009).

resources, so making the best possible use of human resources is critical. Some recent research suggests that people who have lived in different countries as children are more adaptable in later life and therefore they may be more adaptable to international transfers.

International firms do business in a variety of ways: they are involved in licensing, franchising, contracts, joint ventures, strategic alliances, mergers, and so on, as well as simply trading across borders. These structural choices have a critical influence on human resource choices, as the following examples illustrate:

- A licensing agreement relies on a company in a foreign location to produce the parent company's product or service. The licensor (company for whom the product is being produced) is usually concerned with factors such as quality and capacity in the foreign location, and uses its own personnel (PCNs) to train employees and monitor activities at the licensee (company producing the product), but these assignments are usually short term.

- A franchising arrangement involves the franchisor selling the rights to operate a franchise to a franchisee (for example, McDonald's, an American franchisor, sells rights to operate McDonald's restaurants to franchisees in countries around the world). Franchises are usually owned and run by locals (HCNs). The owners and employees often go to the franchisor's headquarters for short-term training courses (McDonald's United States has intensive courses to ensure that all McDonald's restaurants around the world meet the same standards). Managers from headquarters also visit franchisees to provide training and ensure that standards are maintained. Most franchisors supply all or much of the products and systems used by the franchisee, thereby controlling the operations of the franchise.

- A contracting arrangement involves an agreement to provide particular services for a specified period (for example, an engineering firm is contracted to oversee the construction of a bridge, or a management consulting firm is contracted to carry out a survey of employee attitudes). International contracts are usually used where local expertise is not available, and, consequently, this means that foreign personnel from a foreign company are hired on contract to complete a contract. In large projects personnel may come from several different companies and countries (for example, in a World Bank-funded government restructuring contract in Jamaica, there were people from Australia, Canada, the United Kingdom, and the United States all working on the project in Jamaica at the same time). These people are expatriates, but they cannot be considered PCNs because there is not always a parent company in this business structure.

- A joint venture involves ownership of a company by two or more parent companies. For example, an Indian firm and a Canadian company may form a joint venture to operate in India, in Canada, or in a third country, say Taiwan. Again, the distinctions between PCNs, HCNs, and TCNs are not as simple as described earlier. In this example, if operations are in India, an Indian employee is both a PCN and an HCN; if operations are in Taiwan, both Canadian and Indian employees are PCNs, and so on.

- Strategic alliances are arrangements in which two or more firms mutually agree to work together on a particular project of strategic importance to them. For example, the Body Shop, a UK-based franchisor with franchises around the world, might form a strategic alliance with Greenpeace, a worldwide environmental activism organization, to publicize information on endangered species. In this case, there is no parent or host country, and personnel working together on the project would not be classified in this way.

- International mergers involve two companies from different countries becoming one. For example, the Canadian Imperial Bank of Canada and Barclays Bank formed a merger in the

Caribbean to become the First Caribbean International Bank. In a true merger there is no dominant partner, thus there is no sense of one entity being the parent and the other, the host. Nevertheless, in this merger, the new bank was headquartered in Barbados, so in some sense, Barbados was considered the Parent Country. To further complicate the HR question, the Canadian bank later bought a majority share in the new bank, thus essentially meaning that Canada was the parent country; however, by then the public largely considered the bank a Caribbean company.

A particular issue for international companies and developing countries is the "foreign guest worker". Most of these workers come from developing countries and their status is often questionable and their treatment discriminatory. The next section deals with these workers, as a separate category from those discussed previously.

Foreign guest workers

In addition to PCNs, HCNs, and TCNS, throughout the world there are many "guest workers" who have left their country of birth to work in a country where higher pay and a better standard of living exist. These guest workers are different from the TCNs previously discussed, because they work in jobs that members of the local populace choose not to hold: agricultural labor, garbage collection, maid service, repetitive factory work, manual labor, and so forth. For example, if you were staffing a major construction project in the United Arab Emirates (UAE), it is likely that laborers will have to be hired from other countries such as the Philippines, because the labor supply for construction workers in the UAE is small, and the standard of living is high, so very few UAE nationals need to work in manual labor jobs. The Filipino laborers will make more money than they could in the Philippines, and be able to send money home, so they are willing to take the jobs. At the same time, they will be separated from their families for long periods of time and will not be accepted into the mainstream of life in the UAE. Foreign guest workers pose a challenge in many parts of the world, because they do not have the same legal protection that is afforded to locals or other foreign nationals. They are sometimes badly treated, and they are paid substantially less than the minimum wage. As this chapter was being written, there were stories of Indonesian females working as domestic servants in Saudi Arabia who had apparently been tortured and abused, physically and sexually, by their employers. This naturally caused outrage in Indonesia, and there were calls at one extreme for an end to this type of work, and, at least, for greater regulation and supervision of these workers. There were also news reports at the same time about Caribbean migrant laborers on farms in Canada being mistreated. This indicates that migrant workers, or foreign guest workers, may face harsh conditions in a variety of locations. Nevertheless, people in poor countries, seeking work that they cannot find at home, remain willing to go to other countries in order to earn something to be able to provide for themselves and their families.

We often think of foreign guest workers as going from developing countries to developed ones. For example, Mexican agricultural workers in the USA, Caribbean migrants in Canada, African manual laborers in European countries, are all common examples of foreign guest workers. There are also many foreign guest workers who move from one developing country to another developing country. In Barbados, there are Guyanese workers who do many of the less desirable jobs, and Chinese firms have "imported" Chinese workers to African and Caribbean countries, on the basis that they are hard working and more reliable than local workers. The better off African countries host foreign guest workers from poorer African countries, and a similar situation exists among Asian countries.

Foreign guest workers often face discrimination in a variety of areas; for example, they can be deported without notice if an economic downturn occurs, their children may not be able to enter apprentice systems or local universities, their career mobility is virtually nil, and their quality of life is much lower than that of the majority of the citizens of the country in which they work, even though they contribute significantly to the GNP and are the foundation upon which many industries' profits rest. Whether they are illegal aliens or legal short-term residents, the life of foreign guest workers tends to be one of uncertainty, unequal treatment, and no upward mobility. They usually live in isolated "ghettos," and because they may hold different religious beliefs, eat different foods, wear different clothes, and have different cultural values, conflict frequently occurs. Some governments are rethinking their policies toward the use of guest workers because of these concerns.

In the early months of 2011, when substantial unrest started in the Middle East and North Africa, the plight of foreign guest workers in countries such as Egypt and Libya highlighted the uncertain situation of these groups. When fighting broke out in these countries, foreign guest workers were essentially forced to flee, with whatever belongings they had at hand. Their home countries, being among the poorest, were often not able to help them and they had to rely on local people in neighboring countries, who could give them assistance, relief agencies, and third countries, that provided some aid and transportation for refugees. A particular issue was that many of these foreign guest workers were owed money but, due to the unstable situation, they had no way to collect this money. In addition, employers often keep the travel documents of foreign guest workers, and some were unable to retrieve their documents, making them "undocumented" and possibly "illegal" immigrants, even though they were living and working legally.

While companies may not be obligated to provide more than minimal benefits for foreign guest workers, it may be in their self-interest to do so. Foreign guest workers who are treated in ways that they see as equitable are likely to repay their employers with hard work and loyalty. Those who feel that they are treated inequitably will only provide what is absolutely necessary, and find ways to adjust their situation, perhaps through pilferage and the like, and they will move to other jobs or employers if they have the opportunity. Foreign guest workers, given their situation, and the job situation that they faced at home, are likely to see even small benefits as substantial, so by investing relatively little, companies can achieve improvements in the lives of foreign guest workers, and consequently benefit from greater productivity.

In the following sections of this chapter, we turn attention to the management of international human resources. We look at selection and training, compensation, career planning, and retirement.

SELECTING AND TRAINING INTERNATIONAL MANAGERS

In this section, we look at selecting and training international managers. This is becoming an increasingly important consideration for companies from developing countries as they expand internationally. These international companies headquartered in developing countries are facing similar issues to those faced by international companies from developed countries. Much of the literature that was aimed at developed countries in this regard seems to be applicable to developing countries as well.

The selection process for international managers basically involves identifying the important characteristics for a particular position, identifying a pool of potential candidates, evaluating the candidates in terms of the characteristics deemed important, shortlisting the best candidates, reviewing and interviewing the shortlisted candidates, and, finally, selecting the best candidate. The process is never this simple in reality, particularly for an international firm. As the foregoing discussion illustrated, there are both benefits and drawbacks to each of the groups of employees from which one can select. The same is true for any individual – one candidate may have excellent job-related skills and speak several languages but has never worked with people from different cultural backgrounds; another may have moderate job-related skills, speak only her/his native language, but have substantial experience working in multicultural situations. Evaluating these two candidates against each other is complex.

Some international postings may be reserved for certain types of people in some firms. Typically, the finance function and other high level confidential functions (for example, research and development, and corporate strategy) are staffed by parent company personnel; in family-owned firms, which are relatively common in developing countries, this often means family members, for security and confidentiality purposes. Family-owned firms are likely to feel that a family member is more trustworthy than someone from outside of the family, and will want a family member in positions of importance in foreign locations, because of the sense of trust this engenders at home, as well as because the family presence is believed to add to the prestige and image of the subsidiary.

Training is designed to ensure that the selected candidate can perform well. Training can focus around job-related factors or around non-job-related ones, such as an individual's abilities to relate to others (relational) and deal with differences encountered in different locations (cross-cultural adaptation). The following discussion suggests two structured approaches to the selection and training processes that are helpful to managers making human resource choices in international firms. These approaches were designed essentially for developed country firms, but they seem to apply to firms anywhere selecting and training personnel for assignments in another country.

Tung (1981) proposed a selection model that has become well known in the literature. The model relates job characteristics to selection strategies. The model asks a variety of questions about the position and uses the answers to identify the appropriate selection/training. The following is a simplification of this model:

1   Is an HCN available? If so, the position should be filled by an HCN and training should focus on improving technical and managerial skills. If not, ask:
2   What is the degree of interaction required with the host community? If low, focus on job-related training. If high, ask:
    How similar are cultures? If low similarity, focus on cross-cultural training, and include the family. If high, emphasize job-related training (adapted from Tung 1981).

This is a simple but useful model. It can provide a good guide in the selection process. There are, however, some extensions to the model that should be considered:

■   The model assumes that HCNs should be selected if they are available and have the requisite skills. This may be true in many cases, but, as our earlier discussion illustrated, there may be times when non-HCNs are preferred. As noted, PCNs may be preferred, particularly in family-owned firms.
■   If HCNs are used, the model suggests a focus on technical and managerial skills. This focus is appropriate but overlooks the need for the HCN to deal with colleagues in other subsidiaries and counterparts in the parent country. An overlooked aspect of training in much of the literature is the need to train HCNs in cross-cultural skills so that they can deal effectively with their foreign counterparts.

117

■ If a non-HCN is selected, the model focuses on training the candidate and family for the foreign experience. This is, of course, critical, but the employees in the host country are ignored, and it may be equally important to ensure that they and possibly their families receive some training in cross-cultural issues so that they will accept foreign assignees.

From the perspective of the developing country company, a similar approach applies. However, the developing country's pool of candidates may be limited, and this will encourage the use of HCNs and TCNs rather than PCNs. Alternatively, there may be political pressure to use PCNs to establish the parent country's presence in foreign locations. Cultural and social preferences may mean that a PCN goes alone on a foreign assignment, rather than taking the family, and this changes the dynamics of the assignment.

Punnett and Ricks (1989) suggested the following steps for effective selection of international candidates:

■ Begin the selection process by asking what the legal limitations are (it may not be possible to use a PCN or TCN in some situations). If the company is limited to using an HCN regardless of skills and other factors, then the company must deal with this reality.
■ If there are no legal restrictions, identify the needed job-related expertise and experience and develop a pool of candidates with the appropriate expertise and experience from throughout the company, including PCNs, HCNs, and TCNs.
■ Identify non-job-related characteristics, including preference for using a particular group of employees and relational, cross-cultural abilities.
■ Eliminate, from the pool, candidates who do not have the non-job-related characteristics.
■ Remaining candidates should have both job and non-job characteristics and should meet legal requirements. These candidates can be evaluated relative to each other and training tailored to suit the candidate selected.

A key to effective selection is that both job-related and relational/cross-cultural abilities are important. That is, the candidate must be able to do the job, but this is usually not enough in an international situation. The candidate must also be able to relate to others effectively and to adjust to new cultures. The literature has stressed this from an expatriate perspective, but it is also important when selecting among HCNs. This aspect of selection appears to hold for companies whether they are from developed or developing countries. International companies from developing countries can learn from the experiences of those from developed countries, and avoid the problems of high failure rates among international assignees, by incorporating relational and cross-cultural thinking into their selection and training processes. Pacek and Thornily (2004) suggest the following as critical in finding good local managers: establish good links with universities, use locally based headhunters, invest in corporate brand building, hire from other multinationals, and participate in job fairs and career days. These activities are valuable no matter where your company is headquartered.

Human resource choices in an international firm inevitably result in cultural interactions. A firm that uses a staffing policy in which HCNs are used everywhere overcomes this, but only to a certain extent. PCNs may visit these subsidiaries to introduce new products, new policies, and new procedures; to ensure that the subsidiaries are well managed and to evaluate performance; to audit operations and finances; and to train and develop managers and employees. Similarly, HCNs visit the parent country to learn about new products, policies, and procedures; to report on subsidiary performance, operations, and finances; and to attend training and development sessions. Personnel from different subsidiaries also interact for a variety of reasons. Cross-cultural interactions are, thus, a normal part of any international firm's activities. Anyone whose position entails interactions with counterparts from different countries and cultures should have the following characteristics: an ability to get along well with people, an awareness of cultural differences, open-mindedness and a tolerance for foreigners, and adaptability and an ability to adjust quickly to new conditions (adapted from Ricks, 1983: 59). This profile may be more typical of developed country candidates than those from developing countries, simply because candidates from developed countries may have had the opportunity to travel and to interact with people of other cultures. To the extent that this is the case, a rigorous selection and training program for international assignments can be particularly beneficial for international companies from developing countries.

Once a candidate has been selected, training needs to be tailored to deal with the candidate's deficiencies, whether job-related or relational and cross-cultural. Although any individual candidate will have to be evaluated on the basis of a variety of factors, the following outlines the general training needs of the three groups of employees identified.

PCNs particularly need to learn about the host country and how business is done there. The PCN needs to understand specifics of the job that differ from the job at home, including reporting relationships, timeframes, and the subsidiary's relationship to the rest of the organization. The PCN also needs to be familiar with the host's economic, legal, political, and labor environments. Sometimes the most important aspect of PCN training is on the cultural environment and management practices in the host country because these affect every aspect of day-to-day operaions and interactions. Especially important is training PCN personnel to avoid being or appearing judgmental regarding cultural differences.

HCNs particularly need to understand the parent company and what it requires of them. The HCN needs to be familiar with the specifics of parent company policies and procedures, understand the reason for these, and be able and willing to comply with them. The HCN also needs to be able to communicate effectively with counterparts at the parent company. If an HCN appointment is to be successful in terms of the overall organization, the HCN needs to receive training to facilitate subsidiary–parent interactions.

TCNs play an interesting role as "in-betweens." Often, as described, they are specialists and, therefore, being comfortable with the local environment in terms of their particular specialty is vital. TCNs also need to understand the host environment more generally, as well as the parent environment and the interaction between host and parent. Many TCNs, have substantial international experience and this can mean that in-depth, rigorous cross-cultural training can be minimized for that particular group.

The training process

The training process in the literature from developed countries has most often been addressed from the perspective of a PCN and family being sent on an expatriate assignment. In this section concepts of training rigor and matching the rigor of training to the needs of the candidate are introduced. These concepts are often discussed in terms of expatriates, but they are as applicable to the HCN or TCN as well as to the PCN. These concepts are also applicable to companies from developing countries making international assignments; in fact, as noted previously, this may be especially relevant for companies from developing countries. Challenges associated with cross-cultural adjustment arise in all directions.

Cross-cultural training methods have been described as varying from passive with low rigor to participative with high rigor (Black and Mendenhall, 1990). Low-rigor and passive training methods focus on factual issues and include books, lectures, and area briefings. Moderate rigor and somewhat active methods are described as analytical and include films, classroom discussion, and sensitivity training. High-rigor and fully participative methods seek to really involve the candidate in cross-cultural experiences; they are described as experiential and include role playing, simulations, and field trips.

International and cross-cultural training can be relatively expensive. The greater the participation and rigor, the more expensive the training will be. International firms clearly want to optimize training expenses. Tailoring training to the needs of the candidates allows the company to use training resources to best effect. While this is true of all firms, it is likely to be especially important for firms from developing countries, if their access to resources is limited. A tailored approach means that expensive, participative, rigorous training is used only for those candidates who need this and will benefit from it. Using Tung's (1981) model (presented earlier), it seems that as cultural differences increase, and as the need for cultural interactions increase, greater participation and rigor become more critical. On the other side, as the assignee's level of cross-cultural experience and expertise increases, the need for participation and rigor decreases.

In the past, companies tended to provide in-house training for their employees. In the last decade, as many staff functions have been outsourced, international and cross-cultural training has often been undertaken by firms that specialize in this type of training. This seems to be the trend today. International firms should take advantage of the specialized training expertise of these training firms, but this choice also means that the specific needs related to the company could be overlooked. An ideal choice may be both in-company training dealing with company-specific issues paired with outsourced training incorporating in-depth knowledge of particular locations. For companies from developing countries, there may be less availability of outsourced training, because these companies have been established to meet the needs of companies from developed countries. Firms specializing in cross-cultural training are more likely geared to train an American manager to go to an African country than the reverse. This may mean that developing country firms have to use their internal resources for cross-cultural training purposes, but they should still consider the cost/benefit tradeoffs of using outside experts versus developing internal expertise in this area of training. Cross-cultural training specialists are likely to be interested in developing their area of expertise, as there is a growing demand for this expertise from developing country firms. This may also be an area of opportunity – firms in developing countries can provide training for incoming managers as well as for their own companies sending managers on foreign assignments.

Compensation

Compensation decisions in international firms are extremely complex, and this discussion only briefly outlines the issues that have to be addressed. Consider the various groups that have been discussed previously.

PCNs who accept a foreign assignment generally expect to at least maintain the standard of living to which they are accustomed; this includes benefits and pensions. PCNs also expect to be able to live as their local counterparts do in the foreign location, even if this is in effect a higher standard of living than at home, and they usually expect to maintain the accustomed level of pay, benefits, and so on, that they received at home. Many companies deal with PCN compensation on this basis; that is, salary and benefits at least equal to that at home, with premiums to allow a living standard equivalent to that at home or to local counterparts, if appropriate. From the outside, it seems that PCNs get the best of both worlds. This, in fact, is a point of contention when PCN salaries and benefits put them well above their local counterparts. International firms need PCNs and therefore want to compensate them in ways that are fair from the PCN point of view, but they do need to consider the host view as well. In addition to regular compensation and housing/living allowances, PCNs expect additional benefits such as schooling for their children, regular trips home, access to recreational clubs, and so on. Some assignments are seen as unattractive. In these cases, PCNs may require additional incentives, referred to as hardship pay. Altogether, the package for PCNs can be substantial.

HCNs are usually paid on the basis of local salaries and benefits. Some international companies pay at the high end of local scales, so that jobs with these companies are often seen as desirable and prestigious locally. At the same time, some HCNs can feel disadvantaged when they know that PCNs, TCNs, or HCNs in other subsidiaries are being compensated on a higher basis. This provides a new challenge for the international firm – firms are blamed for inflating local prices if they pay above local norms, but they are accused of discrimination if local compensation levels are lower than the parent or other subsidiaries. There is no easy solution to this dilemma, but the firm must seek to be fair in its compensation policies in all locations and must be able to explain the basis on which it decides on compensation. Interestingly, according to Pacek and Thorniley (2004), HCNs are sometimes paid more than their home country counterparts. They say that because of the limited pool of qualified HCNs, multinationals find that they need to offer high salaries and substantial bonuses and benefits to attract desired candidates from a limited group.

TCNs are a particularly difficult blend from a compensation perspective. Should they be paid like PCNs? Should they be paid the equivalent of HCNs? Or should their compensation be equivalent to what they would receive in their home country? The answer is probably a mix; compensation should reflect host country norms, but be adjusted to account for home country expectations and incorporate some of the extra benefits usually afforded to PCNs. This approach sounds reasonable, but has not necessarily been implemented in reality. Some companies seek to attract candidates for international assignments from countries like India for the very reason that they are relatively inexpensive. This may be effective in the short term, but often leads to these candidates feeling disillusioned, with consequences of decreased motivation and performance. Companies need to realize that these employees are expatriates and put into place the needed administrative structures to ensure that the employees succeed.

In compensation decisions, the issue of apparent equity is important. This is especially difficult for international firms because of the different expectations and standards of living encountered around the world. In some locations, it is normal to have a maid, a nanny, and a chauffeur, but the cost of these may be relatively low. In that case, should additional allowances be granted to hire these people, or should the expense come out of one's salary? Many human resource managers indicate that these trade-offs are made on a case-by-case basis. There is some advantage to tailoring the compensation package to the individual's needs, but this is also likely to result in charges of inequity. Compensation remains a major concern for international companies, with no clear evidence regarding best practices.

For companies from developing countries, the compensation issues may be further compli-cated if an assignment is being made from a low-cost developing country to a high-cost developed country. The costs associated with moving a candidate, in such a case, have to be care-fully assessed against the benefits, to ensure that the cost benefit trade off is positive. The costs are tangible and relatively easy to quantify, while the benefits are often intangible and difficult to specify, so this analysis is not straightforward. The complexity may mean that managers prefer not to do the analysis, but, with limited resources, companies from developing countries need to pay particular attention to these tradeoffs.

Promotion, career development, retirement

Selection, training, and compensation issues form the basis for an international assignment. Yet the firm also has to pay attention to what happens to employees over time. Issues of promotion, career development, and retirement are all part of the human resource decision process. As always, these decisions are made complex by their international nature. Consider the following situations:

■ A Canadian employee spends most of her career in Africa. Where will she want to retire? How will her pension funds be invested and paid out?

■ A West Indian from Trinidad works for a U.S. company and serves around the world, from the United Kingdom to the United Arab Emirates and Malaysia. Where are his retirement funds kept? Where are they paid out? How are taxes paid on them?

■ An Italian spends all his working life in the Middle East for a USA company, and his pension is vested in the United States. Can he retire in the Middle East? Must he pay U.S. taxes on his retirement income?

Some of these issues can be worked out by corporate lawyers, but they are complex and need to be considered by human resource managers and employees. For example, American citizens are taxed based on citizenship, while many other nationalities are taxed based on residence. The previous examples illustrate the complexities that are a necessary part of international careers. These examples focused on retirement. Similar issues are inherent in promotion and career development questions:

■ How do within-country promotions compare to promotions to headquarters?
■ Are expatriate assignments really good for your career?
■ How should you evaluate a home country promotion relative to an expatriate posting?

International staffing decisions, like any decision affecting careers and incomes, are among the most sensitive for human resource managers and employees alike. Mistakes, lack of transparency, and perceived inequities can prove costly both in terms of individual motivation and performance, and employee well-being, as well as to the company in terms of overall effectiveness. International companies need to consider this wide array of issues in their human resource choices. These issues are as important for companies from developing countries as they internationalize as they are for their developed country counterparts. Managers going from developing countries to developed ones are likely to face the same culture shock as do managers going to developing countries from developed ones. In the next section we look at some of the issues that are likely to cause culture shock for developing country managers.

CULTURE SHOCK

Where companies face new and different expectations, norms, and even regulations in a host country, their home country managers are likely to experience substantial culture shock. Selection and training of home country managers is particularly critical under these conditions. Home country managers need to thoroughly understand the realities of the host country and be trained so that they are able to accept these realities and work effectively in the host country. For managers from developing countries, it may seem a positive move to be assigned to a developed country, but the culture shock of moving from a developing country to a developed one can be just as great as vice versa.

We have defined developing countries as relatively poor, and developed ones as relatively rich. Within both sets of countries, there are substantially inequalities, with some people being very rich, and some very poor. Managers in developing countries are likely to come from the better off families and those who own the companies and have been able to educate their children well. This means they have probably been among the privileged elite, looked up to, and accustomed to having poorer people to serve them as maids, chauffeurs, cooks, nannies, and so on. Moving to the west, say Canada or the United States, can be a major shock for such a manager, who may find her/his standard of living seriously diminished, and he/she becomes "a small fish in a large pond" rather than "a large fish in a small pond" with less power and prestige than was normal back home. People from developing countries also often have a distorted idea of life in the West, based on television, glossy magazines, and so on. It is a further shock for these people when they discover the less attractive sides of life in a city like New York or Toronto; for example, the homeless who live on the streets of these cities are a distressing surprise to many visitors.

Many developed countries have laws which prohibit discrimination on the basis of a wide variety of factors, including age, gender, race, religion, physical ability, and sexual preference. These laws are not as common in the developing countries. In many developing countries, the following is more likely:

- Age may be respected, but younger people are desired for the 'face' of the organization, so when receptionists are hired, they are expected to be of a certain age, such as under 25.
- Women are often prohibited from working at all, or limited to certain types of jobs or industries.
- Race and religion are considered a normal part of hiring decisions, with preference given to those in the majority or the elite (possibly the minority).
- Facilities for the physically disable are uncommon and it is accepted that these people do not work, or work only in a limited capacity.
- Homosexuality is considered unacceptable, and is often illegal in developing countries, and employing a known homosexual is out of the question.

In some developing countries, because of the previous points, discrimination on the basis of personal characteristics may, in fact, be the accepted norm. Companies from developing countries will typically operate at home according to the norms of the home country. The challenge arises when they become international and face anti-discriminatory legislation that is unfamiliar. Consider a company from a country that does not allow women to be employed with men – if this company expands to Europe or North America, or a variety of other countries around the world, it cannot continue the home country policy of not mixing men and women, as it will face legislative suits in the host country. Of course, the company has to comply with the laws of the host country in which it operates, but this may pose challenges for persons moving from home to work in the host country subsidiary. In the example of men and women, it may be quite difficult for men from the home country when they are required to work side by side with women. These men may also find that their counterparts in other companies are women, and that they are expected to meet with these women for business purposes, and may be invited to mix with them socially. All of this may make them extremely uncomfortable.

An alternative scenario might be a Jamaican male manager sent to Canada to manage a subsidiary. Jamaicans are notoriously homophobic, and aspects of homosexuality are illegal in

Jamaica, as they are in many other countries. Being openly homosexual is absolutely frowned on in Jamaica, and the image of the 'macho' or 'manly' man is promoted. In Canada, the reverse is the case. Homosexuality is quite accepted in Canada; for example, marriage between homosexuals is legal and sanctioned, homosexuals can adopt children and be parents, and managers and executives of some major corporations are openly homosexual, and same-sex partners receive the same company benefits and treatment as any partner. Imagine the discomfort a Jamaican manager will likely feel if he is required to work with a Canadian counterpart who is openly homosexual, and if he is invited to a function where the Canadian and his partner are present, and behave as married partners; for example, holding hands.

These examples underscore the need for good selection and training. The home country manager needs to be flexible enough to adapt to varying conditions, and needs to be sensitive to the cultural differences that will be encountered. The home country manager also needs to be thoroughly trained regarding the reality of the host country, so that differences are expected and understood.

The situation can be even more challenging if the manager's family accompanies her/him on a foreign assignment. The family faces all of the same differences that the manager does, and undergoes the same culture shock, but without the structure of a job and a workplace, or the assistance of colleagues at work who can help explain unexpected occurrences. In many developing countries, an extended family unit is still relatively common, and many families live in family compounds, with communal possessions. This lifestyle means substantial support is essentially always available, and there are others to call on in times of need. These families moving to developed countries may find themselves in a very different environment, essentially on their own and having to make individual decisions with no support systems. It is critical that managers and their companies recognize the need to help the manager's family adapt to the new surroundings and an unfamiliar situation.

SUMMARY

This chapter has looked at how companies from developing countries manage an international workforce. As more developing country firms become international, these issues will become ever more relevant. This chapter looked at various HR choices available to the international firm, and considered the benefits and drawbacks of each group from a developing country firm perspective. A particular aspect of these choices involves foreign guest workers, and the chapter outlined the situation faced by these workers.

The chapter examined staffing issues in an international company, including selection and training, compensation, promotion, career development and retirement. The chapter concluded by looking at culture shock, particularly from the point of view of a manager and family from a developing country going to a developed country.

LESSONS LEARNED

Having completed this chapter you should have developed a critical appreciation of HRM theories and practices, including a recognition that international companies need to consider a wider array of issues in their HR choices, and that these are important for companies from developing countries as they internationalize. You should understand what is involved in the selection process, and identifying the important characteristics for a particular position.

You should be familiar with international organizations' management of a global workforce, and how the management of HR varies between countries. You should also be clear about the challenges of managing a multicultural workforce and how cultural systems influence HRM practices.

DISCUSSION QUESTIONS

1   What aspects of recruitment and selection, training, remuneration and performance management need modification or additional attention in the management of expatriates?
2   Identify and explain factors that influence the effectiveness of HRM in multinational organizations.
3   Discuss the major causes and behavioral outcomes of cultural diversity in international organizations.
4   Describe and discuss the role of culture in the workplace. Do you agree that our cultural heritage affects the way we do business? Explain your response.

EXERCISE

The focus of this activity is determining how the practice of HRM must be adapted in developing countries contexts to ensure cultural appropriateness and effectiveness. In small groups, select a country of your choice and prepare a report recommending how two HRM practices should be designed in order to be effective and culturally appropriate in the domestic culture. Prepare a brief presentation on your country to share your findings with the class. Select the HRM practices to examine from the following list: recruitment and selection, performance management, training and development, remuneration, employment relations.

Chapter 10

Motivation in developing countries

INTRODUCTION

A firm's success and profitability are directly related, to a large extent, to the performance and productivity of the people who work for it; thus, a major component of a manager's role is to ensure that employees are performing at a peak level. This means that managers are concerned with how motivated employees are at work. This is as true in developing countries as it is in developed countries; however, what motivates people will differ from place to place depending on a variety of factors. When one considers the differences between developing and developed countries, such as poverty, lack of education, lack of infrastructure, and so on, one can expect that these factors will all influence motivation.

Motivation is generally described as referring to the inner urges that cause people to behave in certain ways. In the workplace, when we say someone is highly motivated we mean that they work hard to accomplish objectives that are consistent with the organization's goals. When we say someone is demotivated on the job, we mean that they seem disinterested and need to be pushed to perform. It is not really accurate to talk of people being demotivated. People are always motivated in some direction; the question is the direction of their motivation. When someone is demotivated at work, it means that they are motivated in some other, probably non-work, direction; that is, they would rather be doing something other than work. When we say that someone is demotivated, then, we mean that they are not working very hard, and their performance is less than could be expected.

We can hypothesize that in some developing countries many lower-level employees may come to work having had little to eat; and, if someone is hungry, they are likely to seem demotivated, because they are concerned with finding food, rather than working at their job. Also, in some cultures people believe that rewards should be allocated according to need rather than performance; a person with several dependants should receive more pay than someone with none, even though the person with none works much harder and performs at a much higher level. If a manager rewarded the high performer and expected this to be motivating, this would actually be seen as inequitable and would demotivate both parties.

People in all countries, developing and developed experience "motivation". What makes people motivated or demotivated at work is complex because motivation is caused by a mix of psychological and personal characteristics. In this chapter we look at how the characteristics of development may influence motivation. Where there is existing research, we draw on this; however, we also speculate on the possible impact of characteristics of developing countries on motivation. The next section outlines the major theories of motivation.

THEORIES OF MOTIVATION

Motivation has been studied extensively in developed countries, especially in North America; the same is not true in developing countries. Studies of motivation in developing countries are limited to individual studies, examining a particular theory in one location, and often one company or industry. The major theories of motivation that we consider here are based on the studies in developed countries; these theories look at:

- the role of needs in motivation;
- the role of equity, fairness, and justice in motivation;
- the role of rewards in motivation;
- the role of goals and expectations in motivation; and
- the role of delegation and participation in motivation.

Each of these will be explained briefly; then we look at some variations between developing and developed countries that might have an impact on these theories.

Needs and motivation

Need theories are based on the idea that people have certain needs, and their behaviors are designed to help them fulfill these needs. Simply stated, we act in ways that we believe will result in our needs being met. At a basic level, if someone has a need for food (they are hungry), they will seek a means to satisfy this need (for example, they will harvest some available food, cook something, or they might look for a restaurant). Behavior (harvesting food/cooking/looking for a restaurant) thus reflects the need (being hungry). In this example, we would say that the person is motivated by their need for food.

Perhaps the best known of the need theories is Maslow's *hierarchy of needs* (Maslow, 1954). Maslow proposed a hierarchy of needs going from the most basic needs at the bottom of the hierarchy to the highest-level ones at the top. In this model, there are five levels:

1   Most basic: the physiological level deals with survival of the individual and the human race, that is, the need for food, water, shelter, and sex.
2   Next most basic: the security level deals with continued survival, that is, the need for some assurance that food, water, shelter, and sex will be available in the foreseeable future.
3   Mid-level: the social level deals with interactions with others, that is, the need for friendships, relationships, and communication with others.
4   Higher level: the esteem level deals with feeling positive about what one does; that is, the need for praise, recognition, and self-esteem.
5   Highest level: the self-actualization level deals with being the best one can be, that is, the need to do things that are important to us, and to accomplish difficult goals that we set for ourselves.

Maslow proposed that each level of need became important, and thus a motivating force, only when the previous level had been satisfied. The basic, physiological needs were paramount until satisfied. Once someone's most basic needs were filled, they would then focus on security. Once security was achieved, social needs would come to the fore. Once social needs were met, esteem would become important, and finally, when the other needs were met, self-actualization would be the motivating force.

The needs in the hierarchy move from concrete to abstract as one goes up the hierarchy. At the basic level, the survival needs can be clearly defined and delineated for all people. At the highest level, the self-actualization needs are unclear and vary from person to person (for example, one person may aspire to being a high-profile celebrity and making a lot of money, where another sees self-actualization as being achieved through self-sacrifice for the greater good of humanity). The basic physiological needs, as well as the security needs, are likely to be essentially universal – that is, people everywhere share these needs and they will be the dominant motivational force until they are satisfied. So people who do not have enough to eat, whether they are in Australia or Zimbabwe, will be motivated primarily by the need to find food and will behave accordingly. There have been several empirical studies of Maslow's hierarchy in countries around the world, and these have suggested that the idea of a hierarchy of needs is universal, but that the order of the hierarchy can vary. As the need categories become more abstract, they also seem to become more culturally and nationally contingent.

Even with one of the most basic needs, the need for food, there are also cultural variations; in Australia the chosen foods may be quite different from those in Zimbabwe. In some locations, certain foods will be prohibited or preferred, in others, cooking methods prescribed, and so on, usually for religious or cultural reasons. For example, a number of religions – Judaism and Islam, as well as some Christian sects – prohibit eating pork, and the Hindus do not eat beef; in the Far East, insects are commonly eaten, but in North America and Western Europe, the idea of eating insects makes many people shudder. In the Caribbean coal pots are common cooking utensils, while gas barbeques are the norm in the USA.

The order of the needs may also vary. For example, it is possible that in some locations social needs are at the pinnacle because of cultural characteristics. In a country such as China, where hierarchical and social structures are important, maintaining the correct order may be more important than socializing. Alternatively, geography may help determine the importance of various needs. In locations subject to natural disasters, security could be an even more basic need than food and water. The expression of the needs may vary, and the way in which the needs are satisfied may also differ from location to location. As noted above, even at the basic level, food choices vary from country to country and within countries, often for religious reasons. Culture can influence how and when basic needs are satisfied – for example, most cultures have relatively strict rules regarding sex (including when and with whom sex may take place), and these are often tied to religious beliefs. At the higher levels, everyone would agree that culture influences what is meant by esteem or self-actualization; how people choose to meet these needs, as well as their social needs, can vary dramatically.

The expression of needs can also vary because of other characteristics. In communist countries, basic needs are provided by the government, and Warner (2001) talks of the mindsets associated with this dependency. If the government provides only a limited level of basic needs, people may accept this minimal level as normal and not behave in ways to increase satisfaction of this basic need. In the Chinese languages there is no word for *privacy*, so fulfilling social needs might not include this concept. It is also possible that some needs may not be manifested in certain places. Self-actualization, for example, could be inimical to certain religious beliefs because God is the only one able to determine one's fate. The caste system as practiced in India for centuries (note that formally, the caste system is no longer allowed in India) meant that people born into a certain caste accepted this as right, because it reflected earlier lives. Even the untouchables accepted their fate and did the most unpleasant jobs in society because this was their lot in life; they could not seek self-actualization in their jobs, except in the sense of wanting to be born into a higher caste in their next life. Of course, one could argue that their basic needs were not filled, so their higher-order needs for esteem or self-actualization would not come into play.

It seems that people everywhere have needs and that these needs motivate behavior, so in this sense need theories are universal. We should not assume, however, that the importance of these needs is the same everywhere, or that people will choose to satisfy their needs in similar ways. Managers can use the concept of needs to help motivate those with whom they work, wherever they are. To do so effectively, however, means that managers need to figure out which needs are most important and how a particular person or group prefers to satisfy them. Political systems, economics, language, religion, history, geography, and culture all have an impact on needs and their importance and satisfaction.

In developed countries, Maslow's hierarchy is used to illustrate the need to give employees opportunities to meet their higher-level needs on the job in order to motivate them at work. It is assumed that most employed people's lower-level needs are adequately met; they are working and earning, therefore they should be able to find adequate food, water, and shelter, and put a little bit of money aside for emergencies. Their social needs should also be taken care of within the work place as well as outside of work, as there are many opportunities available for meeting others and socializing, whether in person or virtually. Providing opportunities for meeting esteem and self-actualization needs is thus considered to be most important for motivating employees.

In developing countries the situation is very different, and the reverse may hold, at least for a substantial portion of the people. The level of income in developing countries is relatively low, and basic needs may not have been met, and people have little sense of security. Even though people are employed, their wages may be too low to provide adequately for their families, and not enough to put anything aside. In this situation, employees may well be motivated by basic needs, and something like providing lunch on the job could be more motivating than giving someone more responsibility or making a job more intrinsically interesting. Lituchy et al. (2010) reported that respondents in Barbados and Kenya, both developing countries, felt that financial need was the major motivator for non-managers in their countries. Social needs may also be more important at work than is the case in developed countries. Outside of work, people's time may be taken up by going to distant wells to collect water, tending animals and vegetable gardens, looking after family members, and so on. Opportunities to socialize at work may be motivating. Punnett (2009) found that in the Caribbean, workers at a factory in St. Vincent said that they preferred boring, routine, well-known jobs because this allowed them to talk with their fellow workers.

Another theory based on needs, but without the hierarchy, is McClelland's. McClelland (1967) suggested that different needs manifest themselves more or less strongly in different people. McClelland focused on the needs for achievement, affiliation, and power as being most relevant in the organizational context. These needs have been investigated cross-culturally and there is some evidence that they may all be important components of motivation, but there is also reason to question this. Hofstede (1980), for example, noted that the achievement construct is peculiar to the English language. In a study of a larger number of needs (but including achievement, affiliation, and power), Punnett (1999) compared China with North America and found that Chinese respondents scored uniformly lower on all the needs measured. The best explanation of these results was that the more important needs from a Chinese perspective were not being captured in the survey instrument, which had been designed in North America. In China, it may be that needs such as maintaining face, harmony, and *Guanxi* relationships are more important than those felt to be important in North America. Punnett et al. (2007) and Lituchy et al. (2010) found that many Caribbean respondents believed religious beliefs to be an important component of motivation in this context, but this does not appear in most survey instruments. Theories designed in developed countries may exclude needs that are important in developing countries.

As with the upper-level needs of Maslow's hierarchy, the needs studied by McClelland may be exhibited in a variety of ways and can be satisfied by many means. For example, a high need for achievement means that a person has a drive to do tasks that are difficult and to accomplish objectives that are seen as worthwhile. What is relatively difficult in one location may be somewhat easy in another, and what is considered worthwhile can vary substantially. Thus, even if we accept that people everywhere exhibit a need for achievement, the expression of this need is likely to vary from place to place. In many developing countries, infrastructure is limited, so a difficult task may be carrying water from a well that is many miles from one's home, and a woman may feel a sense of achievement for accomplishing this task.

In some locations people value autonomy and will seek to achieve goals on their own. In other locations, structure is valued, and people seek to achieve what their superiors deem important. In general, developing countries are more risk averse than developed countries, higher on hierarchy and more collective. All of these characteristics suggest that autonomy and individual goal achievement will not be particularly motivating in these countries.

Historical and geographic factors play an important role in how needs are exhibited and satisfied. In India, achievement often comes by rising in the bureaucracy, which has been perpetuated from the colonial system. This is quite different from the achievement of the Australian working independently in the outback. The two countries share a British colonial heritage, but India had well-developed systems in place when it was colonized while Australia was largely uninhabited. Many developing countries are former colonies and continue to manifest the top down, centralized, bureaucratic system of the colonial era. Where this is generally well accepted, people may not be motivated by factors such as autonomy on the job.

It seems that the general concept of needs is universal and that people everywhere, in developed and developing countries, have needs that motivate them. The existence of manifest needs is also likely universal – some needs will be more important to some people and will be manifest in their behavior. In order to motivate people effectively, managers have to understand which needs are most relevant in a particular location. The overall concept of needs motivating employees is valid in developing countries, but basic needs may be more relevant than higher-order needs, at least for many people.

Using Hofstede's cultural model, developing countries are generally more collective, and higher on power–distance and uncertainty avoidance than their more developed counterparts. Their needs can be expected to reflect this. People in these countries are likely to be motivated by factors that reflect the group with which they are affiliated, they are likely to respond well to a well-structured hierarchy, and they are likely to seek security and be motivated by a clear understanding of what is expected by their superiors.

Herzberg's two-factor theory and a lot of subsequent work on intrinsic and extrinsic motivational factors, as well as job design, followed from earlier need theories. Herzberg (1959) argued that there are two sets of factors associated with any job and with a person's motivation relative to the job. One set was intrinsic to the job itself – how interesting, challenging, and rewarding the job was – and these were the factors that motivated a person. The second set was extrinsic to the job – physical conditions, money, supervision, coworkers, and so on – and these had to be met for a person to be satisfied, but they did not actually motivate a person. The absence of extrinsic factors could, however, demotivate even though their presence did not motivate. These concepts are appealing because they separate what makes us want to do a job from the conditions in which we do it. This theory is also interesting because, in essence, it separates satisfaction from motivation – that is, because someone is satisfied with their working conditions, it does not necessarily mean that they will be motivated to work hard and perform well. The outcome of Herzberg's theory was literature that focused on designing jobs to be intrinsically motivating. Such jobs incorporated variety and autonomy (making one's own decisions) as well as feedback and understanding of the importance of the tasks one performed (often termed *task significance*).

The distinction between intrinsic and extrinsic job aspects may well be universal, and these aspects may have different roles to play in motivation. The relationship to motivation is not necessarily the same around the world, however. Extrinsic factors essentially relate to the lower-order needs on Maslow's hierarchy and intrinsic factors to the higher-order needs.

In poorer, developing countries, in my experience, extrinsic factors are often valued as motivators more than the intrinsic ones. Workers in these countries often want jobs with little variety and autonomy, and speak of the importance of pay, supervision, working conditions, and other extrinsic factors. In one factory in the Caribbean, workers voted for the company providing uniforms, and against job rotation or job enlargement to include individuals completing their own quality checks. They felt that job rotation would mean they had to learn to do new tasks and that the quality people were good at this aspect and should continue in their specialized role. When asked what they liked about working for this particular firm, they said:

- we can do our tasks with little thought while conversing with our friends and coworkers;
- our supervisor helps do our jobs; and
- the factory is clean.

In this situation in one developing country, job variety, autonomy, and feedback were essentially seen as being inefficient and would likely have been demotivating. Job significance did seem to provide a potential motivating tool; employees were most interested to know, and see physical evidence, that the electronic parts they made were used in computers. Other colleagues with experience in a variety of developing countries have supported the idea that extrinsic aspects of the job may be as much, if not more effective motivators than intrinsic aspects.

The relationship between satisfaction and motivation can also differ from place to place. One can imagine that in some locations a satisfied employee will feel an obligation to work hard and perform well. In many developing countries, managers and employees have a reciprocal relationship, where the person in power is expected to look after the subordinates, and in return subordinates are loyal and work hard. In other places, it is possible that being satisfied would result in a relaxed attitude, which would affect performance negatively – anecdotes suggest that in the tropics, people work less once they are satisfied, and work only until they have made enough money to get by. One can conjecture that if employees were dissatisfied, they might be motivated to work hard, feeling that if they performed well, they could change the situation. Alternatively, hard work could take one's mind off one's dissatisfaction, and so on. There are many potential relationships, and, again, the effective manager needs to assess these relationships to understand how to motivate people at work.

Taylor (2006) writing about the early colonists in North America says that the Iroquois kept the land a wilderness and the colonists thought them improvident and living from hand to mouth, because they were uninterested in accumulating private property. The Iroquois in contrast "considered it foolish and demeaning to labor beyond what they needed to subsist" (p. 17). The Iroquois are described as valuing the collective society and generosity – instead of storing wealth, they accumulated prestige by giving gifts to their family and the less well-off. Their values of generosity, hospitality and reciprocity spread resources across the year, and across the people, achieving a sense of equality. The Iroquois disdained the competitive and acquisitive values of the colonists – Taylor quotes a missionary as saying "they [the Iroquois] wonder that the white people are striving so much to get rich, and to heap up treasures in this world that they cannot carry with them to the next" (p. 17).

The role of equity in motivation

Equity refers to the fairness that people perceive in a situation. Basically, equity theory proposes that individuals consider what they put into a given situation relative to what they get out of the situation and then compare this with the inputs and outcomes of some other(s). If the relationships are judged to be fair or equitable, then the person will seek to maintain the current situation. If they are deemed to be unfair or inequitable, the person will seek to change the situation in the future. An example will serve to illustrate these relationships:

> If a student works hard in a particular course, goes to classes, and hands in all the assignments (these are her inputs in this situation) and ends up with a grade of "B" (her outcome), she will then compare this input–output ratio to that of others in the class. If the comparison seems fair, she will continue to work hard. If, in contrast, others seem to have done little work but ended up with higher marks, the comparison will seem unfair. In this case the student will try to change some of the inputs or outcomes. It is difficult to change other people's inputs or outcomes, so it is most likely the student will try to change her own inputs or outcomes. The student may ask the professor for a better grade (outcome), but if

that does not work, the student may lower her inputs in the future. The impact of a perception of inequity may be to demotivate the student.

In developed countries, equity theory stresses the importance of evaluating and rewarding
people fairly so that hard work is rewarded equitably. Equitable treatment is thus seen as motivating employees and encouraging hard work. At first inspection, it is hard to see how equity would
apply in many developing countries. An earlier example talked of a group in Africa that believes
need should be rewarded over performance. This would certainly seem inequitable in the North
American context. In the previous student example, suppose the professor only gave A's to those
from a certain social class – would this be fair? Certainly not in North America, but conceivably in
some developing countries, where society respects and values a class system, this could be the
expected norm. In India, for example, if a person from the lowest caste was in a class with someone from the highest caste, both might expect that the higher-caste student should be awarded
better marks than the lower-caste student. In Myanmar (Burma) where the government is a military dictatorship, members of that governing elite and their children expect special treatment, and
this likely extends to marks at school. The case would be the same in the workplace; where there
are powerful elites who are accepted as such, members of the elite will get better treatment than
their less fortunate counterparts. This would seem unfair in most developed countries, but may be
considered fair and acceptable in certain developing ones. In essence, status is considered to be a
valuable input, therefore the person of status deserves a better outcome.

If one considers what are believed to be valid inputs and what outcomes are valued, it may be
possible to use the concept of equity to motivate employees in developed countries. For example,
in a location where the number of dependants is believed to entitle someone to greater rewards,
the number of dependants could be considered a valid input; where status because of birth is
accepted as giving rights to certain rewards, this may be a normal input. Other factors that might
be considered valid inputs are age, gender, property, physical characteristics, and so on. In some
places, men and women doing the same work are paid differentially, because women are deemed
to be less valuable than men or because it is believed they need less compensation. Discrimination
on the basis of gender, age, race, religion, language, physical ability, sexual preference, and other
similar factors is unlawful in most developed countries, but accepted in many developing ones.
Where using these differentials is accepted in a developing country, it is not seen as discrimination,
therefore it probably does not act as a motivator/demotivator, as it would in a developed country.

Equity theory in developed countries is also essentially an individualistic concept and equity
is viewed as the individual's inputs and outcomes. In more collective societies the inputs and
outcomes are likely to be evaluated on a group basis. In societies that are high on power–distance,
the decision of the more powerful supervisor is not to be questioned, so attempting to change
decisions that are seen as unjust is unlikely. Further, the superior must be right, and their decisions are made on the basis of information the subordinate does not have, so asking whether it is
fair may not be considered. In developing countries, employees may simply follow the rules and
the instructions of the supervisor, and this avoids uncertainty and is supported by a preference
for clearly defined hierarchies. These may be the factors that are most important and most
motivating in many developing countries.

The role of rewards in motivation

Equity theory incorporates the idea of rewards as a means for motivating employees, assuming
the rewards are distributed fairly. More basically, reinforcement theory ties rewards to behavior
as a means of encouraging desired behavior and discouraging and eliminating undesired behavior.

The idea of reinforcing desired behavior through rewards is that people will repeat behaviors that are rewarded, and behavior that is not rewarded will eventually not be repeated. People often use reinforcement and rewards in daily life; for example, mothers promise children ice cream when they finish their homework (and withhold the ice cream if the homework is not completed); pet owners give their dogs treats when they obey commands (and withhold them when they do not). Reinforcement theory does not incorporate ideas of equity; in fact, to encourage a particular person to change behavior, one might reward them in what would seem to be an inequitable manner. Reinforcement theory in developed countries avoids punishment, as punishment is believed to have undesired side effects. Many developed countries now have laws which prohibit the spanking of children when they misbehave as this is believed to damage them mentally and emotionally.

Encouraging desired behavior through the use of rewards is probably as effective in developing countries as it is in developed ones. Reinforcement in developing countries may appear quite different, however, as rewards may vary, and when and how they are given may not be the same.

Consider *what* we use as rewards:

■   Money is generally considered a valued reward, and increased compensation is used to motivate employees who perform well. In developed countries, however, it is believed that money alone is not enough to motivate employees (although the lack of adequate monetary compensation may be a demotivator). In poorer, developing countries money is likely to be of utmost importance because employees are motivated by basic needs. At the same time, if people work only until they have enough money to pay for necessities, additional compensation will not further motivate them; rather they may stop working.

■   In most developed countries it is considered appropriate to single out individuals who have done a good job (note that there are exceptions among developed countries, such as Japan, where this is not the case). In more collective developing countries, singling out an individual may be used to indicate that he/she has not been performing up to standard.

■   Typically, in developed countries coaching – where the positive aspects of work are recognized and suggestions for improvement given – is considered positive reinforcement. In many developing countries, such as India, straightforward criticism is often preferred, and people expect to be told that they have made mistakes and to be punished for these mistakes.

In developing countries punishment may be an important part of motivation while in developed countries it is generally believed that punishment should be avoided. This second view focuses on rewards and inherently incorporates a belief that people are changeable, and stresses the potential negative impact of punishment. In many developing countries, there is often a belief that if someone behaves in undesirable ways, it is because they are "bad," and that punishment is the only possible way to stop the undesirable behavior. In some Islamic societies the punishment for stealing is amputation of the guilty hand; consequently, theft in these countries is extremely rare, and the idea of rehabilitation is not considered. Reinforcement through punishment works in this case, apparently because the fear of the major punishment deters the undesired behavior.

The role of goals and expectations in motivation

There is substantial evidence that goals help people focus their energies and serve to improve performance. The literature from developed countries has clearly linked specific and challenging goals, once they are accepted, to higher outputs (Locke and Latham, 1990). Goal acceptance is often linked to participation in goal setting, and, in developed countries, participatively set goals are believed to be more effective than assigned goals. Goals on their own appear to stimulate productivity, but they are especially effective when they are linked with desired rewards. Some studies of goal setting in developing countries also indicate that goals are effective in these countries. For example, Punnett (1986) and Punnett et al. (2007) found that in two Caribbean countries, specific and difficult goals increased performance significantly compared to asking employees to "do their best" and Niles (1998) similarly found that goals improved performance in Sri Lanka.

There are, however, factors in developing countries that might mitigate against the usefulness of goals. Using Hofstede's (1980) dimensions, for example; a collective society would likely see group goals as appropriate but would not react positively to the individual goals that are typical in developed countries, a society where people avoid uncertainty might find difficult goals stressful because of the fear that the goals could not be achieved, a society high on power–distance would likely simply expect superiors to make decisions on a day-to-day basis on what needs to be done, and may react more positively to goals set by their boss rather than setting their own goals.

Other factors that are common in developing countries could also affect how effective goals are in improving performance. For example:

- People in postcolonial societies may associate goals with the previous colonial masters and may resent specific and difficult goals, which can be seen as exploitation.
- People in tropical locations often have a "mañana," "soon come," or "jus' now" approach to life, which implies that immediate desires/needs are more important than goals and plans. This approach could make goal accomplishment difficult.
- People who have a low need for achievement may see little value in reaching a challenging goal, and may even be frightened by such a goal.
- Where people feel that they have little control over their environment, the idea of setting a specific target may seem foolish at best and possibly thought of as going against God's will.
- Where people have a short-term orientation, immediate goals will be best, with rewards tied closely to performance; where orientations are longer-term, goals projected well into the future may be used.

Goals may play an important motivational role in developing countries; however, managers will want to experiment with different types of goals to determine what works well in their location. In particular, there is some evidence that the effectiveness of participation in goal setting varies from culture to culture (Audia and Tams, 2002). In many developing countries, decisions are typically made by superiors, who are believed to have the expertise, knowledge, and power to make the best decisions. In this environment, participation in setting goals may actually be intimidating for most employees, and consequently demotivating.

Expectancy theory, as it is usually called, is based on people's expectations about the outcome of their actions. Expectancy theory, simply, proposes that a person looks at a situation and asks:

1   If I try/work harder (put in a lot of effort) will my performance improve? (expectancy 1)
2   If my performance improves, will my rewards increase? (expectancy 2)
3   How much do I value the rewards? (valence)

The answers to these questions ranging from zero to one. If the answer is clearly no, one's score would be a zero, if clearly yes, that would be one, and if in-between, the score would be some fraction to indicate how close to no or yes; for example, a 0.1 is close to no and a 0.9 close to yes. In expectancy theory, motivation is believed to be a multiplicative relationship; that is, motivation = expectancy 1 × expectancy 2 × value (valence). The higher (closer to 1) the score, the higher a person's motivation will be, and, conversely, the lower (closer to 0), the less motivated the person will be. If the answer to any of the three questions is a no, then the person will not put in a great deal of effort. So, if I do not think increased effort on my part will result in increased performance, there is no point in my increasing effort. Similarly, if increased performance will not lead to greater rewards, there is no point to increasing efforts. Finally, if I do not value the rewards, there is no point to increasing efforts. Rewards, of course, are not simply extrinsic (pay, time off, and so on), but may be intrinsic as well (the pleasure of doing a good job, a sense of achievement).

In developed countries, using expectancy theory to motivate employees entails ensuring that people feel they can perform well if they put in the effort, that they have appropriate goals (this links to goal setting), ensuring that performance is rewarded fairly (this links to equity), and ensuring that rewards are valued (this links to needs and reinforcement). Expectancy theory is, thus, considered somewhat holistic, as it incorporates aspects of the other theories.

Expectancy is built around the individual; it integrates individual performance and rewards. Expectancy incorporates rational, linear thinking and control of one's environment; that is, the individual logically evaluates the likelihood of various outcomes and chooses, on this basis, whether to exert effort or not. It is based on egalitarian beliefs and the sense that individuals have options; thus, the individual is not bound to do what a superior wants or expects, and can seek alternatives rather than accept a situation that is seen as unfair or unpleasant. Individualism, control of one's environment, and rational, linear thinking are all part of the developed country context. In developing countries, the context is often essentially the reverse: the group is more important than any individual, the world is controlled by those in positions of power and by the spirit realm, and people's thinking is circular rather than linear; that is, thought patterns do not necessarily go from one issue to the next in a straight line, but may incorporate apparently unrelated issues. Under these conditions, the logic of the expectancy model no longer holds up.

It may be appropriate, nevertheless, to use aspects of the expectancy model even in developing countries, because it seems appropriate, under any conditions, to ensure that an employee's increased effort will result in increased performance, that performance is appropriately rewarded, and that rewards are in fact desired.

The role of delegation and participation in motivation

The developed country management literature is built around the belief that delegation and participation are important positive aspects of effective management. Managers delegate responsibilities to their subordinates and provide subordinates with the authority necessary to carry out the delegated responsibilities. This is based on the idea that employees want to have responsibility and that they appreciate the implicit trust in their abilities and attitudes that accompanies delegation. Further, delegation is seen as an effective means to develop employees' abilities and decision-making capabilities. In addition, participation in decision-making is seen as essential to acceptance of decisions and, consequently, willingness to carry out decisions.

As noted earlier, in developed countries, participative goal setting is believed to be more effective than assigning goals and individuals are expected to accept responsibility for achieving their own goals. The reinforcement literature similarly incorporates employee involvement in designing appraisal and reward systems. Expectancy and equity implicitly assume delegation. Delegation and participation essentially go hand in hand because effective delegation relies on employees accepting the responsibility that is delegated, and acceptance of responsibility is enhanced by participation in decisions, including decisions regarding delegation. Together, delegation and participation provide a work environment conducive to hard work and good performance in developed countries. This environment thus contributes to individual motivation.

The universal effectiveness of delegation and participation is not at all clear. Most developing countries do not have a tradition of either delegation or participation. In these countries, it is assumed that the manager's job is to make decisions, and the subordinate's job is to receive instructions and carry out those instructions. Further, managers are expected to monitor subordinates closely to ensure that instructions are being carried out properly and to correct subordinates immediately if they deviate. People from developing countries that do not have a tradition of delegation and participation believe that managers have the ability to make decisions and that is why they are managers. Equally, they believe subordinates do not have these abilities. Subordinates, therefore, are more comfortable with their managers making decisions and giving instructions. They are uncomfortable if asked to participate in making decisions and take on responsibility beyond the simple performance of assigned tasks. A tradition of non-delegation and nonparticipation makes it difficult for managers or their subordinates to accept and implement delegation and participation.

In addition to cultural forces that militate against delegation and participation, a variety of other factors need to be considered. For example, historically, colonies have been governed from the homeland, and delegation and participation have been discouraged. In colonies and recently independent countries, people may be reluctant to delegate or accept delegation, and they may be uncomfortable with participative management practices. Similarly, in communist countries, decisions tend to be made by the Communist Party leaders, with others accepting these decisions with few questions. Participation from lower levels is not sought for major decisions, and this pattern has become accepted. In organizations the same is likely to be the case.

It is clear that in developing countries delegation and participation are not currently universally accepted as effective management practices. Managers wishing to experiment with delegation and participation in locations where these are not the norm need to implement these approaches cautiously and examine the results carefully.

IS MOTIVATION UNIVERSAL OR CULTURE BOUND?

The previous discussion suggests that there are aspects to theories of motivation produced in developed countries that can be applied in developing countries, but other aspects are definitely affected by characteristics associated with development. Many of the theories apply at a "global" level; that is, the big picture is probably universal. People everywhere have needs, people probably seek some kind of equity, people react to rewards, they work towards goals and have expectations about performance. The details of all the theories, the how and the when of implementing them, are likely to be culturally bound and require specific changes or adjustments to be effective in developing countries. Good managers in developing countries will try a variety of approaches to motivate their employees and will watch the results closely to find those that work best.

Smith et al.'s (2002) work in conjunction with local researchers in a variety of countries, provides some information that can be helpful in understanding the different sources that people use to guide decision making and behavior. They found that:

■ Nations that used participatively oriented guidance sources were those characterized by high individualism as well as autonomy, egalitarianism, low power–distance, harmony, and femininity. These values are most typical in developed countries. In contrast, nations whose cultures relied on superiors and rules were those that were collective as well as high on, hierarchy, power–distance, mastery, and masculinity. This profile is more typical of developing countries, and most of the nations of Africa fit this profile. High power–distance and mastery were also related to reliance on those in power for making decisions.

■ Reliance on "beliefs that are widespread in my nation as to what is right" was one of the least frequently reported of the eight sources of guidance, and variance across nations in scores on widespread beliefs as a source of guidance was greater than it was for the other indices. Widespread beliefs were important in nations such as China, Bulgaria, and Romania but were discounted in others, particularly Hungary and Portugal. Conservatism proved the stronger predictor of reliance on widespread beliefs. Smith et al. (2002) showed that items related to this dimension reflected endorsement of paternalism. It was noted earlier that a form of paternal leadership seems to be accepted in many developing countries.

■ Reliance on unwritten rules was related to Smith et al.'s "loyal involvement." The authors indicated that the items that were most closely linked to loyal involvement referred to loyalty to one's work team and to one's organization, rather than making any specific reference to one's superiors. These values appear to tap a generalized endorsement of commitment to the organization, as contrasted with an individualistic calculation of one's own benefits. Unwritten rules will be important in organizations where informal agreements have emerged from long-established interactions between organization members. They express a local wisdom distilled from continuing dialogue among those who have worked together over time. In this context, reference to superiors would be unnecessary because there would be a shared understanding of what is desirable.

■ Reliance on specialists also varied across nations, in terms of the types of specialists likely to be used and in terms of the financial resources available for their services. The results suggested that outsiders are mostly likely to be hired where utilitarian values prevail.

SUMMARY

Motivation is complex and difficult to understand. In this chapter a variety of developed country motivational approaches have been explored and considered in terms of developing country conditions. It seems that some aspects of motivation may be universal while others are clearly affected by national characteristics. Managers can use the broad concepts of motivation – needs, equity, goals, reinforcement, expectancy, and so on – as a base for understanding motivation in developing countries. They will find that the details of how these broad concepts apply have to be designed for each location.

Motivation is a critical aspect of management no matter where one is. Managers everywhere need to find ways to ensure that employees work hard and perform at peak levels. Especially in today's globally competitive environment, maximum performance can give a firm its competitive edge. Taking the time and making the effort to understand motivation is, thus, central to effective management in developing countries.

LESSONS LEARNED

Having completed this chapter, you should understand that good managers in developing countries will try a variety of approaches to motivate their employees and will watch the results closely to find those that work best. You will also recognize that a variety of developed country motivational approaches have been explored and considered in terms of developing country conditions, but that there is no clear evidence regarding their effectiveness. You will appreciate that managers can use the broad concepts of motivation – needs, equity, goals, and so on, as a base for understanding motivation in developing countries, but that the details of these will depend on the country context. You will also be aware of different incentive systems, and be able to explain the value of aspects of incentives, such as openness, transparency, fairness, consistency and links to performance. You should understand that enhanced motivation leads to improved performance, and that while motivation is an internal state, it is possible to influence it with external changes in the workplace. You will be aware that there has been little research and analysis concerning the evolving state of motivation in developing countries, both in terms of what exists and what is needed, and you should be able to discuss how environmental factors in developing countries might influence motivation.

DISCUSSION QUESTIONS

1   Discuss how national culture influences motivation.
2   Discuss how national culture can influence goal orientation.
3   Explore and review the relationship of national culture to equity and expectancy in developing countries.
4   "Western theories and techniques of motivation do not apply to developing countries." Critically assess this statement. Do you agree with it? If so, explain why. If not, explain why not.

EXERCISE

In small groups, select a particular job with which you are familiar (e.g. secretary, cleaner, manual worker, supervisor). Identify the intrinsic aspects and the extrinsic aspects of the job. What roles do you feel the intrinsic and extrinsic job aspects have to play in motivation? Which do you feel are most important in developing countries? Select one intrinsic and one extrinsic aspect of the job to share with the class, in terms of its contribution to motivation.

Chapter 11

Leadership in developing countries

OBJECTIVES

This chapter examines leadership and explores various theories of leadership in developing countries.

The objectives are as follows:

■ To use characteristics of developing countries to consider what might be most effective in terms of leadership in those countries.
■ To make clear what leadership means in an organization.
■ To differentiate between leadership and management although the terms are often used interchangeably.
■ To examine leadership theories that are common in the Western, developed country literature.
■ To examine how these theories might be different given the identified characteristics of developing countries.
■ To recognize that organizations succeed or fail because of leadership and they cannot function well without effective leaders.

INTRODUCTION

This chapter looks at the critical issue of leadership and explores what we know about leadership in developing countries. It also uses the characteristics of developing countries to consider what might be most effective in terms of leadership in these countries. The chapter begins with a general definition of leadership and what leadership means in organizations; it also differentiates between leadership and management, although the two terms are often used interchangeably. It then examines the leadership theories that are common in the Western, developed country literature and considers how these might be different, given the identified characteristics of developing countries. Wherever possible, literature from developing countries is used to help elucidate the reality of leadership in various developing countries.

THE MEANING OF LEADERSHIP

Leadership is a key component of all organizations. Organizational functioning depends on people within the organization working toward goals that benefit the organization as a whole. When the concept of management and the management processes and activities were introduced in Chapter 4, one of the five major components was leadership – which ensures that staff behaves in desirable ways that lead to achieving plans. Leadership, broadly defined, is the ability to get others to behave as the leader wishes them to behave. There are many processes and structures that enhance organizational functioning, but in the final analysis organizations succeed or fail because of leadership, and they cannot function well without effective leaders. This does not mean that all good leaders will be visible in their capacity as leaders, nor that all leaders are good, nor that all those in leadership positions are in fact leaders. Leadership means different things in different situations, and sometimes the most effective leader is one who appears not to lead in any active sense. Appropriate and effective leadership is influenced by a variety of factors, including culture, politics, religion, history, geography and so on; thus successful leaders adopt a style of leadership that fits the particular situation and environment in which they are leading.

Leadership is often associated with particular positions; for example, the head of an academic department in a university is expected to provide leadership for the department; the chief executive of a firm is the leader for the firm. Leadership is, however, a function of the person who acts as leader to a group of followers, as well as a function of the position or role that a person occupies. For example, a group of people may meet to decide where to go on vacation, and no one is assigned or appointed as leader of the group. Nevertheless, a leader or leaders may emerge and take on the role of ensuring that decisions are made in a timely manner and within the appropriate parameters. Similarly, in organizations leaders may emerge even though they do not hold leadership positions. These can be leaders who encourage others to perform at a certain level, or they can be leaders who are more concerned with social issues and ensure that the group functions harmoniously. Leadership can also be associated with negative organizational outcomes, for example, a slowdown in production or a conflict between certain groups.

Many authors differentiate between leadership and management. Clearly the two concepts are different, and the roles of manager and leader can be separated. Managers are responsible for the running of a unit (department, function, organization, and so on), so they do the necessary planning for their unit, ensure that an organization structure is in place, that the resources are available to achieve plans, and monitor performance and take corrective action to reach desired goals (the traditional management model identifies planning, organizing, staffing, directing, and controlling as the activities of management). Leadership is more than management, however, as it incorporates developing a shared vision throughout a group, and stimulating others to behave in desired ways. While the differences between management and leadership are valid and important, many writers also use the terms largely interchangeably. In this chapter, although the focus is on leadership rather than management, we will often refer to leadership in the context of management and as a function that managers seek to perform along with their other activities.

A fundamental issue in any discussion of leadership is the relative importance of leaders. Leadership in the North American context has a positive connotation; that is, it is considered a desirable characteristic. Dorfman (1996) explained that this view of leadership is not universal. Europeans are less positive about leadership, and in some countries, such as Holland, people believe that leadership should be downplayed. In Japan, CEOs of large, successful corporations credit subordinates with organizational accomplishments and deemphasize their own roles.

The author found that in China leaders played a pivotal role in all situations. In certain developing countries, there seems to be a certain amount of reverence for the powerful or "big man" as leader. In contrast, in some African languages there is no word that is equivalent to "leader" in English, and research has identified the concept of "servant leader" as important (Lituchy et al., the authors ongoing research on leadership in Africa and the African Diaspara) – essentially a leader whose role is to serve for the good of the community.

In the next section of this chapter we will explore various theories of leadership that are commonly accepted in Western, developed countries, and ask if and how these can be transferred to developing countries. In addition we will examine some beliefs about effective leadership that have been investigated in developing countries.

THEORIES OF LEADERSHIP

Leadership has been studied throughout history (often from the viewpoint of state or military leadership). Discussions of the practice and philosophy of leadership can be found in a range of early writing from Homer's *Iliad* to the Old Testament and the essays on Confucius in China. Much of these early discussions, including those relating to the state or the military, has been incorporated into the literature on leadership in an organizational setting. Unfortunately much of the existing literature on leadership is based on Western, developed country theories and practices of leadership. Nevertheless, these theories serve as the basis for the discussion in this section.

Leadership traits

Organizational researchers, in the early parts of the twentieth century, looked at leadership from a *trait* perspective; that is, they sought to identify personal traits or characteristics that could generally be associated with effective leaders. Both physical traits (e.g., height or attractiveness) and psychological traits (e.g., intelligence or emotional stability) were investigated by researchers, but no consistent relationship between traits and effective leadership were identified. Today, people seldom consider traits of this kind in Western leadership studies, but we have little evidence from developing societies regarding the role of physical or psychological traits in leadership effectiveness.

It is possible that certain traits may be relevant in some societies. For example, people refer to the "bearing" (height, stance, and so on) of Nelson Mandela as marking him as a leader even after many years of imprisonment. In a study in African countries (Lituchy et al., 2009), respondents identified tribal affiliations as an important aspect of leadership, and they also identified the need for a leader to be male. It is also likely that certain traits may be considered inappropriate in some locations. For example, if leaders have traditionally come from a tribe, or other group, that is relatively short, then tall people might be frowned on in leadership roles. Lituchy et al. (2009) also found that some respondents believed being a married man was important; so, conversely, we would expect that single men would not be seen as having the appropriate traits to be considered a leader.

While Western research linking traits to effective leadership has not been very helpful in identifying and predicting successful leaders, we must recognize that there are biases in the world that make certain traits salient in spite of this. In many parts of the world, formal leadership revolves around males; in others, status or caste is a prerequisite for leadership; in still others, race or ethnicity determines leadership eligibility. Some readers may wish this were not the case, but it is the reality in many parts of the world and therefore cannot be ignored.

Leadership style

Leadership research in the mid-twentieth century focused on leadership *style*. The prevalent dichotomy was between a task-oriented style and a people-oriented style. In Herzberg's (1968) well-known characterization, the task-oriented style was termed *theory x* while the people-oriented style was termed *theory y*. Herzberg argued that most managers were *theory x* managers who believed that people did not want to work and worked only for economic rewards, thus subordinates could not be trusted or given responsibility; managers focused on the task to be performed and provided discipline if performance was not forthcoming. In contrast, Herzberg argued that people want to work and would respond favorably to responsibility, if trusted. He argued that *theory y* managers, who recognized this and paid attention to people issues, would have satisfied employees who would perform at higher levels. Current research has moved beyond this simple *theory x–theory y* paradigm, but the concept is still relevant for today's managers. Many people still describe managers as falling into these two broad categories. More importantly, from an international perspective, many countries seem to favor the *theory x* approach while others favor the *theory y* approach. Leadership and management are clearly more complex in reality, but this division may provide a simple, initial way to categorize leadership and management in different locations.

A *theory x* management style – that is, a style that focuses on the task and includes close supervision, provides task-related payments, and enforces discipline for infractions – will likely be effective so long as employees, as well as managers, favor this approach. (This is often referred to as a "top-down" approach, recognizing that the locus of most decisions is at the top of the organizational unit.) A *theory y* management style – that is, a style that focuses on people and their satisfaction, delegates responsibility and authority, and encourages performance through rewards – will be most effective when employees are willing to accept responsibility and authority, and managers are comfortable with this approach. *Theory y* is often described as "bottom-up" in recognition of the strong influence of lower levels in the organization on decision-making

A *theory x* approach may be more common in developing countries for a number of reasons, including relative poverty, lower levels of education, and remnants of colonialism and plantation economies. For people who are relatively poor, financial and basic rewards are likely to be most important, and they may not be seeking responsibility and authority; rather they may simply want to concentrate on the work they are doing. A *theory x* management style provides the structure that allows them to concentrate on work without worrying about making decisions. Add to this, lower levels of education, and it is likely that managers are much better educated and trained than their subordinates; thus, they are likely to be in a better position to make decision, and their subordinates are likely to expect and accept this. Many developing countries are former colonies. It was typical of the colonial days that decisions were made by the colonial "masters" and that the people in the colonies were expected to carry out the decisions without question. Colonial rule was, by definition, largely centralized and autocratic. This style of management and leadership has continued past independence and is still the norm in many former colonies. Similarly, in plantation economies, decisions were made by the owners regarding what to plant, when and where, and there was little reason to get input from workers, or involve them in decision making.

Whether *theory x* is an effective management and leadership style in developing countries is not clear, but it does seem to be the norm. Punnett and Greenidge (2009) have argued that in the Caribbean, employees express low levels of power–distance and that this means that a *theory x* style is inappropriate. Carter (1997) identified this mismatch in terms of how workers want to be treated (*theory y*) and how they experience the workplace (*theory x*) as a major reason why Jamaicans "won't work".

143

A substantial amount of research on leadership has been done in India. According to Hofstede's (1980) model, Indian society is high on power–distance and relatively low on individualism. The Indian culture has been described as vertical collectivist, characterized by familialism, patronage, personalized relationships, and obedience to authority (Sinha 1984). Sinha (1994) suggested two key dimensions of leadership in the Indian context – nurturance and task (similar to the people/task dimensions). He described the relatively hierarchical Indian leader as emphasizing task aspects, and some studies have suggested that Indian subordinates prefer this autocratic type of leadership. Sinha's research suggested that the most effective Indian leaders were those who emphasized both nurturance and task. He found that encouraging subordinate participation was valuable and contributed to performance, but that the leader had to work closely with subordinates to nurture their willingness to take responsibility. In essence, a good leader benevolently guides the subordinate, and the subordinate reciprocates with obedience and loyalty.

Contingency theories of leadership

Contingency leadership theories argue that the best leadership style depends on the situation. These theories suggest that there is no one best approach, but that aspects of the environment, as well as the nature of the leader and followers, need to be taken into account to determine the most effective leadership approach. North American contingency theories initially focused on the task–people dimensions. Early contingency researchers (e.g., Fiedler 1967) pointed out that there are situations where task orientation is required; for example, where urgent action is needed (say in a fire), where subordinates do not have much experience, or where superior–subordinate interactions are not very friendly. In other situations, a people or relationship orientation is more appropriate; for example, where time is available for developmental activities, where subordinates are familiar with the task, and where superior–subordinate interactions are cordial. These theories essentially treated leadership style as either task oriented or people oriented.

A further development in the field was the realization that leaders could be both task oriented and people oriented at the same time. Hershey and Blanchard (1969) and Blake and Mouton (1964) described a model where each of the four styles can be effective depending on the situation, and good leaders vary their choice of style to suit the situation. Aspects of the situation that affect choice of style include characteristics of the leader, characteristics of the followers, the nature of the task, and the culture of the group.

According to Dorfman (1996), studies done in different parts of the world suggest that considerate, supportive leaders are generally preferred throughout, but reactions to task orientation are more complex. Interestingly, Dorfman (2004) reports that managers from all countries espoused democratic and participatory styles, but they also had a low opinion of their subordinates' ability to take initiative. It seems that a variety of environmental factors, including culture, politics, geography, history, and so on, shape what any group sees as effective leadership.

Aycan (2004) has described leadership in developing countries as a reciprocal relationship between the leader and her/his subordinates based on relatively high power–distance, as well as high uncertainty avoidance and collectivism. Leaders are expected to take responsibility for the welfare of their subordinates, and in turn subordinates are loyal to their leaders and perform the tasks they are assigned. Leadership in this context is essentially autocratic – subordinates believe that leaders know what needs to be done, and they look up to the leaders simply because they are leaders. But it is benignly autocratic – leaders are concerned for the welfare of their subordinates and make decisions that take this into account.

Participation and democracy

Participation is also an important component of superior–subordinate relationships. Managers who are task oriented are sometimes described as autocratic, those who are people oriented as democratic (the term, democratic, is not to be confused with the political use of the term whereby decisions are made by majority). Democratic leaders, however, are not just people oriented, rather they are leaders who involve their subordinates in making decisions. In the West, in developed countries, it has been argued that people are more committed to decisions when they have participated in making those decisions, thus participation in decision making is often promoted as a positive aspect of leadership. Of course, even in the West participation has its limitations. For example, subordinates can only participate effectively if they have the ability and the desire to do so, and subordinates may only be interested in participating when they believe a decision will directly affect their work/life. Clearly, in developing countries, with low levels of education, participation may not be practical in many decision-making situations. If the leader is believed to know what is best and to be benignly looking out for subordinates' interests, then subordinates likely want the leader to make decisions.

One can picture a range of decision-making styles from autocratic (decisions made by the leader) to democratic (made by the leader and subordinates together) with various levels of subordinate input and influence in between. The appropriate choice would then depend on the situation – the time available, the leader's expertise and experience, the subordinates' expertise and experience, the importance of the decision, the need for subordinates' commitment, and so on. Vroom and Yetton (1973) developed a decision tree that allowed managers to select among different decision-making styles based on aspects of a situation. The styles ranged from the leader making the decision to the decision made by leader and subordinates together, with equal input from all. The variables included in the decision tree are the requirement for quality, the importance of subordinate commitment to the decision, the likelihood of subordinate commitment, the manager's information base, the structure of the problem, the degree to which goals are shared, and the likelihood of conflict among subordinates. For example, a very participative style is suggested if quality requirements are low, commitment requirements high, and participation is likely to increase commitment. In a similar situation where participation is not likely to increase commitment, a more autocratic style is suggested.

Just as various levels of participation are appropriate according to the characteristics of the situation, one can imagine that in different societies the levels of participation that are expected and accepted would vary. If participation in decision making is the norm, then a very autocratic leader is likely to be resented. In contrast, where participation is not the norm, an autocratic leader will be accepted and a democratic one would be resented. For example, in a video dealing with cross-cultural issues in business, there is a scene in which a manager from the UK, working in India, attempts unsuccessfully to get his Indian subordinate to take responsibility for making a decision. The UK manager is frustrated by his subordinate's unwillingness to do so, and the Indian subordinate comments that it is the manager's job to make decisions (that's why he is a manager and that's what he gets paid for) and does not understand why the manager wants him, a subordinate, to do the manager's job.

In Arab countries, the traditional leader was based on a great hero who leads warriors into battle. Leaders are expected to act as fathers and to look after their subordinates, providing and caring for them (Ali 1990). Dorfman (2004) described Arab management as complex, viewed from an American perspective, with a duality of managerial thinking and practice that values modernity while maintaining traditional values. He described the following:

- Establishing a large number of rules and regulations with no attempt to implement them.
- Designing selection and promotion systems based on merit, while hiring and rewarding according to social ties and personal relations.
- Paying employees in the public sector but not requiring them to report for work.

Khadra (1990) described Arab leadership in terms of the prophetic–caliphal model. One type of leader is the prophetic type who is seen to have performed extraordinary actions. Followers revere and love such a leader, and this results in strong attachment to the leader, unity of purpose, and submission to his authority. The second kind of leader is an ordinary or caliphal man. Followers do not have the same attachment to this type of leader, and this can result in conflicts. To avoid that outcome, the leader is expected to use coercion and fear to keep his subordinates in line.

Both autocratic and democratic leaders play an active leadership role and are intimately involved in the decision-making process. A third possibility has also been suggested – that of a laissez-faire leader, one who does not appear to be actively involved. On the surface, one might feel that such an approach is tantamount to abdication of the leadership role. There are, however, situations where this may be the most appropriate approach. Consider a group of highly skilled and motivated scientists working to find a cure for a major disease. This group likely wants simply to be left alone to get on with their work. A good leader for such a group is one who ensures that needed resources are in place and stands ready to provide guidance or act as inter-mediary if this becomes necessary. Our general discussion of the characteristics of developing countries – poor, less educated, high power–distance and uncertainty avoidance – all suggest that a laissez-faire style would be ineffective in most developing countries, except under rare circum-stances such as the scientists.

Charismatic and transformational leadership

Some leaders seem to have an innate ability to attract followers, which we call charisma. Some leaders also seem to have the ability to go beyond sustaining the normal functioning of a company to transforming it and enabling it to operate at new levels. Both charismatic and transformational leadership received substantial attention in the late-twentieth-century literature. There seems to be a general consensus around the world that some people possess charisma that attracts others to them and encourages their followers to behave as the leader wants. Similarly, there seem to be leaders in all locations who can go beyond operational activities, or even strategic ones, and actually engage their followers to transform organizations.

Charismatic and transformational leadership seems to be a universal concept, and such leaders are found around the world, but what makes someone charismatic or transformational is not clear. More importantly, from an international manager's perspective, characteristics of charismatic and transformational leadership are likely to differ from place to place. For example, Mahatma Gandhi and Adolf Hitler are both considered charismatic leaders, yet they represent totally opposing world-views and approaches to society. They seemed driven by their vision of the future, which attracted followers who could share the visions, albeit vastly different.

Charismatic or transformational leadership is not necessarily good, in a moral sense. State leaders such as Genghis Khan, Adolf Hitler, and, more recently, Saddam Hussein might be described as charismatic or transformational, but they would be considered immoral by many students of moral good. Adler (1991) noted that in Germany, because of Hitler, the idea of charisma in leaders has a negative, rather than positive, connotation. Further, in the early twenty-first century, organizational collapses of corporations such as WorldCom and Enron reminded the world that charismatic and transformational leaders are not always good leaders in terms of results for the organization involved.

The major worldwide leadership project (the Globe Project) undertaken by House et al. (2004) provides some evidence that the charismatic and transformational concepts are valid ones around the world (Dorfman 2004). The research suggests that leadership is more than an exchange of rewards for effort; effective leaders share a sense of purpose with their subordinates, which embodies charisma and transformation, and this results in superior performance. Although the concepts may be valid worldwide, they may still be expressed quite differently. Mother Teresa in India was certainly both charismatic and transformational but in an entirely different way from the former, rather flamboyant, Canadian Prime Minister, Pierre Trudeau, who has also been described as charismatic and transformational.

In developing countries, charisma and transformational leadership characteristics may be particularly relevant. If we think of people in these countries as poor and lacking many of the amenities that are common in developed countries, we can believe that they would react positively to a leader who they could admire. A charismatic leader provides evidence that a better life is possible.

Path–goal clarification

An integral aspect of leadership and organizational accomplishment is facilitating organizational members' attainment of goals. Models and theories that deal with this aspect of leadership stress the importance of a leader clarifying goals for followers and ensuring that followers understand the path to these goals, that is, how they can achieve these goals. Path–goal clarification is likely important in many cultures, but there are also aspects that seem peculiarly Western and developed. For example, the concept of setting specific goals and working to achieve them relies on ideas of control of the environment and a causal relationship between a person's activities and the outcomes. People in developing countries may not share a sense of control and causality. People in these countries may feel that outside forces control events and they do not see a necessary relationship between an individual's actions and outcomes. People in these countries may prefer a leader who relies on general directions and a general sense of how to get there. On the other hand, where people are high on uncertainty avoidance, clear goals and a clear sense of how to achieve these goals may provide a sense of certainty and security which will be appreciated in such a society.

Goal setting as a leadership behavior seems to rely on the idea that people have a relatively high need for achievement, and that working towards, and reaching goals will help fulfill this need. The Western literature also emphasizes the importance of participation in setting goals and the acceptance of those goals. Acceptance is seen as more likely where the employee has had a say in what the goals are. Goals are also usually set on an individual basis in the West. In developing countries that are more collective and high on power–distance, participation may not be welcomed, and goals set by superiors for the group as a whole may be more acceptable. In addition difficult goals, advocated in the West, may be intimidating, where need for achievement is not high, and may actually discourage performance.

It seems likely that people everywhere need a sense of what they want to accomplish (goals) and how they can reach these goals (path). The types of goals that will be acceptable, the specificity of these goals, how they are set, who sets them, and the means for accomplishing goals may well differ from location to location. This discussion has given a basic overview of the leadership research in Western, developed countries, in the twentieth century. It has also outlined some issues regarding whether and how these theories may apply in developing countries. Some of this discussion is conjecture, because there is relatively little empirical information available to English speakers on non-Western, developing societies. In the next section, some literature on countries in Africa is briefly examined.

AN EXAMPLE: EVIDENCE OF LEADERSHIP STYLE IN AFRICA

The evidence of leadership in African countries is limited, and only a relatively few countries have been studied. The following information provides a brief idea of some of the contrasts in leadership that have been identified on the continent to date.

Blunt and Jones (1997) suggested that in Africa, the effective leadership styles are more paternalistic than the effective leadership styles in the West and that in Africa, interpersonal relations are placed higher than individual achievement. Mathauer and Imhoff (2006) had similar findings. They found that nonfinancial motivational tools and a more paternalistic leadership style, reflecting "caring" on the part of management, were more effective in African countries.

Hale and Fields (2009) thought that the transformational leadership model is not the most effective leadership model in the African perspective. He found West Africa high on hierarchy, with leaders expected to be powerful and to make decisions. He proposed an effective leadership model for Africa as a blending of transformational leadership theory with servant leadership. Along somewhat different lines, Walumbwa et al. (2005) compared the relationship of transformational leadership to organizational commitment and job satisfaction in the United States and Kenya. They identified African leadership as authoritarian due to high power–distance and hypothesized that this may negate the positive impact of transformational leadership. They found that respondents from the United States rated transformational leadership and satisfaction higher than Kenyan respondents; however, they found that in both cultures the relationship between transformational leadership and commitment and satisfaction was positive.

In contrast to the studies that indicated the importance of hierarchy and power in Africa, Smith (2002) looked at leadership roles, and identified spirituality, time as eternal, importance of ancestors and connection of ancestors and land, strong relationships and communalism as important; he concluded that culture has a significant impact on cultural styles and that in Africa, leaders are expected to be tough, but decisions are holistic and collective. McFarlin et al. (1999), Mangaliso (2001) and Newenham-Kahindi (2009) stressed indigenous leadership styles such as Ubuntu and Indaba – endorsing factors such as supportiveness, relationships, extended networks, as well as spiritualism and tribal destiny. They suggested that trust is based on interpersonal relationships, open discussions involving participation from all employees, and discipline based on how the individual affects the group. Mbigi and Maree (1995) also focused on the concept of Ubuntu, described as a sense of brotherhood among marginalized groups combined with spiritualism.

There seem to be two streams of findings in this African research. One is the powerful leader, who uses his place at the top of the hierarchy to accomplish his objectives; the other is the communal, servant leader, who sees his role as leading for the good of others. Note that the pronoun he is used intentionally here, because of the predominance of males in leadership positions in Africa.

Montgomery (1986) considered issues that African managers face. The most frequent issue was motivating subordinates. The study found that African managers used tight supervision, reprimanding employees, and setting personal examples. This seems to fit with the hierarchical management description, as well perhaps with a sense of community and communalism.

Clearly, cultural values are an important determinant of what works and what doesn't from a leadership perspective. Effective leaders need to fit with the culture. Their leadership style needs to be appropriate for the culture, so that their leadership behaviors are acceptable to their followers. In the following section, Hofstede's cultural values are examined as they relate to leadership.

CULTURAL VALUES AND LEADERSHIP

If we use Hofstede's (1984) cultural value model, we can relate the cultural profile of developing countries to leadership. In Chapter 3, we noted that developing countries were relatively collective, and relatively high on power–distance and uncertainty avoidance. In the following we consider how these may relate to effective leadership. Although there was no clear masculine/feminine value preference in developing countries, a greater disparity in the roles of men and women was identified in these countries, so we also include a discussion of this dimension.

Collectivism

In collective societies people pay more attention to the social context; leaders are not seen as apart from the social context; their role is integral to the social fabric. The result is that subordinates react on the basis of the leader's role and position rather than because of the leader's behavior or style. In addition, in these societies the maintenance of harmonious leader–follower relationships is important, and subordinates will describe leaders in positive terms simply because they have reverence for the position. The leader(s), and followers, see the good of the group as more important than the good of the individual, and decisions are made and accepted on this basis.

High power–distance

In high power–distance societies it is believed that there should be an order of inequality where each person has a rightful place. Organizations have clear hierarchies where those at the top are powerful and those at lower levels have little power, and those at the top are expected to make the decisions and those at lower levels simply carry out these decisions. Powerful people are expected to look powerful and are entitled to privileges, thus leaders should have the trappings that come with leadership (large offices, cars, and so on). Others are a threat to one's power and can rarely be trusted, so information is not shared and input is not sought from subordinates. Those in positions of power are independent and those at lower levels are dependent, thus subordinates are loyal to leaders, follow instructions, and accept what the leader says as right. Approaches such as participative management, may be contrary to the value system of both the powerful and their subordinates.

High uncertainty avoidance

In societies that are high on uncertainty avoidance, people are concerned about the uncertainty that is seen as inherent in life and they seek certainty. This is seen in organizations and leadership in a number of ways. Uncertainty produces anxiety and stress, and leaders can alleviate this by providing security for their subordinates. Expertise is valued because it reduces uncertainty, and leaders will seek input from persons both inside and outside of the organization who can provide valid and reliable information. Consensus provides a sense of security, so leaders will spend time and effort to reach consensus among group members. Conservatism is preferred, therefore younger members and those with divergent ideas are suspect and not trusted. Achievement is defined in terms of security, and leaders are expected to provide a secure work environment for subordinates rather than one that is conducive to advancement within the organization. Rules and regulations, policies and procedures are all important to stability, and leaders are expected to define these clearly and to ensure that all organizational members abide by them.

Masculinity and femininity

Hofstede (1984) described societies as favoring traditional male values or traditional female values. Using his terminology, masculine societies are those that value competition, assertiveness, and achievement. Male and female work roles are often clearly delineated. Feminine societies are concerned with nurturance and the quality of life, and roles are more fluid. In developing countries where male/female roles are differentiated, it is likely that leaders will predominantly be male, and female leaders will embrace traditional male values. It may also be the case that leaders will display the tangible rewards that come from being leader and provide tangible rewards for supporters.

This brief discussion of cultural dimensions is intended only to illustrate some of the differences in leadership style that may arise because of culture. Many other variations can be associated with these cultural dimensions as well as others. This discussion provides a basis for readers to develop their own additional thoughts on appropriate and effective leadership approaches, practices, and styles in their own and other cultural environments.

EXAMPLES OF THE INFLUENCE OF CULTURE ON LEADERSHIP

In this section, a number of situations are posed to illustrate the impact of culture on leadership.

Imagine a manager who has always lived and worked in a country where women are not permitted to work for economic returns (they may carry out such work as raising crops, teaching children, caring for the sick, and so on). If this manager is assigned to work in Canada, he will find working with women difficult. Associating closely with female colleagues will make him uncomfortable. It will be difficult for this manager to accept female colleagues as equals or to report to a female superior. Nevertheless, this manager will have to adjust to the Canadian norms because he will be required to work within a system that strives to treat males and females relatively equally. Similarly, in the reverse situation, a Canadian manager will find it uncomfortable to work in a country where women are not in the visible workforce, and it may be impossible for a female manager from Canada to undertake an assignment in this country.

A Canadian consultant was engaged to carry out a series of training programs in India for academics who wished to be able to undertake management consulting assignments. The programs were well received, but some of the Indian participants expressed a wish for harsher discipline. The Canadian normally focused his comments on how participants could improve performance, but some participants expressed a wish that he focus on what they had done wrong.

The Canadian was concerned with ensuring that the participants felt good about their experience in the training sessions and believed that focusing on improvement was the best approach. Some of the participants believed that more direct criticism of their performance was needed. To some extent, the Canadian style can be seen as reflecting a *theory y* approach, while the participants were expecting more *theory x*.

In the English-speaking Caribbean people are high on uncertainty avoidance, and research has shown that employees seek jobs with a high degree of security (public sector jobs are preferred to private sector ones, even where the latter are better paid). Research has also shown a heavy reliance on rules for making decisions both in Barbados and Jamaica. More generally, developing countries tend to be high on uncertainty avoidance (UAI), and employees in these countries will be concerned with security. Laurent (1983) argued that flexible organizational policies and structures would not work in high UAI countries.

During the 1989 student demonstrations in China, while teaching at the Huazhong University of Science and Technology, in Wuhan, I realized how differently people look at leadership. The students on my campus were well aware of the general student unrest throughout the country and there was a sense of excitement as demonstrations started on the campus. These demonstrations were initially rather small and sporadic. I talked to my students about the situation, and their responses were supportive of the "democracy movement," but they had not yet actively joined the demonstrations. After some time, as the demonstrations were growing, I asked, "Are you going to join the demonstrators?" I expected that some students would say "yes," some "maybe," and possibly some would say "no." The answer I got was "we wait to see what our leaders say." As I sought to understand the situation better, I learned that each unit (e.g., the students studying business) had designated leaders, and these leaders made the decision regarding the unit joining or not joining the demonstrations and student strike. Two days later, I went to class and was politely informed by the students that there would be no class because "our leaders have decided to join the student strike." I had a test to return, and I offered to informally sit in the class so that students could come and get their graded tests; I was again politely told "our leaders have decided to join the strike. There will be no class."

In the following section, a variety of developing countries will be examined in terms of their leadership styles and preferences. This serves to illustrate some of the differences that may be encountered across the developing world.

LEADERSHIP IN SELECTED COUNTRIES

Kessler and Wong-MingJi published a book in 2009 which brought together authors from a variety of countries and regions. These authors looked at mythology in a variety of countries/regions and related mythology to global leadership. The following notes are from chapters in this book that deal with developing countries. These illustrate some thinking on indigenous leadership in a variety of countries.

> *Argentina* – Friedrich et al. (2009) described Argentina as a country of contrasts; times of wealth and tranquility, uncertainties and problems; alternating periods of militarism and democratic leadership. Polarizing events and conflicting feelings are seen as defining the people of Argentina. These changing events make long term planning difficult. The fear of not measuring up to international expectations has resulted in self-acclamation. Effective leaders are charismatic and team oriented. These leaders inspire because of their personal charm, but they also focus on goals that unite the people around them. The culture is

collective, and it is important in the Argentine context to foster the development of employees as people, and to allow social interactions to flourish. For foreigners, social events play a central role in business interactions, and it is important to allow time for lengthier interactions so that trust can be established – and "how you say something is equally important to what you say" (p. 91).

Brazil – Garibaldi de Hilal (2009) described Brazil as a mixture of Western and non-Western, modern and traditional, where personal relationships are as important as more general rules. Brazilians are seen as negotiating between a modern, egalitarian code and a traditional one; consequently the art of breaking the rules (*jeitinho*) is ingrained in the society. The current environment evolved from the colonial plantation economy where patriarchs exercised absolute authority over their dominions. Everyone has a known place in society, and laws apply differentially depending on your social status and family position. Brazilian leaders are considered autocratic with traits of paternalism. They are actively involved in decision processes, but with intense social interactions. The leader is often a godfather figure, where "leadership was based on hierarchical authority supported by a set of clearly defined norms and rules, but where the authority of the leaders prevailed over the rules" (p. 102) – the rule of law is moderated by personal connections, and the concepts of in-group and out-group are very strong.

The Caribbean – Punnett and Greenidge (2009) described the Ananci myth and the prevalence of African practices such as Obeah and Voodoo in the Caribbean. They say that traditional beliefs relied on an important, learned person who had information that others did not have, and could use this either for benefit or harm. They argue that this has led to powerful managers, with access to information that is not shared. This allows managers to make decisions which can affect subordinates in both positive and negative ways. This results in a strong in-group/out-group orientation. Power is also attributed to political leaders, and they are seen as "all powerful". One study in the Caribbean (Punnett et al., 2006) found that managers described their fellow managers as authoritarian, lacking trust, and not communicating with subordinates. Punnett and Greenidge concluded that this style was dysfunctional in the Caribbean context and resulted in "workers who won't work" as described by Carter (1997).

South Africa – Abdulai (2009) argues that it is a myth that ancestral worship underlies the African culture and belief system. He differentiated between worship and ancestral veneration. In the case of the Zulus of South Africa, he says that older people are believed to have wisdom, vision and the ability to maintain harmonious working relations in the workplace; hence they are seen as providing a particular benefit, even if they do not have the requisite expertise. Similarly, the role of kinship is important in hiring decisions. Kinship elicits trust, a source of psychological and emotional support, and fosters teamwork, thus important positions in an organization are likely to be staffed based on kinship ties. Abdulai also describes Ubuntu as offering competitive advantage to businesses by enhancing relationships, communication, decision making, understanding the African attitude towards time, enhancing productivity and efficiency, as well as age and seniority in leadership. Lakhani is quoted as saying that the traditional African philosophy of humanism, caring for people first, shows that leading requires humanity.

The previous illustrations are intended to give a snapshot of differences in effectiveness leadership that exist across the developing world. This is clearly only a snapshot. Throughout this book, we have given examples from different countries to highlight both similarities and differences. These illustrations, more than anything else, suggest the importance of assessing individual countries.

SUMMARY

This chapter examined what the term leadership means, and it looked at various theories of leadership that have been identified in more developed countries. These theories included traits, varying styles, contingency approaches, charismatic and transformational leadership, and path-goal identification. The chapter considered each of these theories and how they might apply in developing countries. Throughout, research from a variety of developing countries was used to illustrate various aspects of leadership in different countries. Some research from Africa was presented, as well as some specific experiential examples, and a selection of literature on other developing countries, based on papers in a book linking mythology and leadership. Hofstede's cultural values as generally experienced in developing countries were also examined from a leadership perspective.

This chapter incorporated research on leadership, from developing countries, wherever possible to illustrate the variations in leadership that exist around the world. The chapter also drew substantially on existing Western theories of leadership, but it examined these theories from a developing country context, to identify what might be effective, and how these established theories might change based on the context.

LESSONS LEARNED

Having completed this chapter, you should understand that successful leaders adopt a style of leadership that fits the particular situation and environment in which they are leading. You will have a better awareness that research suggests that leadership is more than an exchange of rewards for effort, and that effective leaders share a sense of purpose with their subordinates that embodies charisma and transformation. You will appreciate that leadership in any organization seems to incorporate the concept of transformation. You should be familiar with the idea that leadership is a process which allows management to be proactive rather than reactive in shaping the future of the organization. You should be able to suggest alternative strategies where necessary to improve leadership effectiveness, and be aware that rewards for making the organization a better place are important for everyone.

DISCUSSION QUESTIONS

1   Identify and describe organizational environmental differences between your home country and two other countries.
2   Identify and describe the most important ingredients for effective leadership in developing countries.
3   In your home country, describe the leadership traits and styles that seem to be most prominent.

EXERCISE

In small groups, identify an effective leadership style and an ineffective style, for your culture. Discuss why one is effective and the other is ineffective. Prepare a brief skit to illustrate either the effective or ineffective style, and be prepared to explain why this style is effective or ineffective in your culture.

Chapter 12

Special issues for managers in developing countries

⚡

OBJECTIVES

In this chapter a number of special issues associated with the developing world will be examined from the perspective of their impact on effective management.

The objectives are as follows:

- To look at ethics, including issues of corruption.
- To explore differences in ethics between developed and developing countries, and implications for managers.
- To recognize that managers face many ethical issues as they do business and make decisions around the world.
- To understand how ethical issues influence on organizations.
- To understand the role of women around the world.
- To consider implications of health, education, and population dispersion in developing countries.

INTRODUCTION

The final chapter of this book addresses a number of issues that have been mentioned throughout, but warrant additional attention in a book on management in developing countries. These issues are somewhat special to developing countries; for example, ethical questions and corruption, the role of women in developing countries and differential treatment on the basis of personal characteristics, the growing population (especially the young population), and the relatively low levels of health care and education in some countries. In this chapter, we begin by focusing on these issues, from a perspective of their impact on management and effective management. The following headings are used:

- ethics, corruption, corporate governance;
- differential treatment on the basis of personal characteristics;
- health, education, and age.

The chapter concludes with a brief review of all the topics covered in the book, and a look at what we expect in the future. The next section considers ethics, corruption, and corporate governance.

ETHICS, CORRUPTION, CORPORATE GOVERNANCE

In this section we look at three issues which are somewhat related – ethics, corruption, and corporate governance.

Ethics is about what is considered morally appropriate. Around the world, one finds different concepts and approaches to ethics. At home, most ethical rights and wrongs are usually quite clear and well established, but in foreign countries major questions can arise regarding what is right and what is wrong. Ethics is both about fundamental rights and wrongs, as well as what is considered acceptable and unacceptable. For example:

- Lobbying in the United States is considered a normal activity – companies and industries send representatives to "lobby" their government representatives, asking these representatives to make decisions that will positively affect the company or industry, and offering political support in return. In some countries outside of the United States, this practice is considered unethical and equivalent to "buying" influence with the government.
- In Europe and North America as noted in Chapter 3 it is normal to tip restaurant waiters and taxi drivers, but people from many other parts of the world are mystified by this practice, and see it as a form of bribery to get special service, because the waiters and taxi drivers are simply performing an expected service, simply doing their job.
- We also saw that in parts of Africa, Asia, and Latin America, tipping customs officials is considered normal, while North Americans and Europeans see this as bribery because they believe such payments are intended to get preferential treatment.

In classes with a cross-cultural makeup, I have had Indian students (from India) explain to American students (from the USA) that "customs officials are paid very little and rely on the extra payments to make ends meet." The Americans, in turn, have explained that "waiters and waitresses are at the bottom of the ladder, in terms of wages, and need the tips from customers to get by on a day to day basis." Clearly in the case of tipping versus what is bribery, and what is acceptable, depends very much on your cultural background.

Interestingly, law in the USA differentiates between bribes and "grease payments" in foreign transactions. Bribes are illegal, and companies may be prosecuted in the USA for making payments that are construed as bribes, even when they are made in foreign locations. Grease payments, on the other hand, are allowed and acceptable. The difference appears to be the size of the payment as well as the intent. Generally, grease payments are relatively small amounts, and their intent is to keep a system running and ensure that you get what you are entitled to, in a timely manner. For example, if you are entitled to clear your goods through customs and pay a tax of ten percent, the grease payment helps ensure that the goods get cleared and you pay only the ten percent. Bribes, in contrast, often involve substantial amounts, and are intended to get preferential treatment. For example, if several companies are bidding for a multibillion dollar project, one company may pay several million dollars to officials to have the decision go in their favor. Clearly, in this case the company is getting something to which it is not necessarily entitled.

This book has previously discussed the importance of understanding cultural preferences and sometimes ethical issues appear to be culturally determined, but ethics go beyond this because they also express fundamental beliefs about what is universally right and wrong. There are many other ethical issues that managers face as they do business and make decisions around the world. Consider the following:

- In some countries child labor is normal. Children work to help support their families. Their parents may need to remain at home to look after other children, manage livestock, and so on. Many people from more developed countries see child labor as morally reprehensible. Many children are proud of the work they do and their ability to help their families. As a manager in an international firm, how do you handle the issue of employing children?
- Developed countries may ban pesticides because of their potential damage to wildlife or potential for causing a variety of diseases. Some developing countries may wish to continue the use of these pesticides because they increase crop yields. The people of the developing country may be facing severe food shortages, and immediate survival is more important to them than their future or the environment. As a manager in an international firm, how do you react to a request to provide a pesticide, banned in North America, to a developing country?

It is not clear in the two situations described what is right and what is wrong. This is the essence of an ethical dilemma. There are good reasons to employ children where they would be worse off if you did not employ them. There are good reasons to provide pesticides where people would be worse off if you did not provide them. There are also good reasons to stop the practice of child labor and to avoid the use of dangerous pesticides. International managers face such dilemmas and need to weigh the pros and cons carefully. In the two examples given, some ethical answers might include:

- Employ the children, but provide health care and education for them.
- Provide the pesticide for immediate use, if it is the only effective one available, while investing profits to find a safe alternative.

Developed countries, because their legal systems are well developed, generally have rules and regulations in place, which are well enforced, regarding behavior that falls broadly under ethics. For example, these countries have regulations regarding minimum wages, minimum working ages, child protection, freedom of speech, environmental care, preservation of animal habitat, and a wide variety of other activities. These regulations are intended to clearly identify what is acceptable and what is not, and there are penalties associated with contravening them. Developing countries often do not have as well developed legal systems, and, where regulations do exist, they may not be enforced. Ethical or unethical decisions and behaviors, in these countries, therefore tend to be more subjective and individual, and it is more likely that accepted practice includes payments that may be seen as questionable in more developed countries. Where the "rule of man" predominates over the "rule of law", the particular situation is taken into account as well in determining what is considered permissible or ethical. For example, it may normally be unethical to give a customs official an extra payment to get your goods through customs, but if you know that a particular official has had family difficulties, this would be taken into account and a gift would be appropriate; it may be against the law to drive after drinking, but if the person is one of importance, then this law might not be enforced.

Decisions that involve ethical questions are often difficult to make because there are no rules that necessarily apply in all situations. The best advice for managers who want to be ethical is to think carefully about the implications of any decision or activity, and consider all stakeholders, and how they will be affected by the decision or activity. Make the decision or act in a way that leaves one with a clear conscience.

Transparency also seems to be a critical aspect of ethical decision making and actions. Many people argue that when decisions are made so that the reasons for the decisions are clear to all stakeholders, then they will be ethical. The argument rests on the belief that most people will not engage in unethical behaviors if others will know about these actions. In developing countries, the structure may not be in place for transparency – for example, if the press is not free, it cannot, or will not, report activities of powerful people or groups that may be unethical. This has been the case in developing countries where leaders have been accused of taking large sums of money that rightly belong to the country and the people of the country as a whole. Developing countries are believed to be generally more corrupt than developed countries. That is, there is more likelihood of unreported payments and gifts in business dealings. These payments may be to civil servants, government officials, or other businesses.

Transparency International's 2010 Corruption Index of 176 countries (www.transparency. org) listed the most corrupt ten as developing countries (Somalia as worst, followed by Afghanistan, Myanmar, Iraq, Uzbekistan, Turkmenistan, Sudan, Chad, Burundi, Angola) and the least corrupt ten as developed, including Singapore (Denmark as best, followed by Singapore, New Zealand, Sweden, Finland, Canada, the Netherlands, Australia, Switzerland, Norway). As you go through the index, overwhelmingly, the more developed are among the better countries from a corruption perspective, and the developing are among the worse. Of course, there are exceptions, such as Barbados at number 17, but the general picture is one of higher levels of corruption paralleling lower levels of development.

Managers in developing countries can expect that they may face more situations where there is a possibility of unethical or corrupt activities, and that they may be asked to participate in these activities more frequently than would be the case in developed countries. The author believes that corruption leads to an inefficient use of resources, and that developing countries, and managers in these countries, need to use their limited resources wisely and efficiently and effectively. The author would therefore counsel managers to avoid corruption, but at the same time, recognizes that there may be situations where ethically questionable decisions or behaviors are the only way to accomplish desirable objectives and goals.

Many ethical arguments revolve around whether ethics are universal or culturally contingent. Some scholars argue that what is good is good and what is bad is bad, no matter where you are in the world. Others believe that definitions of good and bad change from place to place, and even from one situation to another. For example, in the West, lying is generally considered wrong, yet in some situations, so as not to hurt someone, lying may be considered the ethical thing to do.

As managers, you may believe that ethics are universal or you may feel that a cultural contingency view is closer to reality. If you take the first view, you may find yourself at odds with other managers at times, but if you take the second view, you may find that you are sometimes put in the position of making a decision, or taking an action, which you feel is wrong.

The middle ground is to identify some actions, behaviors, and decisions that are always wrong – that is, cases of universal ethics – and others that are acceptable in some places but not in others. In the first group I would include things like murder, rape, torture, sex with children, and so on. All of these are, to me, fundamentally and universally wrong. In the second group I would include practices like tipping, small gifts, rules applying to relationships between men and women, family customs and relationships, and so on. These differ from place to place, and I am willing to accept the differences. For example, I would consider it wrong in my own environment to segregate men and women socially, but I know that this is normal in other countries for religious reasons, and I would accept it even though I might find it strange. At home, as a woman, I would see nothing wrong with women wearing short skirts and sleeveless tops, but I know this would be inappropriate elsewhere, and in other countries I would advise these women to dress modestly, and cover their hair if need be.

In Barbados, there was a company that employed local Barbadians as well as employees who had immigrated from the Indian subcontinent. The two groups were outraged at each other's dress. On so-called 'dress down day' some Barbadian employees wore shorts and sleeveless t-shirts, which the Asians considered immodest. Some Asian women wore saris, which exposed their mid-sections, which the Barbadians considered vulgar. This situation almost led to a strike!

Managers will need to decide on an individual basis what are universals and what are cultural contingencies, and act accordingly. What we can be sure of is that we will face many situations in foreign countries where what we think is ethical may be seen as unethical, and vice versa. Corruption is a particular form of unethical behavior that managers may encounter. While corruption generally refers to any unethical behavior, it often is used to refer to wrongdoing on the part of the authorities or powerful parties through means that are illegitimate, immoral, or incompatible with ethical standards. Corruption seems to be particularly prevalent in developing countries.

There are a number of reasons why corruption may be more prevalent in developing countries. Developing countries have relatively lower levels of remuneration; thus officials may rely on "extra payments" to make a living wage. Developing countries may not have the available infrastructure (police, regulatory units and so on) to monitor and prosecute those who engage in corrupt practices. Developing countries may be more likely to have powerful ruling elites who believe it is their right, because of their power and position, to receive a variety of payments. Developing countries may have bureaucratic policies and procedures which slow down decisions and actions; thus encouraging the use of extra payments to get around what is seen as "red tape".

These reasons should not be used to excuse corruption. The UN's *World Development Report* (2001) argued that corruption had large costs for development and that there is strong evidence that higher levels of corruption are associated with lower rates of growth and lower per capita incomes. *The Economist* (2002) illustrated the impact of corruption on FDI by correlating FDI inflows with perceptions of corruption and finding a clear link; countries considered more corrupt received much smaller amounts of FDI. It appears that developing countries need to pay special attention to corruption and develop effective anti-corruption approaches if their businesses are to succeed globally. Finding ways to ensure that transactions are transparent in developing countries is especially important. Transparency makes corruption more difficult and less likely.

There is another side to corruption. For every official who receives an inappropriate payment, there is a company, or company official, who makes the payment. Some countries and companies have established rules intended to eliminate corruption. The United States Foreign Corrupt Practices Act makes any payments by United States companies (other than the small facilitation or grease payments) to foreign officials or political candidates illegal. The United Kingdom has enacted legislation extending its anti-bribery laws to cover British nationals and companies abroad. Other developed countries have similar laws. In addition, many multinational companies have "no bribery" policies and codes of ethics that include statements about corrupt practices.

The situation faced by managers in countries where bribery is commonplace is not always straightforward, however. For example:

- In India, a bribe may be expected to get your goods through customs or to be allowed to register at a hotel; managers may have little practical choice but to go along with this practice.

- In Nigeria (once rated as the most corrupt country by Transparency International) bribery is often taken for granted; managers may find themselves receiving gifts that they are unsure whether to accept.
- In the People's Republic of China, corruption is dealt with harshly, but gifts among associates are expected; the difference between a gift and a bribe is not always clear.

A manager from a Canadian company with a subsidiary in Mexico illustrated the difficulty of dealing with corruption in the following story. The Canadian CEO of the Mexican subsidiary went to a party one night. Unfortunately he stayed out too late and had rather too much to drink. On his way home he was arrested and put in jail in Mexico City. The company had a strict "no bribe" clause in its code of ethics and the Mexican police would not release the Canadian unless they received an appropriate sum of money. The solution was to hire a Mexican attorney to make the payment. The managers in Mexico could claim they had not contravened the Canadian code; they had simply paid the attorney. The attorney was happy to receive a fee that also allowed him to pay the bribe to the police. This story illustrates the ease with which rules can be contravened. Even where there are laws and codes of ethics, it remains relatively simple for companies to participate in corrupt activities.

By and large, the developed world seeks more policing of corruption and the developing world is more likely to be the locale for corruption; however, one can argue that business-people from developed countries contribute to the existence of corruption as much as do their counterparts in the developing world, because they are usually the ones making the payments.

From a developing country perspective, it is important to consider the impact that corruption has on the development process. It has already been noted that the existence of corruption is correlated with FDI and that less investment flows to countries that are considered corrupt. Another side to the picture is the distortion that corruption can cause to the economy and development. Corruption means that some people or companies receive special favorable treatment because of the payments they have made. This means that others receive less favorable treatment. Those who get preferential treatment are so treated because of the payments they have made (or other favors they have given) rather than because their projects are the best for the developing countries. Corruption, thus, results in inefficiencies and corrupt countries are not making the best use of their scarce resources. Efficient and effective use of resources is key to economic development, so it seems particularly important that developing countries work to limit corruption and establish transparency in their transactions.

In recent years, corporate governance has become a subject of interest in both developed and developing countries. The role of directors and their responsibilities, as well as the role and responsibilities of auditors, were highlighted in a number of spectacular corporate failures, such as Enron and World Com, both American-based companies. One immediate consequence of the Enron failure was the disappearance of Arthur Andersen, to that point one of the largest and most respected audit firms in the world. Another spin off from these failures has been closer attention to directors around the world, including in developing countries.

While the issues, associated with these roles, have received more attention in developed countries, the impact in developing countries is also substantial. In the past, being a director was often seen essentially as a perk with little real responsibility, or sometimes, a benefit for former politicians. This was particularly the case for small and family owned businesses, where directors were appointed to comply with the law, and to provide a means to support particular family members or friends. This situation is changing, as it has become evident that the legal obligations of directors are real, and that directors can be sued for failure to exercise due diligence in corporate matters, for making bad decisions, or for benefiting inappropriately from corporate activities. This is true of all corporate entities, whether they be private companies, or public bodies, state owned enterprises, para-statal, nongovernmental organizations, charities or, cooperatives.

In developing countries, corporate governance is often not well understood, and directors do not necessarily have a clear understanding, or guidelines, regarding what is expected, acceptable or allowed, and what is not. In particular, conflict of interest can arise easily in these countries. There are often a small number of investors, who come from the privileged class, who serve on various boards. There may also be a limited number of people with the required expertise and experience to serve effectively. This means that the same people serve on several Boards, and they, or their companies, may have the expertise required to carry out specialized projects for these same companies on whose Board they serve. Transparency in these situations is essential, so that it is clear to all stakeholders that any potential conflicts of interest have been addressed.

The next section addresses an issue that is sometimes seen as a specific aspect of ethics – treating people differently because of their personal characteristics. This is often referred to as discrimination, and in the next section, we examine the ramifications of discrimination.

DIFFERENTIAL TREATMENT ON THE BASIS OF PERSONAL CHARACTERISTICS

The differential treatment of certain groups constitutes a particular set of ethical questions. When discrimination is practiced because of factors such as age, ethnicity, gender, race, religion, and so on, the question arises: "Is it ethical to deny someone a particular job because of gender, race, religion, or ethnicity?" In some countries, it is considered acceptable and normal that women do certain jobs or none outside of the home. Yet, this is considered unfair discrimination elsewhere. In general, the developed countries have a series of policies, regulations and laws which specify requirements in terms of what is considered discrimination. In Canada, for example, it is unlawful to discriminate on the basis of these factors, as well as sexual orientation. In Canada, same sex marriage is legally sanctioned, and to a large degree, homosexuality is not an issue in Canada.

From an international perspective, where serious racial or religious biases exist, these need to be taken into account. Sending a Muslim to an anti-Muslim region, a Christian to an anti-Christian location, an Indian to an anti-Indian location, or a Caucasian to an anti-white location may be putting them in serious jeopardy. At best, they will be ineffective on the job because of discrimination. At worst, they may suffer emotional and/or physical harm. Where there are families involved, the situation is even more serious as the families are likely to face discrimination in their everyday life, and possibly harassment or worse.

People with disabilities also pose a special challenge. In North America and Europe, it is often taken for granted that buildings will be accessible for those with disabilities and that these individuals will be treated as equal to others. The same is certainly not the case elsewhere. In many places, people with disabilities are regarded as crippled, with pity the best emotion they encounter. Even where this is not the case, in much of the world little thought has been given to access for the disabled and it is extremely difficult for them to travel or get into and around buildings.

Practices that would be considered discriminatory in many developed countries are more likely to be relatively common in developing countries. Developing countries, by and large, have fewer laws and regulations relating to this aspect of employment and employee relations. In some cases, practices that favor one group or another are well established and accepted, and there is no incentive to change the accepted system. In others, limited infrastructure means that access for the physically disabled does not exist, so discrimination is inevitable.

An interesting question arises for international companies regarding situations that may be seen as discriminatory. Do you follow home country convention or host country convention when selecting personnel for foreign assignments. For example, in the USA it is against the law to discriminate on the basis of sexual preference, but in other parts of the world, particularly the developing world, it is illegal to be a practicing homosexual. Consider the ethical dilemma for an American company if it considers a known homosexual manager for a position in a country where homosexuality is illegal. If the company does not select the manager because of sexual preference, it can be sued in the USA. If it does select the manager, he/she may face social and legal problems abroad. The question arises: "is it still discrimination if the choice is because of the difficulties the person would face in a foreign location?"

A special case of differential treatment that we consider in the next section is the role of women in a variety of countries.

The role of women

Managers moving internationally may be particularly struck by differences in the status of women, especially differences between developed and developing countries. The United Nations (2001) reported that international firms employ about 2 million women in developing countries. This represents a very small proportion of the total labor force in these countries and only about 3 percent of the worldwide employment by international firms. The UN report suggested that the typical role of women in these countries is inferior to that of men. Although the report is more than twenty years old, the situation does not seem to have changed much over the twenty years. The report says, among other things, that:

- In some countries, women are employed, frequently with the whole family, in plantations owned by transnational corporations (TNCs) which often date from colonial times and grow such crops as tea and rubber. Their position in the plantation labor force is inferior to that of men.
- In the service sector, a small proportion of the total employment of women by TNCs is in white-collar occupations in banks and commercial establishments. However, most women employed in services hold low-level jobs as maids, cleaners, waitresses, and salesgirls in hotels, offices, and retail establishments.
- TNCs in export-processing zones (EPZs) have become significant employers of women, who work as low-paid, unskilled or semi-skilled workers. Wages tend to be low, and they are often below those earned by men. Therefore, the practices of TNCs largely reflect prevailing local circumstances. Firms often favor employing women in EPZs because they are seen as more efficient and stable than men and, at the same time, their wages are lower than those for men and it is easier to hire and lay off women.

It is important to recognize that many of these women would otherwise be unemployed, and that they likely prefer to be employed in these jobs than not at all. The inferior role to that of men is also likely accepted by many of the women as culturally normal. This illustrates one of the dilemmas faced by many international managers. The balance between providing employment and exploiting female workers is not always clear-cut. In the following brief discussion, we look at the role of women in a number of developing and developed countries and regions of the world.

The situation of women around the world is that they are not equal in the workplace, but the level of inequality varies. The World Economic Forum's Global Gender Gap Index (Hausmann et al., 2009) compares 134 countries on the equality of women – with scores potentially ranging from 0 to 100. The best countries, all developed countries, score in the low 80s (Iceland, Finland, Norway, and Sweden were the highest scorers at 82.8, 82.5, 82.3, 81.8, respectively). Some developing countries also do quite well; for example, two Caribbean countries (Trinidad and Tobago and Barbados) were among the leaders in the Western hemisphere at nos. 19 and 21, outperforming both Canada and the United States at nos. 25 and 31, respectively. Two African countries, South Africa (no. 6) and Lesotho (no. 10) made the top ten list; the Philippines (no. 9) lost ground for the first time in four years but remained the leading Asian country in the rankings. The bottom of the rankings was made up of developing countries – India (no. 114), Bahrain (no. 116), Ethiopia (no. 122), Morocco (no. 124), Egypt (no. 126), and Saudi Arabia (no. 130) had made improvements relative to their rankings in 2008, while others at the bottom – Iran (no. 128), Turkey (no. 129), Pakistan (no. 132), and Yemen (no. 134) displayed an absolute decline relative to their performance in 2008.

Overall, more than two-thirds of the countries covered in the report showed gains in overall index scores, indicating that the world in general had made progress toward equality between men and women. In contrast, globally, the number of women in senior management in large corporations remained very low – Catalyst (2009) reported that, in the thousand largest companies, only twenty-four women held CEO positions.

In the following sections, we look briefly at some of the attitudes towards women in various countries and regions.

The role of women in business in the Arab world is often difficult for Westerners to understand and accept. Women are described as equal, but with different responsibilities. Once married, for example, women in Saudi Arabia go out only to visit close friends and relatives or to shop, and then they must be accompanied by a male relative. Women make up only about 10 percent of the workforce in Saudi Arabia, not because they are prohibited from working or from certain occupations, but because they are not permitted to work with men. The sexes must be kept segregated. Consequently, most organizations prefer not to employ women. Women who do work are in education, medicine, or social work, where contacts with males can be avoided. The situation is not very different in other countries in the region, even those with less stringent rules governing women's conduct. In Bahrain, for example, women are well educated and given equal opportunity, but affluence and social beliefs have discouraged them from seeking employment. This is changing somewhat with the emergence of a middle class and women interested in entering the professions.

The demonstrations, and unrest, in Middle-Eastern countries in 2011 brought the role of women into focus. Many women participated in the demonstrations in countries such as Egypt. In consequence they argued that they should be well represented in the new governments. What the reality will be is in question, as this book is being written, but it will be a development to watch with interest.

Women's roles in Africa appear to differ (often dramatically) from place to place, and may depend on the particular ethnic or religious group to which they belong. In a number of cases the role of women is clearly secondary and inferior to that of men – Parkin (1978) described one African group as defining women's status as "the producers of men's children" and "confined to domestic activities" while men were the "political leaders and wage earners" (p. 168). Ferraro (1990) described Kenya as one of the most Westernized and progressive African countries but said that the role and status of women remained characterized by traditional distinctions of inferiority, and described African men as having "considerable difficulty seeing women as anything other than wives, mothers, and food producers" (p. 114). Abdulai (2009) speaks of the Zulu, noting that important ancestors are male and that when some educated Zulu women complained that this was a form of discrimination, the response was that these women were feminists who did not respect their own culture. Abdulai goes on to say of the glass ceiling phenomenon "this is not only an African phenomenon but a global one" (p. 216), suggesting that African women in general face similar challenges to their counterparts elsewhere.

Historically, India has been a male-dominated society, in which a woman has been expected to marry, have a family and take care of the household. Traditionally, female children in Indian families did not have access to formal education (Sen, 2005). Recent statistics suggested that only about 2 percent of managers in Indian corporations are women (Saini, 2006). According to Lockwood et al. (2009), the situation is changing as education for girls is increasing, more women are working outside the home, and the number of women attending business schools has increased significantly in recent years. Women are entering professions previously seen as the domain of men, including advertising, banking, engineering, financial services, and the police and armed forces (Budhwar et al., 2005). Nevertheless, women in India still face many of the same challenges in the workplace as women elsewhere. For example, Khandelwal (2002) found that managerial success was more associated with men than with women. Indian male managers are seen as being good leaders, good decision makers, and good bosses, who are effective at handling challenging assignments. These stereotypes have a negative impact on women's ability to progress in management. In addition, the traditional role for women as housewives means that career women face significant work–life balance challenges (Budhwar et al., 2005) and a supportive family is seen as key to professional success (Lockwood et al. 2009).

Countries of the Far East vary in their acceptance of women in business:

- In Hong Kong women are found relatively frequently at all levels of organizations and they are accepted as effective businesspeople. Nevertheless, they are found most often in secretarial positions and males are not found in traditionally female jobs.
- In Malaysia, women have "equal opportunity," but in reality they are sheltered and business is considered the preserve of males.
- In Singapore, increasing numbers of women are entering the workforce, with 80 percent of those between the ages of 20 and 24 working. Professional women are more likely to advance in firms linked with the government, but generally their role is subordinate to that of men.
- In South Korea it is rare for women to be in positions of authority, and their prospects for advancement are slim as many companies have a policy of employing women only until they are 30 or marry.
- In Thailand, women are seen as "the hind legs of the elephant," powerful but following, and are generally working in subordinate positions. This is tempered by educational and social background, which allows some women to hold top positions both in government and private industry.

The situation in the People's Republic of China is somewhat mixed. Virtually all women work, but women in upper-level positions are rare. Traditionally, women were not expected to partake in business activities, but the Communist Party promoted the idea that "women hold up half of heaven" and implemented educational programs that have led to a substantial increase in the numbers of women at work and in scientific professions and government. Women, however, are required to retire at an earlier age than men for "physical reasons" and their advancement and lifetime earnings are consequently diminished.

In looking at a variety of developing countries, Catalyst (2009) reported the percentage of women "legislators, senior officials and managers" in a variety of countries and found the following percentages for selected countries – Peru 27.6 percent, Argentina 23.2 percent, Croatia 20.8 percent, Czech Republic 28.7 percent, Egypt 10.8 percent, Ethiopia 15.7 percent, China 16.8 percent, Vietnam 22.2 percent.

In the more developed world, the situation varies, as the following illustrates:

- Japanese organizations have traditionally seen women as serving in lower-paid, lower-level positions, and even graduates of top universities were hired for clerical positions. In Japan, in 2009 (www.catalyst.org), 41.4 percent of the labor market were women, 61.3 percent were in clerical positions, 46.2 percent in technical/professional, 9.3 percent administrative/managerial and of 43,115 board directors, only 81 were women (.002 percent). More Japanese women have been and are entering the workforce, however, and in 1986 Japan passed a law prohibiting discrimination on the basis of gender. Anti-discrimination legislation is better enforced in the public sector than the private, and women are more likely to be treated equally in government and public offices. While the situation for working women may be improving in Japan, the traditional role of the woman remaining at home after marriage is still accepted by most Japanese.

- The situation is better for women managers in Canada and the United States than in many other locations. Nevertheless, women are more likely to serve in jobs that are subordinate to men's: they are usually the secretaries rather than the bosses, the nurses rather than the doctors, the teachers rather than the principals, the assistants rather than the politicians. In 2009, in Canada (www.catalyst.org), women accounted for 46.9 percent of the labor force but only 5.6 percent of the top earners and, 5.4 percent of CEO's. In the United States (www.catalyst.org), women accounted for 46.5 percent of the labor force but only 6.2 percent of Fortune 500 top earners, and 3 percent of Fortune 500 CEO's. Legislation in both countries prohibits discrimination on the basis of gender and this has encouraged women to seek management positions and organizations to fill these positions with women. At lower and middle management levels women are quite well represented; at top levels, however, there are still relatively few women. The lack of women in top management has been attributed to several factors, including past discrimination, ongoing discrimination, a lack of interest on the part of some women, and a shortage of women with appropriate education, experience and training. Whatever the causes, it seems likely that the situation is changing and that there will be increasing pressure on organizations to admit women to top management ranks. In Canada and the United States, achieving equality in the workforce has focused on demonstrating the equal abilities of men and women. Legislation and social pressure have encouraged organizations to treat men and women largely in the same manner, suggesting that they should be given equal opportunities, training, and compensation for equivalent jobs.

- In the countries of the European Union (EU) the situation varies from country to country. Women are not as well represented in management ranks in Europe as they are in Canada and the United States. Each country has its own regulations and socially accepted views. Integration of the EU and standardization of regulations is likely to result in a more uniform role for women managers throughout the community, although social dissimilarities will likely continue to influence this role in individual countries. The European Community's Foundation for the Improvement of Living and Working Conditions has recently emphasized the need to take positive action for equality in the workplace, and this will likely have a positive impact on women's participation in management throughout the community.

165

One co-author of the gender gap report, Zahidi (in Tonkin, 2009), commented that countries that do not fully capitalize on what is one-half of their human resources run the risk of undermining their competitive potential, observing, "We hope to highlight the economic incentive behind empowering women, in addition to promoting equality as a basic human right" (Tonkin, 2009). In developing countries, the effective use of human resources is often critical to development and increased economic performance. Yet, in these countries, women are often underutilized. This suggests that changes in developing countries to encourage greater participation of women in the business world could potentially have a substantial positive impact. There are good arguments that such discrimination is a misuse of limited resources. That is, by eliminating certain groups from human resource choices, a company limits its choices and does not take full advantage of the potentially available resources.

In the next section we look at health, educational, and age from a developing country perspective. Each of these socio-demographic issues has important implications for development, and how businesses operate in developing countries.

HEALTH, EDUCATION, AND AGE

In general, based on the definitions of developing countries – that is, that they are poorer than developed countries – it is not surprising that in most developing countries health care is limited and illnesses are more common than in the developed world (including higher infant mortality, deaths in childbirth and lower life expectancy). There are exceptions, but this is the case across most of the developing world. Similarly, it is not surprising that educational levels are generally lower in developing countries, with less money devoted to education on a per capita basis, resulting in lower levels of literacy and numeracy. A smaller proportion of people attend primary, secondary, and tertiary school. In addition, in some developing countries, entire groups, such as women or minorities, may be deprived of even basic education. Less obvious is the age dispersion in developing countries. In most developing countries, the population is relatively young, whereas the population is aging throughout the developed world. The implications of these three factors are briefly explored in this section.

The limited availability of health care in many developing countries, coupled with high levels of diseases such as HIV/AIDS, malaria, diabetes, and hypertension, means that health issues are a major concern for companies operating in, or from, these countries. Poor health is likely to result in lower productivity, higher absenteeism and turnover, and higher health care costs for companies that provide health coverage. Higher turnover also means increased training costs and a loss of institutional memory. This can be a major disadvantage for companies from these countries, particularly when they compete with companies from more developed countries. No doubt, these disadvantages are somewhat offset by lower wage and benefit costs, but they nevertheless have to be considered. Companies in developing countries may find it beneficial to address these issues directly, through training programs to encourage healthy lifestyle changes, and through the provision of preventive health care measures.

Limited education also can be a disadvantage for companies in developing countries. Although many jobs in developing countries may be low wage, basic jobs, a lack of literacy and numeracy can make it difficult to carry out even these jobs, especially in today's world, where technology is often a part of even the most basic job. Limited educational levels can mean that it is difficult for companies to carry out more advanced tasks in developing countries. This, in turn, reduces the potential impact of job creation and foreign direct investment in the country. Increasing educational attainment would seem to be a priority for all developing countries, as it should lead to more opportunities for all the people of the country. Companies may also find it worthwhile to invest in education and training in the workplace to improve employee skill levels. The Volkswagen Shanghai model is an interesting example in this regard. In the 1980s, Volkswagen, when establishing its assembly plant near Shanghai in China, decided to include an educational facility in the plant complex. Electrical engineering, mechanics, electronics, automotive chemistry and materials testing and research were among the topics taught in modern classrooms with well equipped labs. The students (factory workers), were issued coveralls with the company logo on them, and, together with the formal training, they developed an exceptionally high morale and work ethic, according to the management of the plant.

In contrast to the health and education issues, the younger population in developing countries can provide an advantage for these countries and companies operating there. A young population means a labor force with many years to be productive. This current younger population is also often familiar with computers and social media. This can be beneficial for companies. Unfortunately, in many developing countries, unemployment remains high, which means the young people are unemployed and not contributing as productively as they could be. Developing countries should find ways to capitalize on their young populations, and companies in these countries may also be able to capitalize on this youthful workforce.

The aging population in the developed world, and the youthful population in the developing world seems to be potentially important from a business and management perspective, but little attention has been paid to this situation. The developing world can provide the labor force that enables the developed world to continue to live comfortably. In turn, this would naturally provide employment and income for the developing world that allows them to improve their overall economic well-being. This is taking place today, as companies in countries such as China, Mexico, and South Africa export more products to the developed world, and the developed world turns more to services and the professions. It may be simplistic, but it may be part of the solution to the existing rich/poor dichotomy in the world's countries.

In 2010, I heard a news story about a Canadian with elderly parents who needed specialized, but nonmedical, care. He felt that he could not afford the care they needed in Canada. He was a yoga instructor and had contacts in India. He found that he could move his parents from Canada to India and employ round the clock care for them in India, at a fraction of the cost of care in Canada. He reported that his parents were happy, with young attentive carers looking after them, and catering to their every need, on a twenty-four-hour basis. He was providing employment for several Indian carers, his elderly parents were well looked after, and he was spending less than if they were in Canada. It seemed that this might provide the basis for building a business in many developing countries. There are many opportunities for companies in developing countries. The former is only one among many. This means that issues of management will be increasingly important in for these countries.

The discussion in this chapter has focused on special issues, from a developing country perspective. It is hoped that this will fully provide insights for readers and will encourage readers to think about a wide array of other issues associated with managing in developing countries, and internationalizing from these countries. The issues selected here are ones that the author finds particularly relevant today; as internationalization continues the nature and complexity of these and other issues will evolve further.

WHERE HAVE WE BEEN AND WHERE ARE WE GOING?

The intent of this book has been to explore management issues from a developing country perspective. To do this, we explored the reality of what it means to be a developing country; that is, the characteristics that differentiate developing countries from more developed ones. We also discussed the terminology of development and explanations of development. This provided the context for considering the process of management and how it might differ in developing countries, from the theories proposed in the developed country literature. A model of management which includes planning, organizing, staffing, leading, and controlling was used as the framework for the chapters on management.

Throughout, we recognized that the models and frameworks were those promulgated in literature from the developed world. This means it is necessary to question the models and frameworks themselves. Nevertheless, it seemed that the models and frameworks could be applied in developing countries, but that the specifics need to be adapted to fit the characteristics of the developing country environment. There is relatively little literature on management in developing countries, but this book has tried to incorporate this literature wherever possible. In addition, I have tried to interpret the information on the characteristics of developing countries in terms of management theories and approaches.

The world's business and economic systems appear to be changing. There has been an enormous interest in developing countries in the past several years, and their integration into the global economy has been steadily increasing. Throughout this book, information supporting this contention has been provided. This means that developing an understanding of management in these countries is increasingly important, for managers within these countries, as well as those from outside, doing business there, or considering it. It is evident that there is relatively little empirical information on management in developing countries generally, or on specific countries. This book provides a step towards a better understanding of management issues in these countries. I hope that the information provided throughout will give readers insights that will be helpful in improving management practice in several directions – within developing countries, for developing country organizations going to other countries, and for organizations from developed countries going to developing ones.

The new interest in developing countries and management in these countries is encouraging. As this book is being completed, there are indications that the economic world order may be changing. There may be substantial developments over the coming decade, and readers should follow these developments with interest as the author will. This also points to the need for more research on managing in developing countries, and I hope the information presented in this book will encourage such research.

Throughout much of this book, there is an implicit acceptance that the world has become "global" and that there is a substantial interrelationship among economies among the countries of the world. We need to take this assumption with a bit of skepticism. An article in *The Economist* (April 2011) reports on Ghemawat's illustration that semi-globalization is at best the reality – many indicators of global integration are surprisingly low: only 2 percent of students are at universities outside their home countries; and only 3 percent of people live outside their country of birth; only 7 percent of rice is traded across borders; only 7 percent of directors of Standard & Poor's 500 companies are foreigners; according to a study a few years ago, less than 1 percent of all American companies have any foreign operations; exports are equivalent to only 20 percent of global GDP, and some of the most vital arteries of globalization are badly clogged – air travel is restricted by bilateral treaties and ocean shipping is dominated by cartels. He provided further information: FDI accounts for only 9 percent of all fixed investment; less than 20 percent of venture capital is deployed outside the fund's home country; only 20 percent of shares traded on stock markets are owned by foreign investors; less than 20 percent of Internet traffic crosses national borders. In ways, the world today is less global than it was a hundred years ago – today's levels of emigration are far lower than a century ago, when 14 percent of Irish-born people and 10 percent of native Norwegians had emigrated; you did not need visas whereas today the world spends $88 billion a year on processing travel documents and in a tenth of the world's countries, a passport costs more than a tenth of the average annual income.

These statistics indicate that we need to be aware of the reality or the world. The press often focuses on issues such as globalization, and we can be extravagant in terms of the impact of these forces. Nevertheless, there are forces at work today that mean the countries of the world have more opportunities to interact, and there are major ways in which countries from developing countries can take advantage of these opportunities. Understanding management in the developing countries is an important area of understanding for the world as a whole. I hope that this book has contributed to this understanding.

SUMMARY

This chapter has looked at some special issues which are particularly relevant to developing countries. There are probably many other issues which could have been highlighted – for example, political developments, technological changes, regional integration, and so on. The choices here reflect the author's interests – that is, ethical issues, differential treatment on the basis of personal characteristics, and the impact of health, education, and age on performance of developing country companies and economic performance. Students and readers are encouraged to consider the impact of other issues as well as those presented here. The chapter concluded with a brief review of the issues covered in the book, and a look to the future. The overall conclusion of this book is that the so-called developing countries are moving to the foreground of the business picture. Issues of management in these countries are becoming more important, and should increase in importance over the coming decades. This book is written in this context, and I hope that readers will find the information presented here informative and relevant. In this changing environment, however, readers will need to constantly update the information base. I hope that the approach taken in this book will serve as a guide for readers in interpreting new information as it becomes available.

In conclusion, I have enjoyed the research and writing of this book. I hope that readers have also enjoyed it, and found it informative. I look forward to comments from readers, who can contact me at eureka@caribsurf.com.

LESSONS LEARNED

Having completed this chapter, you should appreciate the importance of social responsibility and organizational ethics. You should be able to explain the ethical approach to business and investment in terms of profit maximization and return on investment, as well as social effects. You should be able to give examples of personal characteristics that affect managerial decisions, and explain how the role of women in business differs around the world, with examples to illustrate these differences. You should be able to discuss and debate the impact of education and health issues for companies operating in and from developing countries, and discuss the implications of a relatively young population in developing countries.

DISCUSSION QUESTIONS

1   Managing ethics in the workplace holds potential benefits for managers, both moral and practical benefits. Explain these benefits in detail.

2   Explain why corruption may be more prevalent in developing countries.

3   Do you think it is ethical to deny someone a particular job because of race, gender, religion or ethnicity? Explain why or why not.

EXERCISES

1   Your company has several businesses established through the world. As a manager, you have noticed differences in the status of women especially between developed and developing countries. Select three countries where you have found these differences and explain the role of women in these countries. Discuss in small groups and share your findings with the class in the form of a short role-playing presentation.

2   In small groups, identify a current event that is having an impact on business. Discuss the impact of the event, particularly in terms of trade and investment decisions. Be prepared to share your conclusions with the class.

References

Abdulai, D.N. (2009) "Cultural mythology and global leadership in South Africa," in E.H. Kessler and D.J. Wong-MingJi (eds.), *Cultural Mythology and Global Leadership* (Cheltenham, UK: Edward Elgar), pp. 209–24.

Adhikari, D.R. and M. Muller (2001) "Human resource management in Nepal," in P.S. Budhwar, and Y. A. Debrah (eds.), *Human Resources in Developing Countries* (London: Routledge), pp. 91–102.

Adler, N.J. (1991) *International Dimensions of Organizational Behavior* (2nd ed., Boston, MA: PWS-Kent).

Agboolo, A.A. (2011) "Managing deviant behaviour and resistance to change," paper presented at the International Academy of African Business and Development Edmonton, Alberta, May 17–20.

van Agtmael, A. (2007) *The Emerging Markets Century* (London: Simon & Schuster).

Akorsu, A.D. (2010) "Labour management practices in the informal economy of Ghana: A deviation from the HRM orthodoxy?" presented at International Symposium on Human Resource Management in Africa, Nottingham Trent University, September.

Ali, A. (1990) "Management theory in a transitional society: The Arab's experience," *International Studies of Management and Organization* 20(3):7–35.

Alon, Ilan. (2011) "Emerging markets' evolving role in the new economic order," *Insights Academy of International Business,* 10(1):2.

Arnott, R. and J. Stiglitz (1991) "Moral hazard and nonmarket institutions," *American Economic Review* 81(11):179–90.

Audia, P.G. and S. Tams (2002) "Goal setting, performance appraisal, and feedback across cultures," in M.J. Gannon and K.L. Newman (eds.), *Handbook of Cross-Cultural Management* (London: Blackwell), pp. 142–54.

Aycan, Z. (2004) "Leadership in developing countries," in A. Bird, H. Lane, and M. Maznevski (eds.), *The Handbook of International Organizations* (Oxford: Blackwell), pp. 406–423.

Baliga, D.R. and A.M. Jaeger (1984) "Multinational corporations: Control systems and delegation issues" *Journal of International Business Studies* 15(2):25–40.

Baruch, Y. (2001) "Global or North American? A geographical based comparative analysis of publications in top management journals," *International Journal of Cross Cultural Management* 1(1):109–126.

Berkmen, P., G. Gelos, R. Rennhack, and J.P. Walsh (2010) "Differential impact," *Finance and Development* 47(1):29–31.

REFERENCES

Black, J.S. and M. Mendenhall (1990) "Cross-cultural training effectiveness: a review and a theoretical framework for future research," *Academy of Management Review* 15(1):113–36.

Blake, R.R. and J.S. Mouton (1964) *The Managerial Grid* (Houston: Gulf Publishing).

Blázquez-Lidoy, J., Rodríguez, J., and Santisto, J. (2006) "Angel or devil? China's trade impact on Latin American emerging markets," OECD Development Centre Working Paper 252, June.

Blunt, P. and Jones, M.L. (1997) "Exploring the limits of Western leadership theory in East Asia and Africa," *Personnel Review,* 26(1/2):6–23.

Branine, M. (2001) "Human resource management in Algeria," in P.S. Budhwar and Y. A. Debrah (eds.), *Human Resources in Developing Countries* (London: Routledge), pp. 153–73.

Briscoe, D. and R. S. Schuler (2009) *International Human Resource Management* (London: Routledge Global HRM Series).

Broadman, H.G. (2011) "The backstory of China and India's growing investment and trade with Africa: Separating the wheat from the chaff," *Columbia FDI Perspectives* 34, February 17.

Bruton, G.D. (2010) "Business and the world's poorest billion – The need for an expanded examination by management scholars," *Academy of Management Perspectives* 24(3):6–10.

Budhwar, P.S. (ed.) (2004) *Managing Human Resources in Asia-Pacific* (London: Routledge).

Budhwar, P.S. and Y. A. Debrah (2001) *Human Resources in Developing Countries* (London: Routledge).

Budhwar, P.S. and Debrah, Y. (2005) "International HRM in developing countries," in H. Scullion and M. Linehan (eds.), *International Human Resource Management* (London: Palgrave), pp. 259–80.

Budhwar, P.S., D.S. Saini, and J. Bhatnagar. (2005) "Women in management in the new economic environment: The case of India," *Asia Pacific Business Review* 11(2):179–93.

Cappelli, P., H. Singh, J. Singh, and M. Useem (2010) *The India Way – How India's Top Business Leaders are Revolutionizing Management* (Boston, MA: Harvard Business Press).

Carter, K.L. (1997) *Why Workers Won't Work: The Worker in a Developing Economy* (Oxford: Macmillan Education).

Catalyst (2009) "Women CEOs of the Fortune 1000," www.catalyst.org, accessed November 4, 2010.

Chinese Cultural Connection (1987) "Chinese values and the search for culture free dimensions of culture," *Journal of Cross-Cultural Psychology* 18(2):143–64.

CIA World Factbook. accessed at www.cia.gov/library, July 16, 2010.

Contreras, R. (2010) "Competing theories of economic development," University of Iowa Center for International Finance and Development.

Cooke, F.L. (2010) "The changing face of human resource management in China," in C. Rowley and F.L. Cooke (eds.), *The Changing Face of Management in China* (London: Routledge), pp. 28–51.

Cooke, F.L. (2008) "Performance management systems in China," in A. Varma and P. Budhwar (eds.), *Performance Management Systems around the Globe* (London: Routledge), pp. 193–209.

Cunningham, L.X. and C. Rowley (2007) "Human resource management in Chinese small and medium enterprises: A review and research agenda," *Personnel Review* 36(3):415–39.

Cunningham, L.X. and C. Rowley (2010) "The changing face of small and medium-sized enterprise management," in C. Rowley and F.L. Cooke (eds.), *The Changing Face of Management in China* (London: Routledge), pp. 125–48.

Darwin, C. (1859) *The Origin of Species* (London: John Murray).

Das, J., Q. T. Do, K. Shaines, and S. Srinivasan (2009) "Us and them: The geography of academic research" (December 1, 2009). World Bank Policy Research Working Paper Series. Available at SSRN: http://ssrn.com/abstract=1527362 World Bank Policy Research Working Paper No. 5152.

Davies, J.B., S. Sandström, A. Shorrocks, and E. N. Wolff (2011) "The level and distribution of global household wealth," *Economic Journal,* Royal Economic Society, 121(551):223–54.

Debrah, Y.A. and P.S. Budhwar (2001) "Conclusion: International competitive pressures and the challenges for HRM in developing countries," in P.S. Budhwar and Y. A. Debrah (eds.), *Human Resources in Developing Countries* (London: Routledge), pp. 238–54.

Developmentgateway.org, accessed November 29, 2006.

Dorfman, P. (1996) "International and Cross-Cultural Leadership," in B.J. Punnett and O. Shenkar (eds.), *Handbook for International Management Research* (1st ed., Oxford: Blackwell), pp. 267–349.

Dorfman, P. (2004) "International and cross-cultural leadership," in B.J. Punnett and O. Shenkar (eds.), *Handbook for International Management Research* (2nd ed., Ann Arbor, MI: Michigan University Press), pp. 265–335.

Dowling, P. (2007) *International Human Resource Management: Managing People in a Multinational Context* (Cincinnati, OH: South-Western College Publishing).

Doz, Y. and C.K. Prahalad (1984) "Patterns of strategic control within multinational corporations," *Journal of International Business Studies* 15(2):55–72.

Economist (2002) "Bribery and business" (March 2–8):63–5.

Economist (2006) "Carmaking in India" (December 16–22):64–5.

Economist (2006) "Dubai's financial center" (December 16–22):69–73.

Economist (2006) "Steel the prize" (November 25–31): 64–5.

Economist (2006) "The new titans" (September 16–22):1–28.

Economist (2010) "The world turned upside down" (April 17); p3 of a special report on innovation in emerging markets.

Economist (2010) "They may be giants" (May 15); p3 of a special report on banking in emerging markets.

Economist (2010) "Banyan - the elusive fruits of inclusive growth" (May 15): 50.

Economist (2011) "The case against globaloney – At last some sense on globalisation", April 20 www.economist.com, accessed May 26, 2011.

Economist Intelligence Unit (2000) (www.eiu.com).

Economist Intelligence Unit (August, 2009) "Survive and prosper: emerging markets in the global recession."

Economist Intelligence Unit (2010) "Brand and deliver: Asia's new corporate imperative," accessed at www.economist.com January 21, 2011, 5.

Erez, M. (1986) "The congruence of goal-setting strategies with sociocultural values and its effects on performance," *Journal of Management* 12:83–90.

Erez, M. and P.C. Earley (1987) "Comparative analysis of goal-setting strategies across cultures," *Journal of Applied Psychology* 72(4):658–65.

Ferraro, G.P. (1990) *The Cultural Dimension of International Business* (Englewood Cliffs, NJ: Prentice-Hall).

Fiedler, F. (1967) *A Theory of Leadership Effectiveness* (New York: McGraw-Hill).

Friedrich, P., A. Hatum, and L. Mesquita (2009) "Cultural mythology and global leadership in Argentina," in H. Kessler and D.J. Wong-MingJi (eds.), *Cultural Mythology and Leadership* (London: Edward Elgar), pp. 79–92.

Garibaldi de Hilal (2009) "Cultural mythology and global leadership in Brazil," in H. Kessler and D.J. Wong-MingJi (eds.), *Cultural Mythology and Leadership* (Northampton, MA: Edward Elgar), pp. 93–107.

Gokgur, N. (2011) "Are resurging state-owned enterprises impeding competition overseas?" *Columbia FDI Perspectives* 36 April 25.

Gwartney, J. and R. Larson (2002) *Economic Freedom of the World* (Vancouver, BC: Fraser Institute).

Hale, J.R. and D.L. Fields (2009) "Exploring servant leadership across cultures. A study of followers in Ghana and the USA," *Leadership* 3(4):397–416.

Hausmann, R. L. Tyson, and S. Zahidi (2009) *The World Economic Forum's 2009 Global Gender Gap Index* (Berkeley CA: University of California Press).

Henry, P.B. and C. Miller (2009) "Macroeconomic narratives from Africa and the diaspora – Institutions versus policies: A tale of two islands," *American Economic Review: Papers and Proceedings* 99(2):261–7.

Hershey, P. and K. Blanchard (1969) *Management of Organizational Behavior: Utilizing Human Resources* (Englewood Cliffs, NJ: Prentice-Hall).

Herzberg, F. (1959) *The Motivation to Work* (New York: John Wiley).

REFERENCES

Herzberg, F. (1968) "One more time: How do you motivate employees?" *Harvard Business Review* (January–February):53–62.

Hill, C. and G.R. Jones (2007) *Strategic Management: An Integrated Approach* (Boston, MA: Houghton Mifflin).

Hoff, K. and J.E. Stiglitz (2001) "Modern economic theory and development," in G.M. Miller and J.E. Stiglitz (eds.), *Frontiers of Development Economics* (Oxford: Oxford University Press), pp. 389–458.

Hoff, K. and J.E. Stiglitz (2010) Modern economic theory and development (www.4shared.com).

Hofstede, G. (1980) *Culture's Consequences: International Differences in Work Related Values* (Beverly Hills, CA: Sage).

Hofstede, G. (1984) *Culture's Consequences* (Beverly Hills, CA: Sage).

Hofstede, G. (1991) *Cultures and Organizations: Software of the Mind* (London: McGraw-Hill).

Horwitz, F.M. (2010) "Evolving human resource management in emerging markets," keynote address to International Symposium on Human Resource Management in Africa, Nottingham Trent University, September.

House, R.J., P. Hanges, M. Javidan, P. Dorfman, and V. Gupta (2004) *Culture, Leadership and Organisations. The GLOBE Study of 62 Societies* (Thousand Oaks, CA: Sage).

House, R.J. (1971) "A path–goal theory of leadership effectiveness," Administrative Science Quarterly (September).

Huang, T.C. (2001) "Human resource management in Taiwan," in P.S. Budhwar and Y. A. Debrah (eds.), *Human Resources in Developing Countries* (London: Routledge), pp. 56–74.

International Monetary Fund (2011) (www.imf.org)

Kamel, M. and G.T. Wood (2001) "Human resource management in Saudi Arabia," in P.S. Budhwar and Y. A. Debrah (eds.), *Human Resources in Developing Countries* (London: Routledge), pp. 135–52.

Kamoche, K. (2001) "Human resource management in Kenya," in P.S. Budhwar and Y. A. Debrah (eds.), *Human Resources in Developing Countries* (London: Routledge), pp. 209–21.

Kamu, A. (2010) "An investigation into the prevalence of HRM practices in SMEs – Sierra Leone an example," presented at International Symposium on Human Resource Management in Africa, Nottingham Trent University, September.

Kaufman, R. and B.J. Punnett (2009) "Specific marketing problems for small countries," paper presented at Academy of Marketing Sciences, Baltimore, May.

Kekic, L. (2009) "The global economic crisis and FDI flows to emerging markets," Vale Columbia Center on Sustainable International Investment: Columbia FDI Perspectives, October 8.

Kessler, E.H. and D.J. Wong-MingJi (2009) *Cultural Mythology and Global Leadership* (Northampton, MA: Edward Elgar).

Khadra, B. (1990) "The prophetic–caliphal model of leadership: An empirical study," *International Studies of Management and Organization* 20(3):37–51.

Khandelwal, P. (2002) "Gender stereotypes at work: Implications for organizations," *Indian Journal of Training and Development* 32(2):72–83.

Khanna, T., K.G. Palepu, and J. Sinha (2005) "Strategies that fit emerging markets," *Harvard Business Review* June:63–76.

Khiji, S. E. (2001) "Human resource management in Pakistan," in P.S. Budhwar and Y. A. Debrah (eds.), *Human Resources in Developing Countries* (London: Routledge), pp. 102–20.

Kiggundu, M. (1989) *Managing Organizations in Developing Countries* (West Hartford, CO: Kumavian Press).

Kolk, A. (2010) "Social and sustainability dimensions of regionalization and (semi)globalization," *Multinational Business Review* 18(1):51–72.

Landler, M. (2009) "Seeking business alliances – Clinton connects with India's billionaires," *New York Times* July 18.

LaPorta, R. and A. Schleifer (2008) "The unofficial economy and economic development," National Bureau of Economic Research Working Paper No. 14520.

Laurent, A. (1983) "The cultural diversity of Western conceptions of management," *International Studies of Management and Organization* 13(1–2):75–96.

Laza, K. (2009) "The global economic crisis and FDI flows to emerging markets," Perspectives on topical foreign direct investment issues, the Vale Columbia Center on Sustainable International Investment, No. 15, October 8, London.

LeDuc, B. (2005) "How to find your best niche market," Web Engaged Marketing News, February, accessed at inetready.com, May 25, 2011.

Lewis, W.A. (1955) *The Theory of Economic Growth* (New York: Taylor & Francis).

Lituchy, T., B.J. Punnett, D. Ford, et al. (2011) "Leadership and motivation in Africa and the diaspora: Some evidence from Kenya, Barbados, Canada and the United States," revised and resubmitted to *International Journal of Human Resource Management,* June, 2011.

Lituchy, T., B.J. Punnett, D. Ford, and C. Jonsson (2009) "Leadership effectiveness in Africa and the diaspora," Eastern Academy of Management International Proceedings, Rio, Brazil, June.

Locke, E.A. and G.P. Latham (1990) *A Theory of Goal Setting and Task Performance* (Englewood Cliffs, NJ: Prentice-Hall).

Lockwood, N.R., R. Sharma, and S. Williams (2009) "Perspectives on women in management in India," *Society for Human Resource Management* 1–12.

Maddison, A. (1982) *Phases of Capitalist Development* (Oxford: Oxford University Press).

Mangaliso, M. P. (2001) "Building competitive advantage from Ubuntu: Management lessons from South Africa," *Academy of Management Executive* 15(3):23–32.

Maslow, A.H. (1954) *Motivation and Personality* (New York: Harper).

Mathauer, I. and I. Imhoff (2006) "Health worker motivation in Africa," *Human Resources for Health* 4:24.

Mbigi, L., and Maree, J. (1995). *Ubuntu: The Spirit of African Transformation Management* (Randburg: Knowledge Resources).

McClelland, D.C. (1967) *The Achieving Society* (New York: Free Press).

McFarlin, D.B., E.A. Coster, and C. Mogale-Pretorius (1999) "South African management development in the twenty-first century: Moving toward an Africanized model," *Journal of Management Development* 18(1):63–78.

Mellahi, K. and G.T. Wood (2001) "Human resource management in Saudi Arabia," in P.S. Budhwar and Y. A. Debrah (eds.), *Human Resources in Developing Countries* (London: Routledge), pp. 135–52.

Montgomery, J.D. (1986) "Levels of managerial leadership in Southern Africa," *Journal of Developing Areas* 21:15–30.

Morris, I. (2010) *Why the West Rules – For Now* (Toronto: McClelland and Stewart).

Napier, N.K. and V.T. Vu (1995) "International human resource management in developing and transitional countries: A breed apart?" *Human Resource Management Review* 8(1):39–77.

Newenham-Kahindi, A. (2009) "The transfer of Ubuntu and Indaba business models abroad – A case of South African multinational banks and telecommunication services in Tanzania," *International Journal of Cross Cultural Management* 9(1):87–108.

Niles, F.S. (1998) "Achievement Goals and Means: A Cultural Comparison," *Journal of Cross-Cultural Psychology* 29(5):656–67.

Ovadje, F. and A. Ankomah (2001) "Human resource management in Nigeria," in Budhwar, P.S. and Y. A. Debrah (eds.) *Human Resources in Developing Countries* (London: Routledge), pp. 174–89.

Pacek, N. and D. Thorniley (2004) *Emerging Markets: Lessons for Business Success and the Outlook for Different Markets* (London: The Economist in association with Profile Books).

Park, H.W. (2001) "Human resource management in South Korea," in P.S. Budhwar and Y. A. Debrah (eds.), *Human Resources in Developing Countries* (London: Routledge), pp. 34–55.

Parker, I. (2010) "The poverty lab," *New Yorker,* May 17:79–89.

Parkin, D. (1978) *The Cultural Definition of Political Response: Lineal Destiny among the Luo* (London: Academic Press).

Perez-Bates, L.A., M.J. Pisani, and J.P. Doh (2010) "A perspective on international business scholarship: Is it regional or global?" *Multinational Business Review* 18(1):73–87.

Perkins, D.H., S. Radelet, D.R. Snodgrass, M. Gillis, and M. Roemer (2001) *Economics of Development* (5th ed., New York: W.W. Norton).

REFERENCES

Peterson, M., P. Smith, S. Smith, and S. Schwartz. (2002) "Cultural values as sources of guidance and their relevance to managerial behavior: A 47 nation study," *Journal of Cross-Cultural Psychology* 33(1):188–208.

Poon, I. H-F, J.Q. Wei, and C. Rowley (2010) "The changing face of performance management in China," in C. Rowley and F.L. Cooke (eds.), *The Changing Face of Management in China* (London: Routledge), pp. 149–74.

Porter, M. (1980) *Competitive Strategy: Techniques for Analyzing Industries and Competitors* (New York: Free Press).

Porter, M.E. (1988) *The Competitive Advantage of Nations* (New York: Free Press).

Prasad, A., ed. (2003) *Postcolonial Theory and Organizational Analysis: A Critical Reader* (London: Palgrave).

Punnett, B.J. (1986) "Goal-setting: An extension of the research," *Journal of Applied Psychology* (February):171–2.

Punnett, B.J. (1999) "The impact of individual needs on work behavior: China and North America," *Journal of Asia-Pacific Business* 2(3):23–44.

Punnett, B.J. (2004a) *International Perspectives on Organizational Behavior and Human Resource Management* (Armonk, NY: M.E. Sharpe).

Punnett, B.J. (2004b) "Management in developing countries," in Martha Maznevski, Mark Mendenhall, and Harry Lane (eds.), *The Handbook of Global Management* (London: Blackwell), pp. 387–405.

Punnett, B.J. (2004c) "Niche markets and small Caribbean companies," report prepared for Fulbright Foundation, December.

Punnett, B.J. (2009) *International Perspectives of Organizational Behavior and Human Resource Management* (Armonk, NY: M.E. Sharpe).

Punnett, B.J., A. Corbin, and D. Greenidge (2007) "Goal setting and performance: Extending the global reach," *International Journal of Emerging Markets* 3:215–35.

Punnett, B.J., E. Dick-Forde, and J. Robinson (2006) "Culture and management in the English-speaking Caribbean," *Journal of Eastern Caribbean Studies*, June 31(2):44–7.

Punnett, B.J., J. Duffy, S. Fox, A. Gregory, T. Lituchy, Silvia Inez Monserrat, M.R. Olivas Lujan, and N.M. Fernandes dos Santos (2006) *Successful Professional Women of the Americas: From Polar Winds to Tropical Breezes* (Northampton, MA: Edward Elgar).

Punnett, B.J. and D. Greenidge (2009) "Culture, myth and leadership in the Caribbean," in E.H. Kessler and D.J. Wong-MingJi (eds.), *Cultural Mythology and Leadership* (Northampton, MA: Edward Elgar).

Punnett, B.J., D. Greenidge and J. Ramsey (2007) "Job attitudes and absenteeism: A study in the English-speaking Caribbean," *Journal of World Business* 2:214–27.

Punnett, B.J. and A. Morrison (2006) "Niche markets and small Caribbean producers: A match made in heaven?" *Journal of Small Business and Entrepreneurship* 19(4):341–54.

Punnett, B.J. and D. Ricks (1989) *International Business* (London: International Thompson Press).

Ray, D. (2008) "Development economics," in L. Blume and S. Durlauf (eds.), *The New Palgrave Dictionary of Economics* (2nd ed., London: Palgrave Macmillan).

Ricks, D. (1983) *Big Business Blunder* (Columbus, OH: Grid).

Robinson, R. (1978) *International Business Management* (New York: Holt-Saunders).

Rosling, H. (2011) "The wealth and health of nations," accessed May 18, 2011 (at www.gapminder.org).

Rostow, W.W. (1960) *The Stages of Growth: A Non-Communist Manifesto* (Cambridge: Cambridge University Press).

Rowley, C. and F.L. Cooke (2010) "Setting the scene for the changing face of management in China," in Rowley and Cooke (eds.), *The Changing Face of Management in China* (London: Routledge), pp. 1–27.

Rugman, A.M. (2001) "The myth of global strategy," *AIB Insights* 2:11–14.

Rugman, A.M. and A. Verbeke (2008) "A new perspective on the regional and global strategies of multinational service firms," *Management International Review* 4:397–411.

Saini, D.S. (2006) "Labour law in India," in H.J. Davis, S.R. Chatterjee, and M. Heur (eds.), *Management in India: Trends and Transitions* (New Delhi: Response Books), pp. 60–94.

Sala-i-Martin, X. (1997) "I just ran two million regressions," *American Economic Review* 87(2): 178–83.

Schuler, R., P. Budhwar, and G.W. Florkowski (2004) "International human resource management," in B.J. Punnett and O. Shenkar (eds.), *Handbook for International Management Research* (Ann Arbor, MI.: University of Michigan Press), pp. 356–414.

Sen, A. (2005) *The Argumentative Indian: Writings on Indian History, Culture and Identity* (New York: Farrar, Straus and Giroux).

Shrestha, L.B. (2000) "Population aging in developing countries," *Health Affairs* May–June:204–14.

Sinha, J.B.P. (1984) "A model of effective leadership styles in India," *International Studies of Management and Organization* 14(3):86–98.

Sinha, J.B.P. (1994) "Cultural imbeddedness and the developmental role of industrial organizations in India," in *Handbook of Industrial and Organizational Psychology*, vol. 4, 727–64 (Palo Alto, CA: Consulting Psychologists Press).

Smith, B. (2002) "Worldview and culture: Leadership in Sub-Saharan Africa," *New England Journal of Public Policy* 19(1):243.

Smith, P.B., M.F. Peterson, S.H. Schwartz, et al. (2002) "Cultural values, sources of guidance and their relevance to managerial behavior," *Journal of Cross-Cultural Psychology* 33(2):188–208.

Smyth, R. and Zhai, Q. (2010) "The changing face of state-owned enterprise management," in Rowley, C. and Cooke, F.L (eds.), *The Changing Face of Management in China* (London: Routledge), pp. 101–24.

Tayeb, M. (2001) "Human resource management in Iran," in P.S. Budhwar and Y. A. Debrah (eds.), *Human Resources in Developing Countries* (London: Routledge), pp. 121–34.

Taylor, A. (2006) *The Divided Ground* (New York, NY: Alfred A. Knopf).

Thomas, A. (1996) "A call for research in forgotten locations," in B.J. Punnett and O. Shenkar (eds.), *Handbook for International Management Research* (Cambridge, MA: Blackwell), pp. 485–506.

Tirole, J. (1996) "A theory of collective reputations with applications to the persistence of corruption and firm quality," *Review of Economic Studies* 63:1–22

Tonkin, S. (2009) accessed at samantha.tonkin@weforum.org, November, 2010.

Tung, R. (1981) "Selection and Training of Personnel for Overseas Assignments," *Columbia Journal of World Business* 16(1):68–78.

UN Daily News (2010) "Invest more in the developing world, UN urges gathering of global business leaders," United Nations News Service, June.

United Nations (1998) *World Population Prospects* (New York: United Nations).

United Nations (2000) *Entering the 21st Century: World Development Report* (Oxford: Oxford University Press).

United Nations (2001) *World Development Report* (Oxford: Oxford University Press).

United Nations (2002) *Human Development Report* (Oxford: Oxford University Press).

United Nations (2005) *Human Development Report* (Oxford: Oxford University Press).

United Nations (2010) *World Investment Report* (Oxford: Oxford University Press).

United Nations Center on Transnational Corporations (1988) *Transnational Corporations in World Development: Trends and Prospects* New York: United Nations).

United States. Council for International Business. (1985) *Corporate Handbook to International Economic Organizations and Terms* (New York: U.S. Council for International Business).

Vroom, V.H. and P.H. Yetton (1973) *Leadership and Decision Making* (Pittsburgh, PA: University of Pittsburgh Press).

Walumbwa, F.O., B. Orwa, P. Wang, and J.J. Lawler (2005) "Transformational leadership, organizational commitment, and job satisfaction: A comparative study of Kenyan and US financial firms," *Human Resource Development Quarterly* 16(2):235–56.

Warner, M. (2001) "Human resource management in the People's Republic of China," in P.S. Budhwar and Y. A. Debrah (eds.), *Human Resources in Developing Countries* (London: Routledge), pp. 19–33.

REFERENCES

www.wikipedia.org, accessed September 6, 2006.

www.globalchange.umich.edu accessed May 18, 2011.

www.happyplanetindex.org accessed September 20, 2010.

www.heritage.org accessed January 28, 2008.

www.transparency.org (2010) "2010 Corruption Index," accessed May 21, 2011.

www.transparency.org accessed 18 July, 2010.

Yang, K.S., K.K. Hwang, and U. Kim (eds.) (2005) *Scientific Advances in Indigenous Psychologies: Empirical, Philosophical and Cultural Contributions* (Cambridge: Cambridge University Press).

Index